Earthkeeping
and Character

Exploring a Christian Ecological Virtue Ethic

Steven Bouma-Prediger

Baker Academic

a division of Baker Publishing Group
Grand Rapids, Michigan

Published by Baker Academic
a division of Baker Publishing Group
PO Box 6287, Grand Rapids, MI 49516-6287
www.bakeracademic.com

Printed in the United States of America

Library of Congress Cataloging-in-Publication Data
Names: Bouma-Prediger, Steven, author.
Title: Earthkeeping and character : exploring a Christian ecological virtue ethic / Steven
    Bouma-Prediger.
Description: Grand Rapids, MI : Baker Academic, a division of Baker Publishing Group, [2020] |
    Includes bibliographical references and index.
Identifiers: LCCN 2019011774 | ISBN 9780801098840 (pbk.)
Subjects: LCSH: Human ecology—Religious aspects—Christianity. | Ecotheology.
Classification: LCC BT695.5 .B685 2020 | DDC 241/.691—dc23
LC record available at https://lccn.loc.gov/2019011774

20   21   22   23   24   25   26   7   6   5   4   3   2   1

green press INITIATIVE

To my mother, Jean Prediger,
and in memory of my father, Curtis Prediger,
with gratitude for lives well lived

Contents

Acknowledgments

I would like to acknowledge with gratitude a number of people who helped me with this book. Their comments, questions, and suggestions improved both its substance and its style. First, my fellow members of the Religion Department at Hope College, in our departmental colloquia, read and discussed various chapters of this book and offered much sound advice. Many thanks to Barry Bandstra, Wayne Brouwer, Angela Carpenter, Jenny Everts, Steve Hoogerwerf, Lynn Japinga, Phil Munoa, Jared Ortiz, Rakesh Peter Dass, Jeff Tyler, and Boyd Wilson. It is a privilege to work with such talented scholars, committed teachers, and supportive colleagues.

And a hearty thank you to all at Hope College whose vision and diligence have made it such a wonderful place to write a book such as this—past presidents Jim Bultman and Dennis Voskuil, former provost Rich Ray and current department chairperson Jeff Tyler, longtime office manager Pamela Valkema and die-hard third shift Lubbers Hall janitor Scott Plaster, to name just a few.

I have had the opportunity to try out various parts of this book at venues all over North America. Thank you to the following for their invitations: Ted Koontz and Janeen Bertsche Johnson at Anabaptist Mennonite Biblical Seminary, Markku and Leah Kostamo at A Rocha Canada, Fred Van Dyke and Jon Terry at the Au Sable Institute for Environmental Studies, Darin Davis at Baylor University, Roland Hoksbergen and Matt Heun and Dave Koetje and David Smith and Dave Warners for various events at Calvin College, Matt Bonzo at Cornerstone University, Richard Middleton at Northeastern Seminary, Sid Ypma and Paul Heintzman at the University of Ottawa, Loren Wilkinson at Regent College in Vancouver, BC, Derek McNeil at the Seattle School of Theology and Psychology, Mark Liederbach and Seth Bible at Southeastern Baptist Theology Seminary, Richard Kyte at Viterbo University, and

Jonathan Moo at Whitworth University. Many people—too numerous to mention here—have offered their comments at conferences and gatherings at which I was speaking about some part of this book. Thank you one and all for your kind invitations and the many insights that came from being with you.

A number of brave souls (bless them, good scholar-friends) read the entire manuscript and offered their comments. Special thanks to Steve Hoogerwerf, David Stubbs, and Brian Walsh. This book is much better because of your insightful comments and perceptive questions.

A big thank you to former Hope student Lauren Madison, who served as my research assistant for two summers and whose very fine work has been incorporated into this book, especially in chapter five. My gratitude, also, to many other students whom I have had the privilege to teach—at Hope and on other college and university campuses here in North America and in Belize and New Zealand. Your questions and comments on the ideas I develop in this book have, among other things, reminded me of the timeliness of this topic.

The good folks at Baker Academic have once again been a joy to work with. Melisa Blok, Erika Genz, Bob Hosack, Regula Noetzli, and Mason Slater have, each in their own way, helped make the publication of this book possible. And I am sure there are others there whose labors on my behalf I do not know. To all of you at Baker Academic, thank you very much.

As with all my previous books, I owe a debt of gratitude to my wife, Celaine, and my daughters Anna, Chara, and Sophia. Thank you, thank you, thank you.

This book is dedicated, with much gratitude, to my mother and in memory of my father—exemplars of many of the virtues central to the Christian faith. May each of us be inspired by someone we know whose life embodies the dispositions we need in order to be caretakers of God's good earth.

Abbreviations

General

alt.	altered
chap(s).	chapter(s)
ed(s).	edition(s)
e.g.	for example
esp.	especially
et al.	and others
i.e.	that is
p(p).	page(s)
rev.	revised
trans.	translation
v(v).	verse(s)
vol(s).	volume(s)

Old Testament

Gen.	Genesis
Exod.	Exodus
Lev.	Leviticus
Num.	Numbers
Deut.	Deuteronomy
Josh.	Joshua
Judg.	Judges
Ruth	Ruth
1–2 Sam.	1–2 Samuel
1–2 Kings	1–2 Kings
1–2 Chron.	1–2 Chronicles
Ezra	Ezra

Neh.	Nehemiah
Esther	Esther
Job	Job
Ps./Pss.	Psalm/Psalms
Prov.	Proverbs
Eccles.	Ecclesiastes
Song	Song of Songs
Isa.	Isaiah
Jer.	Jeremiah
Lam.	Lamentations
Ezek.	Ezekiel
Dan.	Daniel
Hosea	Hosea
Joel	Joel
Amos	Amos
Obad.	Obadiah
Jon.	Jonah
Mic.	Micah
Nah.	Nahum
Hab.	Habakkuk
Zeph.	Zephaniah
Hag.	Haggai
Zech.	Zechariah
Mal.	Malachi

New Testament

Matt.	Matthew
Mark	Mark

Luke	Luke	1–2 Tim.	1–2 Timothy
John	John	Titus	Titus
Acts	Acts	Philem.	Philemon
Rom.	Romans	Heb.	Hebrews
1–2 Cor.	1–2 Corinthians	James	James
Gal.	Galatians	1–2 Pet.	1–2 Peter
Eph.	Ephesians	1–3 John	1–3 John
Phil.	Philippians	Jude	Jude
Col.	Colossians	Rev.	Revelation
1–2 Thess.	1–2 Thessalonians		

Introduction

Ecological Ethics Reframed

> What sort of person would do a thing like that?
>
> Thomas Hill Jr.[1]

> But lacking the qualities of virtue, can we do the difficult things that will be necessary to live within the boundaries of the earth?
>
> David Orr[2]

What Sort of Person?

The day was picture perfect. A brilliant sun was shimmying up a clear blue sky, birds were singing to their hearts' content, and the temperature was in the low fifties. My group of hikers—five Hope College students and one other instructor on a ten-day canoeing and backpacking expedition in the Adirondacks of upstate New York, as part of a May-term course called Ecological Theology and Ethics—broke camp and hit the trail toward our evening's destination. As we rounded the bend in the rocky trail, we could not believe what met our eyes. The campsite by the trail was trashed. Litter was everywhere. Half-burned wood from the fire ring was strewn hither and yon. Large pieces of metal, hard to identify, were leaning up against an old log lean-to that was thoroughly inscribed with knife carvings. Birch trees were stripped of their bark all the way around. After a long astonished silence, one of my students uttered the words in my mind: "What sort of person would do a thing like that?" What kind of person would trash such a beautiful place? With this heartfelt cry, my student gave voice to an ancient but until recently neglected approach to ethics: virtue ethics. Ecological virtue ethics to be precise.

Thomas Hill had a similar experience. That is, he found himself uttering the same probing question: What sort of person would do a thing like that? In 1983 Hill, a philosopher at the University of North Carolina at Chapel Hill, authored an essay now recognized as pivotal in the development of contemporary environmental virtue ethics. Hill writes:

> A wealthy eccentric bought a house in a neighborhood I know. The house was surrounded by a beautiful display of grass, plants, and flowers, and it was shaded by a huge old avocado tree. But the grass required cutting, the flowers needed tending, and the man wanted more sun. So he cut the whole lot down and covered the yard with asphalt. . . .
>
> It was a small operation, but it reminded me of the strip mining of large sections of the Appalachians. In both cases, of course, there were reasons for the destruction, and property rights could be cited as justification. But I could not help but wonder, "What sort of person would do a thing like that?"[3]

This question evokes not a discussion of duties or rights or consequences but a focus on character traits—virtues and vices. What character traits (vices) allow someone to destroy a beautiful place? And what character traits (virtues) prompt indignation on seeing such a degraded place and fuel the desire to make it better?

Hill insightfully observes that even if there is a convincing case to be made, based on a careful cost-benefit analysis, for asphalting over the yard or strip-mining the mountain, there is something more at stake, evident in our underlying uneasiness about such destructive action. Something important is missed in asking merely, "Are the rights or interests of plants neglected?" or "What is the intrinsic value of a tree or forest?" Hill argues that we must turn from "the effort to find reasons why certain acts destructive of natural environments are morally wrong to the ancient task of articulating our ideals of human excellence. Rather than argue directly with destroyers of the environment who say, 'Show me why what I am doing is *immoral*,' I want to ask, 'What sort of person would want to do what they propose?'"[4]

In short, Hill shifts the terms of the discussion from doing to being, from actions to attitudes, from conduct to character. In this seminal essay, Hill describes the centrality of virtues such as humility and self-acceptance—two virtues that help us acknowledge that we are the sort of creatures that we are. This shift of questions and terms represents a reframing of ecological ethics away from the traditional approaches that focus on rights, duties, or consequences in favor of the ancient tradition of virtue ethics.

Ethics Reframed

This recovery of the virtue ethics tradition should come as no surprise. In our more reflective moments, most of us wonder about the kind of person we have become and the kind of person we aspire to be. Perhaps celebrating a new birth or lamenting the loss of an old friend, contemplating a job change or witnessing a wedding, reading an obituary or attending a funeral, we ask: Who am I, really? What personal character traits am I proud of? Courage and compassion, humility and honesty, generosity and graciousness? And which traits do I wish would magically disappear? Impatience and insensitivity, stinginess and self-deprecation, avarice and apathy? Character traits lie at the heart of who we are. They mark us—for good and ill, to our credit and to our shame—as the unique people we are.

So an ethics of character is not new or foreign to our lives. Parents strive to nurture in their children commonly sought virtues such as courage and compassion, honesty and hope. Teachers endeavor to form students in certain ways, for example, by discouraging plagiarism and promoting academic integrity, even if the teachers think (falsely) that they are not in the business of moral formation. Business owners set policies designed to cultivate certain virtues—for example, honesty, diligence, and inventiveness—and thus promote particular practices and behavior in the workplace. In short, character formation is taking place all the time, for better or for worse. What is new is that in recent years more scholars have given virtue ethics their attention, and scholarly discussions have shifted to recapture the virtue ethics tradition.

So what I propose in this volume is a reframing of ecological ethics. I develop an ecological ethic centered on the virtues by drawing on the rich resources of the Christian faith tradition. In so doing I join a growing chorus of scholars (philosophers, theologians, and ethicists) who advocate virtue ethics,[5] including many Christian scholars.[6] I also join an increasing number of scholars (again mostly philosophers, theologians, and ethicists) who espouse some form of environmental ethics.[7] There are, however, not many scholars who focus on the intersection of virtue ethics and environmental ethics—namely, environmental virtue ethics.[8] That is, there are relatively few who emphasize character traits (both virtues and vices) with respect to environmental issues. And within the field of environmental virtue ethics, there are, as yet, few whose work draws explicitly on the Christian tradition.[9] With this book I offer my contribution to our understanding of ecological virtue ethics. Beyond mere understanding, important as that is, I hope this volume will, to use the words of David Orr in the second epigraph to this chapter, help nurture "the qualities of virtue" that will enable us to "do the difficult things that will be necessary to live within the boundaries of the earth."

Why the title *Earthkeeping and Character*? And what exactly is meant by the subtitle *Exploring a Christian Ecological Virtue Ethic*? Of the many words and phrases used to express our care for our home planet, in my view the word *earthkeeping* best captures our human vocation to serve and protect the earth. Coined by Loren Wilkinson and his coauthors in their groundbreaking book,[10] the term *earthkeeping*, with its reference to the earth, is concrete, unlike the more abstract term *world*. Also, earthkeeping focuses on where we actually live, this blue-green orb called Earth, unlike the hopelessly expansive term *creation*. This focus on the earth, furthermore, includes the entire biosphere and all the interlocking systems and creatures that are an integral part of this thin slice of life-filled existence, thereby emphasizing both human and other-than-human creatures, unlike the term *nature*, which tends to assume a split between human and nonhuman. Finally, the compound word *earthkeeping* accurately names our biblical calling as humans to preserve and protect (as well as use) the earth (Gen. 2:15). In short, earthkeeping captures our calling to care responsibly for our home planet. The third word in the title, *character*, points to the tradition of ethics most concerned with virtues and vices and the crucial role they play in our attempts to care for the earth.

The subtitle, among other things, names the academic territory: ecological virtue ethics. While the commonly accepted term for the field is *environmental virtue ethics*, I favor the term *ecological virtue ethics*. So when referring to the larger world of scholarship in ethics, I use the more common term, even though I think the term *environmental* is a poor choice of adjective. Words matter. As an ancient Chinese proverb puts it, "Whoever defines the terms wins the argument." There will be more later (in chap. 1) on why *ecological virtue ethics* is my preferred term.

The subtitle also states my perspective as a Christian scholar on this academic field of study. Unlike some who argue that religion should be eradicated or at least kept private, I argue that the Christian tradition has much to offer contemporary ecological ethics, as do other religions each in their own way.[11] The Bible has more to say on earthkeeping than many people (including many Christians) realize, and the Christian tradition is deep and rich when it comes to virtue ethics. My treatment of this topic, however, is a series of explorations, much like being a backpacker in the Sierra Nevada or a canoeist in Quetico. What follows are excursions from a journey, like a series of day trips designed to reconnoiter new terrain.

What does this bookish exploration look like? In chapter 1, I map the territory. In other words, I lay out the big-picture landscape of ethics in our time, provide an anatomy of virtue and the virtues, outline the development of ecological virtue ethics, and articulate my own approach to ecological virtue ethics. A kind of primer in Christian ecological ethics, this chapter lays the groundwork for all that is to follow.

In chapter 2 we explore what it means to live with amazement and modesty. In a culture that all too often sucks the amazement right out of us as we proceed up the educational ladder, how do we recover our ability to recognize and appreciate the marvels of life on earth?[12] In a culture that seems to assume that humans are divine, what does it mean to acknowledge honestly that we are not gods or demigods?[13] If we took our creatureliness seriously, what virtues would we deem necessary? Wonder and humility are two such virtues. These habitual dispositions are at the very core of what it means to acknowledge that we are creatures of God—humble humans from the humus (to paraphrase Gen. 2) standing amazed by the world of wonders in which we find ourselves.

In chapter 3 we explore what it means to live with strength of mind and discernment. In a culture where bumper stickers proclaim, "Whoever dies with the most toys wins" and "You are what you drive,"[14] what would it look like to live with fewer things because we are able to restrain and retrain our desires with a spirit of gratitude for what we already have?[15] And in a culture that often mistakes data for knowledge, thinks education means regurgitating information, and confuses intelligence and insight, what does it mean to live wisely and well?[16] Self-control and wisdom name the countercultural virtues needed here. These character traits enable us to discipline our disordered desires and discern what is genuinely good and true.

In chapter 4 we explore what it means to live with respect and care. In a culture in which lives, both human and nonhuman, seem increasingly cheap and disposable, where disrespect for all that is other than ourselves seems more and more prevalent, what does it mean to live as people animated by justice?[17] In a culture that promotes cynical indifference, where apathy all too often accompanies our foggy awareness of the latest plunderings of our home planet, what would it mean to cultivate care for human and nonhuman alike?[18] Justice and love name the virtues we need in this (or any) culture. Respect for rights and care for needs succinctly describe these habitual dispositions. These two virtues lie at the core of every discussion of ethics.

In chapter 5 we explore what it means to live with fortitude and expectation. In a culture of growing apprehension and seemingly endless anxiety, what would it look like to face our fears and act with a resolute spirit, without either acting recklessly or being paralyzed by fear?[19] In a culture rife with false hopes, with prophets (and profits) of easy credibility lurking everywhere, what does it mean to resist both despair and presumptuousness and, in contrast, embrace with confidence the expectation of God's good future of shalom?[20] In these circumstances, courage and hope are the virtues needed to enable us to live through our fear and overcome the temptation to despair.

Finally, in chapter 6 we explore how we become people of praiseworthy character—people who embody the virtues described in chapters 2–5. In a culture of bogus hero worship, of hollow media personalities, of spurious role models who seem to embody the glittering vices, how do we become people of virtue? How do we become people marked by awestruck wonder and unheralded humility? Grateful self-control and winsome wisdom? Passionate justice and boundless love? Tenacious courage and clear-eyed hope? As Aristotle, among others, reminds us, the aim of studying the virtues is not theoretical but practical.[21] That is to say, our goal is not only to learn about the virtues but also to become more virtuous. May that goal be realized in your reading of this book.

"What Sort of Person?" Revisited

The day was picture perfect. A brilliant sun was shimmying up a clear blue sky, the robins and cardinals were singing to their hearts' content, and the temperature was in the low fifties. My group of hikers—Hope College students and one other instructor on a May-term course called Ecological Theology and Ethics—broke camp and hit the trail toward our evening's destination. Late in the day, after many miles on the rocky trail, we rounded the bend and could not believe what met our eyes. The campsite by the trail was absolutely beautiful. There was no litter in sight. A stack of firewood was neatly placed next to a small fire ring. The old log lean-to was in tip-top condition. Tall white pines provided a protective canopy overhead. After a long astonished silence, one of my students uttered the words in my mind: "What kind of people would have done this?" In other words, what kind of respectful, humble, loving people must have cared for this place for many years? With this heartfelt affirmation, my student gave voice to exactly what I was thinking. And she gave voice to an important way of thinking about ethics—ecological *virtue* ethics.

1

Mapping the Territory

On Virtue and Vice

If, then, the virtues are neither passions nor faculties, all that remains is that they should be states of character.

Aristotle[1]

What you see and hear depends a good deal on where you are standing. It also depends on what sort of person you are.

C. S. Lewis[2]

A Student, His Grandparents, and a Poem

He sat in the back row, quiet as the proverbial mouse. At first he said little or nothing in class, appearing to be the stereotypical introvert. But in his papers and exams, he was anything but quiet. It was clear he had done all the reading, giving careful thought to my "questions to ponder," and was thinking deep and long about the issues raised in class. The class was Ethics and Christian Discipleship, an introductory religion course at Hope College. Populated mostly by second- and third-year undergraduate students, many of whom were taking it to fulfill a general education requirement, this semester-long course covered the basics of Christian ethics in the first five weeks. Then in the remaining ten weeks we examined a variety of ethical issues—for example, social justice in the presence of poverty and racism, peacemaking in the face of violence, and earthkeeping in a world of ecological degradation.

According to Andre, this was the very first time he had any instruction in ethics. Like most of his college-age friends, Andre had gut-level feelings about what was right and wrong, but he was ignorant about ethics and unsure what was at stake. Nothing in his K–12 education in public schools (or, sadly, Sunday school classes at church) had touched on these issues. When I reminded Andre that one of the purposes of education is to expand the frontiers of your knowledge, he laughed. But as the course progressed, I sensed he was growing more interested in the subject matter of the class.

When we got to the section on environmental issues, Andre became especially excited. He had heard of various topics such as species extinction and global warming but had not studied them. He dove into the reading with great enthusiasm. Indeed, he became more vocal in class discussions and argued eloquently as a member of a team debating a case study on greenhouse gases. It was as if he had become a different person from the quiet, reserved, and seemingly disengaged student sitting in class on day one.

Andre chose to write his ethical analysis project paper on an issue of more than passing interest to him. His maternal grandparents owned a farm, and he had grown up visiting this farm. In fact, as a high-school student, he worked on the farm during the summers. Andre knew the land, the cows and horses, the dogs and cats, the neighbors. He also knew that farming was changing, with fewer and fewer small family farms able to survive in a world where the mantra was "Get big or get out."[3] His grandparents had been tempted to "Get big" by renting more land, but that would require buying larger machinery, using more fertilizers, and hiring extra help; they were not comfortable with such radical changes to their simpler way of life. Getting big didn't seem right—for them or for the land—so they decided to pass on the chance to get big, betting they would not be forced to get out. Andre knew one more thing: his grandparents were getting older and hoped, if possible, to pass on the farm to someone in the family.

So Andre wrote his paper on the ethical issues concerning his grandparents' farm. He listed the various consequences (good and bad) of different possible courses of action, going beyond the typical cost-benefit analysis to include costs and benefits not usually included in neoclassical economics. He identified various moral and legal rights at stake and clarified the ethical duties and obligations implicit in those rights. All of this was helpful. But at the end of the day, Andre said what struck him the most about this family case study were the character traits embodied by his grandparents. Beyond the rules and rights, the duties and consequences, were the virtues that marked his grandparents: humility and wisdom, frugality and gratitude, diligence and perseverance. Andre ended his paper, fittingly, with a poem by Wendell Berry.[4]

The clearing rests in song and shade.
It is a creature made
By old light held in soil and leaf,
By human joy and grief,
By human work,
Fidelity of sight and stroke,
By rain, by water on
The parent stone.

We join our work to Heaven's gift,
Our hope to what is left,
That field and woods at last agree
In an economy
Of widest worth.
High Heaven's Kingdom come on earth.
Imagine paradise.
O dust, arise!

Ethics in Our Time and Place

What is morality, and what exactly is ethics? For the sake of clarity, let's begin with a few basic distinctions. First, what is moral must be distinguished from what is nonmoral. Some judgments have to do with moral rights and wrongs, with what is morally good and bad, while other human judgments do not concern moral matters at all. They are, rather, nonmoral. So, for example, to say that I am wearing a really bad tie is to make not a moral judgment but rather an aesthetic judgment. Commenting that my canoeing technique is not very good is not a moral judgment but a claim about my athletic ability. So we must distinguish between the moral and the nonmoral. Second, what is moral must be distinguished from what is immoral. To say that my act of stealing that bicycle was immoral is to claim that it was not morally right and that I am morally blameworthy. To state that helping that lost child find his way back home was "the moral thing to do" is to make a judgment that my action is morally good and praiseworthy. Third, morality is not the same as ethics. Morality has to do with what is good or bad, right or wrong, with respect to our action or behavior, while ethics is the academic discipline that studies morality. Ethics, in the usual understanding, is the study of what is morally good and bad, morally right and wrong, and how and why we make such judgments.[5]

But implicit within this understanding are assumptions about the kind of people we are and aspire to be—a vision of the character traits deemed necessary to live a good life. Indeed, one of the primary meanings of the Greek word *ethos*, from which we get the English word *ethics*, is "character." So an alternative way to define ethics is to say that it is about the study of people with good (and bad) character. As David Cunningham puts it, "Ethics concerns the study, evaluation, and formation of *people of good character*."[6] In other words, ethics can also be defined in terms of character traits (virtues and vices) that result in conduct that is morally good or bad, right or wrong.

In all human cultures, various traditions of moral discernment and ethical decision making have arisen. Patterns of thought and habits of practice have developed over time. In short, ethical theories came to be. For the last 250 years in Europe and North America, the prevailing ethical theories focused on obligations, rights, and goods. In technical language, ethical theory has been dominated by deontology and teleology. For deontology (from the Greek words for the study of that which is needful or obligatory), the central ethical question is: What are our obligations? In other words, what are our duties with respect to others (in most cases other humans)? And this question is often tied to a related question: What are our rights? What legitimate claims do we have, and what duties follow from those claims? For deontology, the good is defined in terms of the right.

For teleology (from the Greek words for the study of goals or aims), the central question is: What are the ultimate goods, and which human actions produce those goods? In other words, what actions will produce the greatest balance of good over evil? Consequentialism is the more common name for this approach since what is morally right and wrong is determined by an assessment of good and bad consequences. In contrast to deontology, teleology defines the right in terms of the good.

The most common form of consequentialism is utilitarianism, which holds that an action is morally right if and only if it brings about the greatest balance of good over bad consequences for the greatest number of recipients. For most versions of utilitarianism, the recipients include only humans, though in recent years the scope of what matters has expanded.[7] So the relevant ethical question for utilitarians is: If I (or my company, school, city, or country) did this action, what would be the costs and benefits for the greatest number of people? This kind of consequentialism, often understood solely in terms of an economic cost-benefit analysis, is, as many argue, the predominant ethic of our age.[8]

These two ethical theories, however, have their critics. Two of the main criticisms are nicely summarized by Clive Barnett, Philip Cafaro, and Terry Newholm:

Both consequentialist and deontological approaches are open to two related criticisms. First, both present models of ethical conduct that appear to be far too stringent in the demands they make on the capacities of ordinary people—consequentialist arguments seem to imagine it is possible to collect, collate and calculate all sorts of information and chains of causality prior to, or even after, action. While utilitarian considerations might be relevant in relation to evaluating collective public decisions, they seem rather unrealistic as complete models of personal choice. Similarly, deontological approaches seem to present an implausible picture of actors rationally judging the degree to which each of their actions conforms to a very abstract principle of universalization. This criticism . . . is related to a second problem with both consequentialist and deontological approaches. They end up presenting models of ethical conduct that are rather inflexible, leaving little room for the complexities and ambivalences of ethical decision making. They therefore present a highly abstracted model of the ways in which people are implicated and involved in their actions.[9]

In other words, each of these ethical theories has an inadequate anthropology—a faulty view of the human person and what it means to be human. It simply is not the case that most people most of the time, when making an ethical judgment, stop to identify and collect and reflect on all the possible good and bad consequences of each hypothetical action. It is false to assume that most people most of the time, when deciding on whether and how to act, measure the degree to which each of their possible actions meets some philosophically derived principle of obligation. These ethical theories have a highly implausible view of human nature.

There is much support for this critique. Many scholars from across the academic disciplines have shown that we humans are much more than Cartesian thinking things.[10] As Mark Johnson puts it, the pervasive view "that regards moral reasoning as consisting entirely of the bringing of concrete cases under moral laws or rules that specify 'the right thing to do' in a given instance" is "quite mistaken." Indeed, the Moral Law Folk Theory, as Johnson calls it, "is premised on bad psychology, bad metaphysics, bad epistemology, and bad theories of language."[11] As he argues more recently, "What we call 'mind' and what we call 'body' are not two things, but rather aspects of one organic process, so that all our meaning, thought, and language emerge from the aesthetic dimensions of this embodied activity."[12] So Johnson concludes, "Acknowledging that every aspect of human being is grounded in specific forms of bodily engagement with an environment requires a far-reaching re-thinking of who and what we are, in a way that is largely at odds with many of our inherited Western philosophical and religious traditions."[13] Our cognition is embodied in ways we are only now beginning to understand.[14] And since every ethic is rooted in assumptions about human nature—a philosophical and/or theological anthropology—the fact that our cognition is embodied has important implications for how we do ethics.

Furthermore, while these two different ethical theories—deontology and utilitarianism—have dueled for two centuries, with each side claiming victory, for all their differences they have one thing in common: each theory assumes that ethics, at its roots, is about doing and not being, primarily about conduct and not character. As Charles Taylor, among others, notes, "The dominant philosophical ethics today, divided into the two major branches of Utilitarianism and post-Kantianism, both conceive of morality as determining through some criterion what an agent ought to do. They are rather hostile to an ethics of virtue or the good, such as that of Aristotle. And a Christian conception, where the highest way of life can't be explained in terms of rules, but rather is rooted in a certain relation to God, is entirely off the screen."[15] But what if the more important question is "What kind of person should I be?" rather than "What should I do?" What if character rather than conduct is more fundamental?

Despite the dominance of the deontological and utilitarian approaches to ethics, an increasing number of people are asking precisely these questions. In an essay on the Anthropocene and its meaning in our time, John Vucetich, Michael Paul Nelson, and Chelsea Batavia conclude that "robust arguments have already been made for how and why the key to wise relationships to nature depends on a set of virtues that include precaution, humility, empathy, and rationality. . . . Those virtues will be vitally important in any new epoch." Despite these claims about the importance of virtues in our time, however, with honesty and no little amount of anxiety, they admit that "we live in a culture with too little capacity or interest in those virtues."[16]

Social scientists Olivia Bina and Sofia Guedes Vaz also argue for the centrality of the virtues. In light of "the current market-driven and globalized socio-economic system," they argue we need "a more holistic understanding of what it means to be human." A virtue ethic, in their view, provides just such an understanding. Indeed, in emphatic terms, they insist "virtues need to be reclaimed as a central dimension of what it means to be human, starting from how we educate the future generations, if they are to contribute to a life that is good for them, for the planet, for all children, and all species."[17] An ecological ethic, based on a more informed and accurate view of human nature, must focus on character more than conduct.

Virtue ethics is the third of the three main traditions of ethical discourse in Western culture. Areteology is the fancy name, from the Greek words for the study of (*logos*) excellence or virtue (*aretē*). Areteology focuses more on being than doing, emphasizes attitudes rather than actions, and takes character to be more basic than conduct. Virtue ethics names the tradition of ethical reflection prominent in the ancient Greco-Roman world and also in the Bible. So those registering a minority report against the modern hegemony of deontology and teleology are tapping into a well-established tradition, eclipsed only in the last few centuries by these other two approaches.

The most influential scholar to argue in recent years that virtue ethics must be reclaimed is Alasdair MacIntyre. First published in 1981, his book *After Virtue* is one of the most articulate and insightful discussions of ethical theory in its generation.[18] It has proven to be of immense importance and influence in moral philosophy and in Christian ethics. MacIntyre shows how virtue ethics was eclipsed in the history of Western thought and argues cogently for why it should be retrieved and revived. This is not the place to restate those arguments. Suffice it to say that the era in which deontology and teleology were seen as the only options available is now (thankfully) long gone.

One is tempted to view these three approaches to ethics as mutually exclusive; however, there is no good reason to do so. For example, philosopher Philip Cafaro states, "I take deontology and virtue ethics to be the two halves of a complete ethics, rather than competing, comprehensive ethical theories. The one describes and grounds our duties toward others, the other describes and explains our own possibilities for self-development and personal excellence."[19] Writing about climate change ethics, Tim Hayward argues for an approach that incorporates all three ethical traditions—rights, consequences, and virtues. In his discussion of "ecological citizenship," he insists that "a focus on the virtues—as a complement to ethics of duty, rights, or utility, and proposals such as carbon allowances, or allowances even against a wider range of ecological services—would seem to be a necessary factor in thinking about what individuals should do."[20] And in his introductory text on environmental ethics, Ronald Sandler outlines all three approaches when discussing normative theories and suggests that "perhaps the 'right' deontological view, consequentialist view, and virtue ethics view will converge on similar values, rules, and principles as they are continually revised and improved in response to new information and challenges from each other."[21]

One masterful combination of all three perspectives in ethics is evident in the work of Lewis Smedes.[22] Without dumbing down the nuances or avoiding the points of tension, Smedes skillfully threads into a single cloth all three of the main Western ethical traditions: deontology, teleology, and areteology. His process of ethical decision making embraces all three approaches in its four basic parts: face the facts, respect the rules, consider the consequences, and be responsible. Bruce Birch and Larry Rasmussen do something similar in their approach to Christian ethics. They view character formation (virtues) and decision making (duties and consequences) as complementary parts of a single ethic.[23] Similarly, my beloved Hope College colleague Allen Verhey long argued that conduct and character must be combined in doing Christian ethics.[24] More examples could be cited, but the point is clear: these three ways of doing ethics need not be viewed as mutually exclusive.

In my view, the three traditions of doing ethics can and should be seen as complementary. Conduct (habits over time) shapes character (virtues and vices), and character (dispositions to act) informs conduct (for better and worse). Indeed, virtues cannot be conceived except by reference to rules about what actions are morally permissible, and rules are powerless without the dispositions to act morally. Put succinctly: duties are impotent without moral virtues, consequences are blind without moral rules, and virtues are unfocused without moral goods. Deontology, teleology, and areteology are mutually interdependent. An adequate ethic must include all three.

This squares with the Christian tradition. For most Christian ethicists (and most Christians), an adequate Christian ethic includes duties (the Ten Commandments, Jesus's greatest commandment), goods (shalom, the kingdom of God), and virtues (Jesus's beatitudes, Paul's fruit of the Spirit). Christians have a commonly agreed-on moral exemplar in Jesus and a clearly envisioned *summum bonum* or greatest good: shalom (Old Testament), the love of God and love of neighbor (Gospels), the reconciliation of all things (the apostle Paul).

Thus duties and rights are in the service of a *telos* or goal that involves the formation of virtuous character. Paraphrasing Smedes's four-part process of ethical decision making: we must follow certain moral rules while simultaneously paying attention to the consequences of our actions; or alternately, we must make decisions according to the anticipated consequences while simultaneously following the moral rules. Each is necessary but not sufficient. And while following the rules and considering the consequences, we must each be responsible as a person of moral character. We must ask ourselves whether we have used discernment (wisdom), whether the action we intend supports our commitments (integrity), whether we are willing to go public (courage).[25]

In sum, ethics in our time and place is complicated. There are different moral traditions and ways of thinking about what ethics is. Deontology and utilitarianism have dominated ethical theory in the recent past, leaving areteology in the shadows. It is time, however, for us to retrieve the virtue ethics tradition. The most fundamental question is not "What are my duties?" or "What would be the consequences?" but "What kind of person should I be?" While obligations and consequences are important in ethics, virtues are even more central. In the chapters that follow, I develop an ecological ethic that emphasizes the virtues, drawing extensively on the Christian tradition. But first we need more on the nature of the virtues. What exactly is a virtue?

Virtue and the Virtues

One significant reason for giving primacy to virtues and thus adopting a virtue-based approach to ethics is quite simple: what we do depends on who we are. As indicated previously, doing is contingent on being. Our actions arise from our desires and affections, our dispositions and inclinations—in short, our character. James K. A. Smith captures this point well: "Much of our action is not the fruit of conscious deliberation; instead, much of what we do grows out of our passional orientation to the world—affected by all the ways we've been primed to perceive the world. In short, our action emerges from how we *imagine* the world. What we do is driven by who we are, by the kind of person we have become."[26] What we do is driven by who we are. And who we are—the kind of person we have become—is best described by traits of character such as virtues and vices. This approach implies a critique of much contemporary ethics as too intellectual, too focused on rational principles and conscious deliberation. Such ethical theory has failed to notice or understand the pre-reflective and preconscious basis of (moral) action. While rational reflection is important, the simple fact is that most of our actions are pre-reflective, a result of having an intuitive, embodied feel for the world—a kinesthetic way of being in the world shaped over time by habits and routines.[27]

Furthermore, the kind of person we have become depends on the stories with which we identify. We are, to use the words of Jonathan Gottschall, "the storytelling animal."[28] What does this mean? Barbara Kingsolver puts it well: "Storytelling is as old as our need to remember where the water is, where the best food grows, where we find our courage to hunt." Contrary to what many believe, stories are useful beyond mere entertainment. Indeed, stories are, according to Kingsolver, "as persistent as our desire to teach our children how to live in this place that we have known longer than they have."[29] Narratives engage that part of us that most shapes our desires—namely, the imagination. Stories, including "legends, myths, plays, novels, and films," best speak to this imaginative core of our being because they paint a "more affective, sensible, even aesthetic *picture*" than do lectures or textbooks.[30] As many biblical commentators have remarked, Jesus was on to something in using parables for the instruction of his followers.

As an example, imagine two young students introduced to issues of ecological degradation.[31] John is given a pamphlet about deforestation in the Amazon.

He reads about the importance of these rain forests to global environmental health, looks through the predictions, and even memorizes statistics. Meanwhile, Joanna is given Dr. Seuss's *The Lorax*. She may not be able to spout off statistics, but she understands the impacts of human greed on the voiceless. The story gives her a clear sense that some things matter beyond their usefulness or economic value—that there is much to lose by "biggering and biggering" our businesses. Both of these students are introduced to the same topic, though in critically different ways. Both methods have value, and taken together they provide a student with a more thorough understanding of the matter. But taken alone, most of us would wager that Joanna is more likely to "speak for the trees."[32]

Stories shape our character, and all human action is shaped in terms of narratively formed character. Smith again articulates well the central insight: "And that shaping of our character is, to a great extent, the effect of stories that have captivated us, that have sunk into our bones—stories that 'picture' what we think life is about, what constitutes 'the good life.' We live *into* the stories we've absorbed; we become characters in the drama that has captivated us."[33] In the succinct words of MacIntyre, "I can only answer the question 'What am I to do?' if I can answer the prior question 'Of what story or stories do I find myself a part?'"[34] In other words, a founding story is not a husk that can be shucked to get to the kernel inside but is indispensable to knowing who we are. As Stanley Hauerwas reminds us, "We do not tell stories simply because they provide us a more colorful way to say what can be said in a different way, but because there is no other way we can articulate the richness of intentional activity—that is, behavior that is purposeful but not necessary."[35] There is, in short, a "narrative quality" to human action.[36]

So a virtue is a narratively formed praiseworthy character trait. But we find ourselves living in a world of competing narratives—competing understandings of what virtuous living looks like. For example, one strand of folk wisdom states that "cleanliness is next to godliness." But what is cleanliness? That depends on what narrative most profoundly shapes that home. An American family shaped by the 1950s' medically inspired preoccupation with germs and sanitation will have a different idea of cleanliness than a family in Belize in 2015. Indeed, Jesus found himself in a lot of trouble over the matter of cleanliness because he in some ways understood the story of the Jewish covenant differently from the Pharisees. We may agree that it is good to be clean, but the stories we indwell give us different understandings of what that actually means.[37]

In addition, virtues are shaped by practices. As Stanley Hauerwas and David Burrell put it, "In allowing ourselves to adopt and be adopted by a particular story, we are in fact assuming a set of practices that will shape the ways we relate to our world and destiny."[38] With the indwelling of a particular story comes a particular set of practices—of communal, embodied rhythms and routines—that shape and mold our dispositions. In other words, the meta-narratives or big stories we hear and with which we identify—of manifest destiny, of material prosperity, of an outrageous carpenter from Nazareth— shape our character by enlisting us to engage in certain practices—reciting the Pledge of Allegiance, shopping at the mall, saying the Lord's Prayer. These practices shape the kind of person we become—our virtues and vices—and hence the actions we engage in.

And sometimes we see practices embodied in a person who displays for us what a life of virtue concretely looks like—for example, a well-known saint such as Mother Teresa or a well-loved if little known relative such as Uncle Peter. Such people are models of virtue who inspire us to live such lives ourselves. So we alter our own life narratives by cultivating the virtues of our most admired exemplars. When it comes to matters ecological, Aldo Leopold, Henry David Thoreau, and Rachel Carson are some of the most commonly mentioned exemplars of an ecological virtue ethic.[39]

So stories and practices and exemplars shape character. Furthermore, our practices over time color the way we see ourselves and the world. There is a connection between virtue and vision. As Gilbert Meilander says, "What duties we perceive—and even what dilemmas—may depend upon what virtues shape our vision of the world."[40] We see the world differently, depending on how we have been formed by the virtues that constitute our character. C. S. Lewis captures this point well in *The Magician's Nephew*, book 6 of The Chronicles of Narnia. The creation of Narnia by Aslan looks and feels very different for wicked Uncle Andrew than it does for the children. While the children find Narnia alluring and understand the words spoken by the animals, Uncle Andrew shrinks back in fear and hears only barking and howling. Because of his evil character, he is blind to what the children see and misconstrues both Aslan the creator and what is created. As the narrator comments, "For what you see and hear depends a good deal on where you are standing; it also depends on what sort of person you are."[41] What you see and hear depends on your character.

In summary, a virtue is a story-shaped, praiseworthy character trait formed by practices over time that disposes us to act in certain ways. It is a habitual disposition to act with excellence, molded by the narratives we identify with and the exemplars we follow. By soaking in the stories of particular communities, engaging in their practices, and looking to their role models, we know what is truly good and how to live well.

Environmental Virtue Ethics and Its Critics

In recent years, significant work has been done in the field of environmental virtue ethics.[42] Some date the beginning to the 1983 publication of Thomas Hill's pivotal essay, "Ideals of Human Excellence and Preserving Natural Environments,"[43] mentioned at the beginning of the introduction. In this essay Hill describes a new neighbor who destroys his bushes and trees and paves over his flourishing yard with asphalt. Hill asks: What sort of person would do a thing like that? His answer: only someone whose character is malformed, someone who lacks the proper virtues. Hill argues that such a focus on character is sorely needed in contemporary environmental ethics, and he proposes proper humility as one such virtue.[44]

With subsequent work by Philip Cafaro, Geoffrey Frasz, Ronald Sandler, and Bill Shaw (to name only a few of the principal contributors), the field of environmental virtue ethics is becoming well established. Evidence for this claim includes the publication of anthologies such as *Environmental Virtue Ethics*, monographs such as *Character and Environment: A Virtue-Oriented Approach to Environmental Ethics*, and environmental ethics textbooks such as *Environmental Ethics: Theory in Practice*,[45] which includes informed and robust sections on environmental virtue ethics. One additional sign that the field has developed its own identity is that it now has its own acronym—EVE.[46]

One of the most insightful contributions to EVE is by Philip Cafaro. In his catalog of environmental virtues, Cafaro lists care, patience, persistence, self-control, humility, respect, and self-restraint.[47] Along with these moral virtues, Cafaro lists intellectual virtues such as attentiveness and wonder, aesthetic virtues such as appreciation and creativity, physical virtues such as stamina and hardiness, and what he calls "overarching virtues" such as wisdom and humility. Cafaro approaches environmental virtue ethics by focusing on human excellence and flourishing. He identifies Henry David Thoreau, Aldo Leopold, and Rachel Carson not only as moral role models but also as virtue ethicists who describe what human flourishing means for the natural world. Among these luminaries, Cafaro finds common themes such as appreciation of the wild and the embodiment of virtues, including humility and wisdom.[48]

One of the most significant contributions to date is by Ronald Sandler in his book *Character and Environment: A Virtue-Oriented Approach to Environmental Ethics*. Sandler offers a comprehensive theory of environmental virtue ethics. He sets forth reasons for what makes a character trait an environmental virtue, presents his vision of human and nonhuman flourishing, argues for why some nonhuman organisms and the land itself ought to be included in what counts morally, describes how virtues inform moral decision making, and makes a case for why his pluralistic virtue-centered approach to environmental ethics meets various criteria of adequacy, rebutting criticisms along the way. Finally, as if that were not enough, Sandler applies his environmental virtue ethic to the issue of genetically modified crops, thereby demonstrating its ability to provide insight into this controversial topic.

This is not the place to offer a full analysis of Sandler's book. Let me merely give you a taste of its depth and breadth by summarizing his typology of environmental virtues. There are six categories, each with five virtues. The *virtues of sustainability* are temperance, frugality, farsightedness, attunement, and humility. These character traits dispose us to promote and maintain over time certain kinds of goods such as clean air and safe water. The *virtues of environmental activism* are cooperativeness, perseverance, commitment, optimism, and creativity. These character traits incline us to advocate in the social and political world for pollution regulations and land protections. The *virtues of communion with nature* are wonder, openness, aesthetic sensibility, attentiveness, and love. These character traits enable us to enjoy certain natural goods such as the beauty of a sunset or the call of a songbird. The *virtues of environmental stewardship* are benevolence, loyalty, justice, honesty, and diligence. These enable us to appreciate places in the natural world and motivate us to maintain such places, whether local greenways or national parks. The *virtues of respect for nature* are care, compassion, restitutive justice, nonmaleficence, and ecological sensitivity. These character traits are conducive to promoting the good of living things, whether a famous endangered species or an individual's much-loved pet. Finally, the *land virtues* are love, considerateness, attunement, ecological sensitivity, and gratitude. These are character traits that make us into good citizens of what Aldo Leopold called the land community.

Sandler has put forward a thought-provoking environmental virtue ethic. Well informed and creative, it is currently the most comprehensive description of such an ethic. Whatever its shortcomings, there is much we can learn from it.[49]

There are a number of criticisms of virtue ethics in general and environmental virtue ethics in particular.[50] One common complaint is that "virtue ethics decision-making resources are not robust enough to generate specific guidance in concrete cases."[51] More precisely, some argue that virtue ethics "does not give us an algorithm that can lead to certainty in our ethical decisions"; thus, virtue ethics "may prove unnerving to people who have counted on their religious or secular ethics to give them principles that will lead to feelings of certainty that one's actions are right."[52] In other words, virtue ethics can tell us what kind of person we ought to be, but it cannot tell us enough about what we should do in specific situations.

But what ethical perspective actually provides an algorithm that leads to certainty in ethical decision making? As C. D. Meyers avows, "There are no simple procedures that we can robotically apply to a situation that will tell us what is right and wrong." None of the theories (deontology, teleology, areteology) can deliver on this unrealistic expectation. But what about the more modest goal of specific guidance in concrete circumstances? The critics assume that virtues have little to offer here, but that is simply not the case. Meyers, again, puts it well: "Resolving difficult moral dilemmas requires common sense, intuition, cumulated life experiences, and sensitivity. Highly virtuous persons will have keener moral perception and thus be better able to discern the right course in difficult cases."[53] In other words, paraphrasing Aristotle, being a person of virtue will help you do the right thing, at the right time, in the right way, to the right extent. There is no inherent conflict between seeking guidance in moral decision making in particular situations and adopting a virtue ethic. Indeed, as Jason Kawall demonstrates, it is possible to provide "rules of thumb" for meeting the epistemic demands of environmental virtue.[54] In sum, a virtue ethic can be helpful in the process of making difficult decisions. This first criticism is misplaced.

Another criticism is that there is no adequate way to provide the kind of agreed-on specifications of the virtues that environmental virtue ethics theory requires. As Sandler puts it, "What is distinctive about virtue ethics is that the normative content is provided by the virtues and vices." Thus, "it is through articulating what the virtues and vices are that the theory generates an account of what sort of people we ought to be and what we ought to do in concrete situations."[55] But, the critic argues, there must be some more or less universally accepted set of virtues and agreed-on definitions of these virtues. And yet different cultures espouse different moral virtues. Indeed, most of us need look no further than our own culture to find competing worldviews with different ethical norms and moral virtues. So the goal of having a common understanding crashes on the rocks of moral plurality, and hence virtue ethics is impossible.

There is no doubt that plurality (and pluralism) in ethics is a significant issue.[56] However, it is not clear that this hamstrings all efforts to articulate an environmental virtue ethic. As Sandler correctly notes, "It is fallacy to infer from the fact of disagreement to the conclusion that no view is more justified than another." Just because people disagree does not mean every view is equally justified or that no moral claim is warranted. "It is possible," as Sandler argues, "to evaluate different specifications of virtue based on the quality of the empirical information and reasoning in support of them, as well as their consistency with other ethical beliefs."[57] In other words, cultural or ethical differences do not necessarily entail the kind of epistemic or moral relativism in which anything goes. There are criteria, based on a shared view of what sort of people we ought to be, that allow us to specify certain virtues though we must acknowledge that these criteria (and our views of moral exemplars) are not worldview-independent—that is, somehow untouched by the pre-theoretical beliefs and underlying narratives that form us. Our views on the virtues are inevitably shaped by a particular place and time.[58]

A third criticism is that virtue ethics is anthropocentric. With its focus on humans becoming virtuous, virtue ethics pays insufficient attention to the natural world. In the words of Holmes Rolston III:

> Sometimes we ought to consider worth beyond that within our selves. It would be better, in addition to our preferences, our self-development, our self-interest, our concern, to be virtuous, to know the full truth of the human obligation— to have the best reasons, as well as the good ones. If one insists on putting it this way—emphasizing a paradox in responsibility—concern for nonhumans can ennoble humans. . . . Noblesse oblige. But those who act responsibly with concern for their nobility miss the mark. The real concern is for the other benefited. Genuine concern for nonhumans could humanize our race all the more.
>
> That is what the argument about environmental virtue ethics seems to be trying to say, but if taken as the whole truth, it confuses a desirable result with the primary locus of value. A naturalistic account values species and speciation intrinsically, not as resources or as a means to human virtues.[59]

With virtue ethics, Rolston warns, "we seem to make love of nature tributary to self-love. But when we frame nature up in terms of what it can contribute to our virtue, this puts nature in the wrong reference frame."[60] Insisting on the objective value of the other-than-human world, Rolston argues that "the wild does not become valuable if and when it results in something valuable for me. It is valuable for what it is, whether I am around or not."[61] Insofar as environmental virtue ethics sees the natural world merely as a means to the end of human virtue formation, it remains too anthropocentric and thus is not truly an environmental ethic.

While this criticism might apply to some forms of environmental virtue ethics (e.g., a eudaemonistic virtue ethic that defines flourishing only in terms of the human person), it certainly does not apply to those forms of environmental virtue ethics that define flourishing more broadly, such as Sandler's inclusion of the flourishing of nonhuman creatures and the land. One distinguishing mark of most environmental virtue ethics is the expansion of the vision of flourishing to include much more than human flourishing. Christians tutored by Scripture should shout a loud "Amen" to this move. The last chapters of the book of Job are only one of many places in the Bible where an anthropocentric ethic is blown to smithereens. Indeed, Job teaches us that deep engagement with God's good earth is itself an education in virtue.[62] In sum, there is nothing inherently anthropocentric about environmental virtue ethics. Thus this criticism is not valid.

A fourth concern is that virtue ethics fails to take seriously the sociopolitical systems in which we find ourselves. To change the unjust systems in which we live, it is argued, we need to focus on rights and duties and thus some form of deontology. For example, in her summary of environmental virtue theory, Marilyn Holly wonders "what sort of political virtue theory would implement environmental Virtue Theory in sound public policy and legislation about protecting the environment" given that "at present environmental Virtue Theory and general Virtue Theory . . . do not have a political virtue theory to go with them."[63] In other words, virtue ethics fails to ask what virtues are needed for the *polis*—what dispositions are necessary to live together in communities. In a similar vein, Brian Treanor observes that "despite philosophical precedent and the recent interest of some virtue ethicists, the connection between the individual and the community remains underappreciated."[64] In other words, environmental virtue ethics seems unconcerned about the larger social and political systems that must be engaged for the flourishing of all creatures to be advanced.

This criticism, however, overlooks a long tradition of virtue ethics that criticizes and attempts to reform our sociopolitical systems. The practice of certain virtues by people who embody them has challenged the oppressive empires of the world and has had a positive impact on our political life (the life of the *polis* or city-state). For example, self-control (otherwise known as temperance) is typically considered a personal virtue, since its immediate goal is the flourishing of a particular person, but self-controlled people almost always benefit their communities (human and nonhuman) by consuming no more than what they need. They have a positive effect on the common good of the *polis*. Those who exemplify the virtue of justice—whether Jeremiah or Jesus, Mahatma Gandhi or Martin Luther King Jr.—call into question oppressive sociopolitical systems.

Is justice a personal or a public virtue? That distinction is not helpful. So-called personal virtues benefit the public, and so-called public virtues benefit individual people. While our thinking about virtues often pigeonholes virtues as private, any dichotomy between private (or personal) and public ethics must be rejected, since such dualisms assume a kind of individualism that simply does not reflect reality.[65] As Treanor affirms, "There is no sharp line distinguishing public virtue from personal virtue; because we are social beings, all virtues have both personal and public effects."[66] In short, it is not the case that virtue ethics cannot take seriously sociopolitical systems. That those who advocate environmental virtue ethics have not made these connections clearer should serve as a challenge for us to do better in the future.

In sum, none of these criticisms are cogent. Virtues actually help in moral decision making. It is possible to specify virtues on the basis of a shared vision of the good. Virtue ethics is not necessarily anthropocentric. The virtues (and virtue ethics) have a crucial role to play in challenging and reshaping unjust political systems. While these criticisms may not be convincing, those of us who do environmental virtue ethics still have much to learn. One resource is the Christian faith. To that we now turn.[67]

Christian Ecological Virtue Ethics

Before I describe my approach to ecological virtue ethics, I offer, as promised, a word on terminology. Many people ask why I use the adjective *ecological* rather than the more commonly used term *environmental* when speaking of this kind of ethics. In brief, I am persuaded by Wendell Berry, among others, that the terms *environment* and *environmental* ought to be abandoned. In Berry's insightful and persuasive words:

> The idea that we live in something called "the environment," for instance, is utterly preposterous. This word came into use because of the pretentiousness of learned experts who were embarrassed by the religious associations of "Creation" and who thought "world" too mundane. But "environmental" means that which surrounds or encircles us; it means a world separate from ourselves, outside us. The real state of things, of course, is far more complex and intimate and interesting than that. The world that environs us, that is around us, is also within us. We are made of it; we eat, drink, and breathe it; it is bone of our bone and flesh of our flesh. It is also Creation, a holy mystery, made for and to some extent by creatures, some but by no means all of whom are humans. . . . None of this intimacy and responsibility is conveyed by the word *environment*.[68]

In short, the words *environment* and *environmental* fail to accurately describe the world in which we live. In fact, they distort our understanding of the world and thus contribute to the all-too-common belief that we humans are separate from the rest of the natural world. The adjective *ecological*, in contrast, is from the word *ecology*, which in Greek means the study (*logos*) of the house or home (*oikos*). The etymology of the word *ecological* points to the very real yet often unacknowledged fact that this earth is our home. Furthermore, the word *ecological* reminds us of the science of ecology, which is the study of the relationships between living organisms and the complex systems that connect them. In sum, in contrast to the term *environmental*, the term *ecological* reminds us of the interconnectedness of the world in which we live. It firmly tethers our minds to the unimpeachable fact of our inescapable embeddedness in this world.

In chapter 6 of my book *For the Beauty of the Earth*, I describe a set of fourteen ecological virtues.[69] My method there was, first, to read the biblical story with care. From that reading, certain theological motifs emerged, and from those motifs, I derived ethical principles and practical moral maxims. From these reflections, I then identified a set of virtues: respect, receptivity, self-restraint, frugality, humility, honesty, wisdom, hope, patience, serenity, benevolence, love, justice, and courage. I argued that these are crucial dispositions if we are to care properly for the world in which we live. Over the years, many readers (and reviewers) commented that this chapter was both unique and helpful. So the book you are now reading is in some ways a sequel, written in response to readers who wanted more on ecological virtue ethics.

My approach in this book is somewhat different from that of *For the Beauty of the Earth*. In each of the subsequent chapters here, I begin with a story that illustrates in some way the importance of an ecological virtue. I then provide some background on each of the virtues of that chapter: wonder and humility, self-control and wisdom, justice and love, courage and hope. Drawing on the wisdom of many thoughtful writers—scholars and activists, historians and scientists, poets and novelists—my aim is to gain greater clarity about what these virtues are. In the middle of each chapter, I turn to the Bible and the history of the church—the two main sources for those who do Christian theology and ethics. No reputable Christian approach to ethics of any sort can or should ignore Scripture or tradition. I do not assume that you, dear reader, have any prior knowledge of Christianity or that you share my own faith commitment. But it is important to acknowledge honestly that there is no ethic from nowhere. Every ethic is rooted in a particular religious or philosophical perspective of some sort. I wish to be clear about mine. More importantly, I wholeheartedly believe that the faith tradition of which I am a part has much to offer the field of ethics.

With all this background, I then describe the virtues and explain what makes the virtues in question ecological virtues. While similar in many ways to the virtues as usually conceived (e.g., as naming a particular habitual disposition to act excellently), the virtues I describe here are different in some way that warrants using the term *ecological virtue*. I employ various arguments. In the case of love, it is the expanded scope of moral concern, beyond an anthropocentric ethic that includes only humans, that calls for the use of the adjective *ecological*.[70] In other words, what makes a virtue an ecological virtue is its expanded focus on nonhuman creatures such as sandhill cranes or on particular places such as the greater Yellowstone ecosystem. Other ecological virtues, such as humility and justice, have a distinct meaning as ecological virtues because what is required for human flourishing is reconceived to include the flourishing of more than just humans.[71] In other words, these virtues are ecological virtues because of the ecologically informed vision of what traits make a person an excellent human being, for example, courage as a kind of endurance. Finally, virtues such as self-control and wonder are ecological virtues because they capture the character traits of moral role models such as Henry David Thoreau and Rachel Carson.[72] In other words, what makes these virtues ecological virtues is that they describe exemplary earthkeepers. In each of these cases, the adjective *ecological* helps distinguish these virtues from those to which we usually refer.

The penultimate section of each chapter describes people who embody these virtues. What do these ecological virtues look like embodied in real life? Who are some of the moral exemplars, famous or little known? Given the importance of role models in virtue formation, and of the practices that form such people, this is a vital part of any ecological virtue ethic. Finally, given the role of narrative in shaping our character, each chapter ends as it begins, with a story.

A Student, Her Grandparents, and a Poem

She sat in the front row, hard to miss. Almost always the first to poke her hand in the air to ask a question, she was a stereotypical extrovert. Her papers gave evidence that my questions were hitting home. It was clear she had done all the reading, giving careful thought to my "questions to ponder," and was diving deeply into the issues raised in class. The class was Earth and Ethics, an introductory religion course at Hope College.

With thirty-five mostly first-year undergraduates in the room, this course introduced the study of religion and ethics through the lens of environmental issues. It had a heavy dose of environmental science up front, with students learning basic ecology and discovering more about their own campus ecology by doing scavenger hunts (in groups of four outside of class) to find, among other things, the residence hall that uses geothermal heating and cooling, the bicycle repair station, and the place where the compost goes. This was followed by an introduction to the study of worldviews, including the exploration of different maps of the world (Upside Down, Peters Projection, New Zealand at the center) and an analysis of the contemporary American worldview. The final weeks of this half-semester course involved the reading and discussion of texts from four religions (Judaism, Islam, Buddhism, and Christianity), with a focus on their views of the natural world and our relationship to it. It was a popular course.

According to Alyssa, this was the first time she had received any formal instruction in ethics. Like most of her college-age friends, she had gut-level feelings and some inchoate thoughts about what was right and wrong, but she was new to ethics and not sure what was at stake. Nothing in her previous education had introduced her to religion and the intersection of "earth" and "ethics." When I reminded Alyssa that one of the purposes of education is to expand the frontiers of your knowledge, she laughed. But as the course progressed, it was clear she had taken a keen interest in the subject matter.

When we got to the section on ecological virtues, Alyssa became even more entranced by the subject matter. She intuitively understood some of the virtues, such as courage and honesty, but others, such as benevolence and frugality, were new to her (at least in name). She realized she misunderstood others: for example, why humility has two vices (hubris and self-deprecation) and not just one. She debated with me in and out of class about whether apathy or malice was the contrary to love, and she asked probing questions about whether justice, wisdom, benevolence, and love really do have only one corresponding vice.

Alyssa chose to write her worldview response paper on the topic of "the good life." This assignment asked the student to define the life most worth living by describing the character traits of someone deemed to be a good person—someone who exhibits the good life (all in no more than three pages!). Alyssa had no problem thinking of someone who fit the bill. Her maternal grandparents quickly came to mind as exemplars of the good life. Oppa and Omma, as she affectionately called them, lived nearby and had regularly taken care of her when she was young and her parents went through an ugly divorce. They were now in their eighties. Grandma was in ill health and needed daily care, which Grandpa tirelessly and joyfully gave. Their selflessness and loving concern for each other, as well as for their children and grandchildren, was as clear as a bell.

With insight and passion, Alyssa eloquently wrote about the virtues she saw embodied in their common life. Marriage-saving virtues such as respect and humility. Community-building virtues such as courage and justice. Life-essential virtues such as love and hope. And ecological virtues such as frugality and simplicity. Her paper was a joy to read. Indeed, it was itself an expression of gratitude—a telling mark of a good person living a good life. Like Andre, Alyssa, too, ended her paper with a poem, by (you guessed it) Wendell Berry.[73]

> Whatever is foreseen in joy
> Must be lived out from day to day,
> Vision held open in the dark
> By our ten thousand days of work.
> Harvest will fill the barn; for that
> The hand must ache, the face must sweat.
>
> And yet no leaf or grain is filled
> By work of ours; the field is tilled
> And left to grace. That we may reap,
> Great work is done while we're asleep.
>
> When we work well, a Sabbath mood
> Rests on our day, and finds it good.

2

Living with Amazement and Modesty

Wonder and Humility

What is the value of preserving and strengthening this sense of awe and wonder, this recognition of something beyond the boundaries of human existence? Is the exploration of the natural world just a pleasant way to pass the golden hours of childhood or is there something deeper?

Rachel Carson[1]

Humility trains us in the art of being creatures. It does so by teaching us to be honest about our need, grateful for the gifts of others, and faithful in the service of healing the many memberships of creation.

Norman Wirzba[2]

The Night Sky

We had been on the road for twelve hours. On a hot August day, I and my co-leader Heidi and ten high-school students had packed ourselves and eight days' worth of personal gear into the fifteen-passenger van. And now, traveling north from Chicago, we were on our last leg, winding our way from Ely, Minnesota, east on Fernberg Road to the outfitters' place on Moose Lake. As we turned from the pavement onto a one-lane dirt road, I rolled down the driver's window, felt the cool night breeze on my skin, and took a deep, pine-scented breath that smelled fresh and clean. After a mile or so, we finally came to a stop in the parking lot of Canadian Border Outfitters. I opened the door, stumbled out of the van, and looked up.

To this day, decades later, in my mind's eye I can see that night sky. I had never before seen so many stars—and so brightly shining. The stars were beyond counting and so brilliant it seemed I could reach up and touch them. On this cool, crystal-clear night, with no light pollution for miles and miles, the stars evoked wonder.[3] Everyone in that trusty old van—even the teenage guys who were well practiced in "being cool" and not expressing emotion—had the same reaction: slack-jawed awe and an immediate and involuntary "Aaah." Emblazoned in my memory is that night, the first of many over the years that I would spend paddling and camping in the Boundary Waters Canoe Area Wilderness in northeastern Minnesota.

With this sense of amazement came a sense of my smallness. I was both astonished and humbled, struck by wonder and overcome with humility. In the vast expanse of space, with those lights in the sky literally taking me back in time, I felt like an insignificant nothing—a dot in some pointillist painting. A line from Psalm 8 popped into my mind: "What are human beings that you are mindful of them?" (v. 4). Indeed, what are we humans in the vast expanse of God's mind-boggling universe? We are humble humans from the humus[4] on a tiny planet in one solar system among many in a galaxy of enormous size in a universe that is literally beyond our imagination. Wonder and humility—conjured by this expanse of the heavens on a clear summer night.

Later that same trip we were treated to an amazing display of the aurora borealis—the northern lights. Visible on the northwest horizon, this atmospheric event educed yet more wonder as we watched the colors dance and whirl and play. In the words of Sigurd Olson, the bard of the Boundary Waters:

> The lights of the aurora moved and shifted over the horizon. Sometimes there were shafts of yellow tinged with green, then masses of evanescence that moved from east to west and back again. Great streamers of bluish white zigzagged like a tremendous trembling curtain from one end of the sky to the other. Streaks of yellow and orange and red shimmered along the flowing borders. Never for a moment were they still, fading until they were almost completely gone, only to dance forth again in renewed splendor with infinite combinations and startling patterns of design.[5]

Spellbinding these northern lights were, an evocation of wonder. And every night on that canoe trip we would look to the north in search of another such celestial illumination. Already our appetite was whetted for more.

Wonderings about Wonder

When it comes to literature on wonder and the natural world, the first name that comes to mind for many people is Rachel Carson. Though best known for her last and most famous book, *Silent Spring*,[6] Carson wrote many other books, including *The Sense of Wonder*.[7] Originally published under the title *Help Your Child to Wonder*, this slim volume is, as the original title suggests, designed to help parents foster wonder among their children. Reflecting on her interactions with her nephew, Carson comments:

> A child's world is fresh and new and beautiful, full of wonder and excitement. It is our misfortune that for most of us that clear-eyed vision, that true instinct for what is beautiful and awe-inspiring, is dimmed and even lost before we reach adulthood. If I had influence with the good fairy who is supposed to preside over the christening of all children, I should ask that her gift to each child in the world be a sense of wonder so indestructible that it would last throughout life, as an unfailing antidote against the boredom and disenchantments of later years, the sterile preoccupation with things that are artificial, the alienation from the sources of strength.[8]

So wonder is the antidote to boredom and disenchantment. Carson goes on to observe:

> I sincerely believe that for the child, and for the parent seeking to guide him, it is not half so important to *know* as to *feel*. If facts are seeds that later produce knowledge and wisdom, then the emotions and the impressions of the senses are the fertile soil in which the seeds must grow. . . . Once the emotions have been aroused—a sense of the beautiful, the excitement of the new and the unknown, a feeling of sympathy, pity, admiration, or love—then we wish for knowledge about the object of our emotional response.[9]

Wonder has to do with a sense of the beautiful, an excitement for the novel and unknown, a feeling of sympathy and admiration and even love for the object of one's attention.

Without using the language of virtue, Rachel Carson nevertheless assumes that wonder is a virtue. For example, she observes that "exploring nature with your child is largely a matter of becoming receptive to what lies around you. It is learning again to use your eyes, ears, nostrils and finger tips, opening up the disused channels of sensory impression."[10] How do we become more receptive? How do we learn again to open up our senses? Carson offers specific advice on how to proceed. She notes how a magnifying glass can bring a new world into sight, how powerful the sense of smell is in evoking long-lost memories, and how touch is a potent if little-used sense. Carson more than hints at the need to cultivate our abilities to perceive the world around us when, for example, she says, "Hearing can be a source of even more exquisite pleasure but it requires conscious cultivation."[11] "Conscious cultivation" is the language of virtue.

Annie Dillard also has her eye on wonder. Her award-winning book *Pilgrim at Tinker Creek* is, among other things, a treasure trove of musings on wonder. For example, after she happens upon the sight of a mockingbird making a steep vertical descent only at the last second to land upright on the grass, she writes, "Beauty and grace are performed whether or not we will or sense them. The least we can do is try to be there."[12] She remarks, "I'm always on the lookout for antlion traps in sandy soil, monarch pupae near milkweed, skipper larvae in locust leaves." Understanding one's surroundings is "a matter of keeping eyes open,"[13] of taking care to notice small things like coneflowers and field mice.

But there's more to it: Dillard makes a concerted effort not just to see but to alter the way she sees. "I see what I expect," she muses ruefully.[14] So she attempts to open her eyes to all the possibilities of beauty and intricacy around her. Such attentiveness is necessary to develop the capacity for wonder. Trying to be there with eyes open and always being on the lookout are Dillard's shorthand ways of speaking of wonder as a virtue. Wonder requires study and attentiveness and diligence. To develop the capacity for wonder requires a lifetime of dedication.[15] The ability to see and be amazed by features of the natural world requires a disposition developed over time by attention and practice.[16]

So what exactly is wonder? *Wonder*, as a noun, is anything that causes astonishment. A wonder is some event or place or thing that evokes amazement. "It's a wonder you weren't killed," we may say after a miraculous escape from a dangerous automobile accident. "Iguazú Falls is one of the wonders of the world," we exclaim after visiting this spectacular series of waterfalls on the border of Paraguay and Brazil. As a verb, *wonder* denotes a state of amazement or astonishment evoked by that which is beyond what we expect or think possible, as in "She wondered at the virtuosity of the musicians," or "He marveled at how effortlessly the dolphins swam and frolicked together." Wonder is rapt attention in the presence of something awe-inspiringly mysterious or novel. Hence, wonder often includes a sense of surprise: "She was amazed at how many seeds came out of that small sequoia cone."

Sam Keen posits a helpful typology of wonder.[17] There are three kinds: ontological wonder, sensational wonder, and mundane wonder. Ontological wonder is amazement that there is anything at all—that there is being (*ontos*) rather than nothingness, something rather than nothing. Sensational wonder is the astonishment felt when first gazing at some wonder of nature, such as the Grand Canyon or Iguazú Falls, or some wonder of human culture, such as the Great Pyramid of Giza or the Golden Gate Bridge. Mundane wonder is marveling at something familiar or commonplace, such as a morning frost or a baby's smile. As William Brown comments, mundane wonder is "the familiar becoming new and fresh or downright strange." In whatever form, wonder "grabs us, shakes us, puzzles us, disturbs us, or embraces us (or all of the above)"; thus, "wonder draws us in."[18]

As indicated above, contrary to what many think, wonder is a virtue. It is not an ability given at birth—what Aristotle calls a "faculty" given "by nature";[19] if it were, it would have no need for cultivation over time. While wonder may seem to be an innate capability given at birth and particularly present in children of a certain age, it must be cultivated by practice over time. It is this adult disposition of attentiveness, awareness, and openness to what is new and beyond our expectations that I refer to when speaking of wonder. In short, the virtue of wonder is the cultivated capacity to be amazed or astonished.

All these ruminations prompt further reflection on wonder as a character trait. As Lauren Madison puts it, "What kind of person is purposeful in the effort to seek and perceive these things? What kind of person is then affected by what they see?"[20] What kind of person seeks out and is able to perceive the amazing inhabitants, events, and places in this world of wonders?[21] How is such a disposition to wonder cultivated? And how is wonder related to humility? Is humility, as some suggest, a necessary condition for the cultivation of wonder? Let's turn to a discussion of wonder's close cousin.

Musings on Humility

"I'm humble and proud of it." So goes the one-liner about humility. Being humble is not something about which you can be proud, lest you fall afoul of what philosophers call a performative self-contradiction: the very claim to be proud of your humility proves that you are not, in fact, humble. But humility is slippery. For example, a kind of false humility is found in expressions such as "I am humbled to accept this award," ". . . to serve as your president," or ". . . to have scored the winning basket." The speaker may be sincere, but all too often we smell some false humility when hearing those words. And then there is the "humblebrag"—a boast disguised as a complaint—such as "I've got to stop saying yes to every interview request."[22] We seem to want to be (or at least appear) humble, but what exactly is humility?

Aristotle was not big on humility. Like most Athenian men of his status in his time, he believed pride was a virtue. Great men (and he only discussed men) who are worthy of great things can and should be proud; that is, they should exhibit justifiable self-respect and self-esteem based on the honor due them. Great men who do great things merit honor and thus justifiably exhibit pride. Indeed, pride "seems to be a sort of crown of the virtues."[23]

However, Aristotle's views are more nuanced than this. Because he believes that pride must be proportionate to accomplishments—"The proud man . . . claims what is in accordance with his merits"[24]—he acknowledges a kind of improper pride. Indeed, two vices are correlative to the virtue of pride. The person who "thinks himself worthy of great things, being unworthy of them, is vain," while the person "who thinks himself worthy of less than he is really worthy of is unduly humble."[25] Vanity is inordinate or unjustified self-esteem, while undue humility is insufficient or unjustifiably low self-image. So for Aristotle proper pride is the mean between the extremes of vanity and undue humility.

For the desert fathers and mothers in the early centuries of the church, humility was the foundation of the spiritual life. Abba Anthony, who began living in the Egyptian desert in AD 285, believed humility was the antidote to the snares of the devil.[26] Abba Poeman compared humility to the air we breathe, that without which we cannot survive: "As the breath which comes out of his nostrils, so does a man need humility and the fear of God."[27] Augustine, as is well known, found pride to be the primordial sin, and thus humility the preeminent virtue.[28] For him, humility meant having a proper sense of one's creatureliness and brokenness, and thus one's dependence on God. Benedict of Nursia devoted the longest chapter of his influential *Rule of St. Benedict* to humility—insightfully (and famously) tracing the twelve steps—and thereby laid the foundation for centuries of cenobitic monastic life centered on humility, which is, in sum, having a proper estimation of oneself before God and neighbor. We are not gods but sinful creatures. Following in Benedict's footsteps, Bernard of Clairvaux, the great twelfth-century French mystic and abbot, wrote a whole book on humility, *The Steps of Humility and Pride*, in which humility is defined as "a virtue by which man has a low opinion of himself because he knows himself well."[29]

Medieval theologian Thomas Aquinas (died 1274) very carefully took the insights of Aristotle and reframed them in light of the Christian faith. Aquinas described humility as the virtue that "temper[s] and restrain[s] the mind, lest it tend to high things immoderately." Humility prevents us from becoming conceited or self-important. According to Aquinas, a humble person "restrain[s] himself from being borne toward that which is above him," since "he must know his disproportion to that which surpasses his capacity."[30] Humility is the habitual disposition that prevents us from thinking we are worthy of something we are not. Hence, the vice of deficiency contrary to humility is pride. Those lacking humility exhibit arrogance based on an inflated and false sense of self.

But Aquinas, like Aristotle, warned against another vice—the vice of excess. In this case, a person fails to recognize and accept his or her proper worth. This is the vice Aristotle called "undue humility." This vice was clearly exemplified for me when I complimented a student of mine who had won a national championship in swimming, only to have her respond, "It's no big deal." Instead of acknowledging her accomplishment, she downplayed this significant achievement. I was expecting her to say something like, "Thank you. This is a high honor. I worked long and hard to achieve this goal, and I am grateful to my coach, my teammates, and God for the opportunity and ability to swim at this level." In short, self-deprecation is not a virtue. Humility is not to be confused with low self-worth.

In either form—arrogance or self-deprecation—the vices contrary to humility share a common preoccupation with the self. Constantly focusing on oneself, even in self-judgment, promotes the notion that the self is of the utmost importance—more important than God or the rest of creation. Lisa Gerber identifies such self-absorption as the underlying malady, regardless of whether it results in arrogance or self-criticism.[31] In contrast, the truly humble person honestly assesses his or her own abilities and acknowledges both accomplishments and limitations, but without the self-centeredness of either arrogance or self-deprecation. To gain even greater understanding of wonder and humility, let's take a brief look at the Bible.

Biblical Insight into Wonder and Humility

Many biblical texts come to mind when thinking about wonder. Let's start with the creation story in Genesis 1. A carefully crafted text designed not to provide a scientific explanation of cosmic or human origins but rather to instruct us on where we are and who we are, Genesis 1:1–2:4 evokes wonder, for those who read it rightly.

With respect to the worldview question "Where are we?," three insights are germane to our discussion of wonder and humility.[32] First, from Genesis 1 we learn that God is the Creator of all things. The merism "the heavens and the earth" (*hashamayim ve'et ha'arets*) indicates that the heavens and the earth and everything in between—all things—come to be as a result of God's creative Word and energizing Spirit. Also, verses 1–2 of chapter 1, meant to apply to all that follows, form an inclusio with verses 1–3 of chapter 2 (like bookends), again emphasizing that everything is formed by God. In addition, both the regions of the cosmos (days 1–3) and their various inhabitants (days 4–6) are created by God. None of the celestial beings—sun or moon or stars—have the power to create. And though living beings procreate, none (e.g., light, the dome, humankind) have the power that God has to create. The God described here brings all things into existence. This is a thing of wonder. And this God sustains all things. Another thing of wonder. And we humans are not God. A prompt for proper humility.

Second, the Genesis 1 creation narrative reminds us that not all agency resides with God. While God is the ultimate Creator—artistically fashioning the cosmos and bringing things into being out of nothing—God's means of creating often involves sharing power. The earth is invited to "sprout forth" (*tadshe'*) vegetation, and it does so, yielding plants and trees of every kind (Gen. 1:11–12). The waters are invited to "swarm forth" (*yishretsu*) swarms of living creatures (v. 20). The sun and moon are given the job of ruling the day and night (v. 16). And humans are given the delegated, royal responsibility of ruling (*radah*) the earth. God is not the only agent in this story. Creation has the genuine ability to act. God calls and creatures respond. This, too, ought to evoke wonder—and humility, since our actions have real consequences.

Third, Genesis 1 teaches us that creation is a cosmos. The chaotic, to be sure, exists, but the universe is a place of order and structure, purposefully and lovingly designed by God. Indeed, the universe takes shape as the chaotic waters (*tohu vabohu* and *tehom*) are bounded, and despite the ongoing vulnerability of the earth to these chaotic forces, the world remains a cosmos because of God's sustaining breath. Even the orderliness of the very form of the story, evident, for example, in repetition and symmetry, bespeaks the order of the creative process. Everything has its habitat and niche. As Bernhard Anderson states, "The wonderful order and regularity of the cosmos, in which every creature, animate and inanimate, has its assigned place and function in a marvelous whole, evoke aesthetic feelings of wonder and reverence."[33] This portrayal of cosmic fittingness evokes wonder. William Brown concludes, "There is much wonder to behold in Genesis 1. God for one: the divine collaborator at work enlisting the elements of creation to create life according to all its various 'kinds.' Creation for another: a finely tuned, life-hosting world cast as God's living temple generously endowed with the natural capacities to bear and sustain life in all its diversity. And as for human beings, we are nothing less than God's walking, talking theophanies on earth."[34]

Many of the psalms also evoke a sense of wonder about the world in which we live and the God who made and sustains it. Have you ever seen something in the natural world that gave you goose bumps, silenced you, or evoked instantaneous praise? The psalmist has. For example, consider these words from Psalm 104:

> You make springs gush forth in the valleys;
>   they flow between the hills,
> giving drink to every wild animal;
>   the wild asses quench their thirst.
> By the streams the birds of the air have their habitation;
>   they sing among the branches.
> From your lofty abode you water the mountains;
>   the earth is satisfied with the fruit of your work. (vv. 10–14)

> The trees of the LORD are watered abundantly,
>   the cedars of Lebanon that he planted.
> In them the birds build their nests;
>   the stork has its home in the fir trees.
> The high mountains are for the wild goats;
>   the rocks are a refuge for the coneys.
> You have made the moon to mark the seasons:
>   the sun knows its time for setting. (vv. 16–19)

As the psalmist surveys the heavens and the earth and contemplates the wonders of creation, he erupts in praise: "O LORD, how manifold are your works! / In wisdom you have made them all; / the earth is full of your creatures!" This doxology in verse 24 serves as the climax to this prayer/song. Plants and animals both domestic and wild, ocean depths to mountain heights, predators and prey—all evoke wonder and offer praise. As poet Gerard Manley Hopkins famously put it, "Creation is charged with the grandeur of God."[35] Creation is a wonder that bespeaks God's glory. In this psalm, creation is like one grand symphony, intended to give praise to God, its maker and sustainer, and we humans are to make beautiful music and help give voice to creation's praise.[36] This awesome task and joyful responsibility are made possible only if we acknowledge with gratitude to God that we live in a wonder-full world.

Psalm 148 is another of the so-called nature psalms from the Psalter. What do you make of these lines?

Praise God, sun and moon;
   praise God, all you shining stars!
Praise God, you highest heavens,
   and you waters above the heavens! (vv. 3–4 NRSV alt.)

Praise the LORD from the earth,
   you sea monsters and all creatures of the deep,
fire and hail, snow and frost,
   stormy wind fulfilling God's command! (vv. 7–8 NRSV alt.)

Mountains and all hills,
   fruit trees and all cedars!
Wild animals and all cattle,
   creeping things and flying birds! (vv. 9–10)

Can sea monsters and cedar trees, snakes and sandpipers give praise to God? What is with this talk of nonhuman creatures praising God? Is this just a figure of speech? Is this just an example of the psalmist getting a bit carried away?[37]

This joyous psalm invites all creatures—in heaven and on earth—to offer praise to God the Creator and Redeemer. Angels and shining stars. Mountains and fruit trees. Humans young and old, female and male, rich and poor. All creatures are called to sing praise to God. This creational doxology is not commanded. It is not sought by appeal to duty or obligation. Praise is simply fitting for creatures—each of us in our own creature-specific way. Wonder-evoked praise is a natural response of gratitude to God's ever-present grace.

As in the Old Testament, so also in the New Testament, many passages come to mind when thinking of wonder, not least many of the stories about Jesus. Whether speaking in parables or healing the lame or commanding the sea to be still, Jesus evoked wonder. Indeed, perhaps the most wonder-full text is from the Gospel of John: "The Word became flesh and pitched his tent among us" (John 1:14, my translation). Or, as Eugene Peterson fetchingly translates it, "The Word became flesh and moved into the neighborhood" (Message).[38] But along with this summary of the mystery of the incarnation comes the equally profound wonder evoked by the Gospel narratives of the cross and resurrection. Pick your narrative. Wonder fills the stories of Jesus.

One text that attempts to describe succinctly this wonder-full good news (and itself evokes a profound sense of wonder) is a poem included in one of the letters from the apostle Paul. In Colossians 1:15–20, Paul writes of Jesus the Christ:[39]

He is the image
  of the invisible God
  the firstborn of all creation
    for in Him were created all things
    in heaven and on earth
    things visible and invisible
      whether thrones or dominions
      whether rulers or powers
    all things have been created
    through Him and for Him

And He is before all things
  and all things hold together in Him
And He is the head
  of the body, the church

He is the beginning
  the firstborn from the dead
  so that he might become in all things himself preeminent
    for in Him all the fullness
    was pleased to dwell
    and through Him to reconcile all things to Him
      whether things on earth or things in heaven
    by making peace through the blood of his cross.

One can only marvel in wonder at the person and work of Christ as described in this ancient hymn. Christ is the firstborn because in him were created all things in heaven and on earth, things visible and invisible. This includes the heavenly and earthly realities of our world that some suppose are ultimate: thrones, dominions, rulers, and powers.[40] All heavenly principalities and powers are subordinate to Christ. All earthly kings and rulers are subject to Christ. These "powers" are not ultimate; they do not have the last word. All things have been created and continue to exist through him and for him. Christ is the agent by whom and the goal for whom creation exists.

But there is more. Christ is before all things, and all things are held together in him.[41] Christ comes first—in both time and status. And, most amazing yet, all things cohere, hang together, in Christ. Christ is the sustainer of the universe and the unifying principle of life. The world hangs together not by virtue of any heavenly power. Creation coheres not because Caesar reigns; rather, all things hold together in and through and for Christ.[42]

But there is yet more. Christ is the beginning.[43] Not only is Christ the firstborn of all creation; he is also the firstborn from the dead. Christ has been raised from the dead—the firstfruits of those who have died.[44] Christ is the founder of a new people.[45] With his death and resurrection, the new age has begun. And this cosmic reconciliation has been effected by a curious kind of peacemaking. This peace is secured not through violence or conquest or the merciless bloodletting of others—this is no *Pax Romana*—but through the blood of his cross. This is a very different peace—the shalom of the kingdom of God—and a very different peacemaking, one in which a person voluntarily suffers for others and in so doing absorbs evil. Joseph Sittler captures the profound meaning and scope of this text better than anyone:

> For it is here declared that the sweep of God's restorative action in Christ is no smaller than the six-times repeated *ta panta*. Redemption is the name for this will, this action, this concrete Man who is God with us and God for us—and all things are permeable to his cosmic redemption because all things subsist in him. He comes to all things, not as stranger, for he is the firstborn of all creation, and in him all things were created. He is not only the matrix and *prius* of all things; he is the intention, the fullness, and the integrity of all things: for all things were created through him and for him. Nor are all things a tumbled multitude of facts in an unrelated mess, for in him all things hold together.[46]

These are truly audacious claims. But if true, what a world of wonders we live in! And how important that we cultivate the virtue of wonder in order to see the world for what it truly is, giving thanks to the Triune God—its Maker, Sustainer, and Redeemer.

Turning now to humility, what insight does Scripture provide? The Bible speaks often of humility. As expected, many of these texts are from the Wisdom literature of the Old Testament (e.g., Ps. 90; Prov. 15:33; 18:12). But one of the most important places to learn of humility is the book of beginnings, for the first chapters of Genesis describe what it means to be human. More exactly, Genesis 1–2 powerfully describes human finitude. In Genesis 2, the narrative tells us (v. 7) that the human creature is formed out of the ground and made alive by God's life-giving breath. We are earth creature (*'adam*) because we are clumps of earth (*'adamah*) animated by the Spirit of God. And lest we forget, the text reminds us "to dust [we] shall return" (3:19). We, like all God's creatures, are finite.

The finitude of humanity is also powerfully portrayed in the book of Job. Often overlooked in this tale of human misfortune in light of the greatness of God is the very end of the story (chaps. 38–41). Listen again to one portion of these concluding chapters:[47]

At long last, God addresses Job. Speaking from a whirlwind, with an onslaught of questions piled one on the other, God responds to Job's lament and his complaint. But God's response is strange and seemingly not to the point. God's first response is all about cosmology and meteorology and hydrology and animal husbandry and ornithology.

First, earth and sky. "Where were you, Job, when I laid the foundation of the earth? Who was it, Job, who marked the boundaries of the sea? Have you, Job, commanded the morning to come? Were you around, O Job, when the primordial waters were fixed in place? Have you journeyed to the underworld or traveled the expanse of the earth? Did you separate light from darkness? And what about the weather? Do you, Job, know where the snow and hail are stored? Have you knowledge of where lightning comes from or whence the east wind roars? And what, O Job, of the rain? Have you brought it to the desert? Do you provide water to the wasteland? Is it you who begets the ice and frost and snow? Have you, Job, placed the Pleiades in the sky, or fixed Orion and the Great Bear in their celestial circuit?"

Then, animals and birds. "Can you, Job, provide food for the hungry lion? Do you provide for the raven its prey? Do you, Job, know when the wild mountain goats give birth or the wild deer have their young? Is it you, O Job, who let the wild ass go free or made the ox forever wild? And what of the ostrich? Was it your design that it leave its eggs on the earth and deal cruelly with its young? Was it according to your wisdom, Job, that the hawk soar south or the vulture suck the blood of the slain?"

After this cascade of questions, God demands an answer: "Anyone who argues with God must respond." Job has publicly reproached God, and now God awaits his answer. Job simply states, "I am small." And so he places his hand over his mouth. Having spoken once, of things he claimed to know but really did not, he will not make the same mistake twice. He has forcibly been shown the limits of his knowledge and power. And so after declaring that he would approach God "like a prince," Job engages in an act of self-humiliation. He now knows his place, and it is not at the center of things.

In the deluge of questions asked by God from the whirlwind, Job is forcibly reminded of his finitude and his ignorance. Job has not commanded the morning or entered the storehouses of the snow or provided prey for the ravens. He does not know when the mountain goats give birth or who let the wild asses go free. That the hawk soars and the eagle mounts up is not Job's doing. Job's power and knowledge are definitely limited. Thus he should be humble.

We are finite. It might seem that this rather obvious point needs no special attention; however, we humans have a penchant for forgetting this central feature of our existence. Indeed, we have a deep desire to avoid looking our finitude, especially our temporal finitude or mortality, straight in the face.[48]

To acknowledge the limited nature of our existence produces anxiety and raises the question of whether death is the end of one's life or whether there is Someone who is sufficiently able and willing to preserve our life beyond biological death and in whom we can rest despite our fear and anxiety.[49]

But we are not only finite; we are faulted. These two are not the same. Finitude is a good feature of human existence. It is simply how God made us—a characteristic of our humanity to (joyfully) accept. Faultiness, however, is not God's intention. The brokenness we know in ourselves, and the effects we see all around us, we acknowledge with regret and seek with God's grace to overcome.

Brokenness is also powerfully depicted in the Genesis narrative. In chapter 3, we learn that Adam and Eve desire to transcend their creaturely finitude and become, like God, omniscient. But in this attempt they fail to trust in God and thus become estranged. Their relationship with God is broken. They become estranged from each other (they attempt to pass the blame). They lose touch with their own true and best self (they hide and conceal their actions). And they become out of joint with the earth (working the earth becomes burdensome). In these four ways, they and we are alienated. In short, our lives are interwoven with a contagion called sin, which we knowingly and unknowingly perpetuate. The Bible confirms what we know in our hearts: the world is not the way it is supposed to be.[50]

In sum, we are limited in power and knowledge as well as space and time. We are 'adam from the 'adamah, humans from the humus. We are not God, though we are God's. And we are alienated from God, other humans, ourselves, and the earth. Though we are not God, we all too often think and act as if we were. Given the limitations of our knowledge and power, we must be circumspect and exercise forethought. Given our stubborn unwillingness to admit such limitations, we must strive to be honest and be willing to be held accountable for our actions.

Humility is mentioned often in the New Testament. For example, Luke recounts that Paul describes his life as "serving the Lord with all humility and with tears" (Acts 20:19). In a well-known passage from his letter to the church at Philippi, Paul urges his sisters and brothers, "Do nothing from selfish ambition or conceit, but in humility regard others as better than yourselves" (Phil. 2:3). And Peter exhorts the elders in the churches in Asia Minor, "All of you must clothe yourselves with humility in your dealings with one another, for 'God opposes the proud, but gives grace to the humble'" (1 Pet. 5:5). Humility (*prautēs*) is a mark of those who follow Jesus.

These biblical texts enrich our previous reflections on wonder and humility. This earth of which we are a part is a world of wonders, created and redeemed by a wonder-working God. So, astonished amazement and proper modesty are fitting responses for creatures such as us living in such a world. Wonder and humility are appropriate responses to the work of God in Christ through the Holy Spirit.

Ecological Wonder and Humility

Let's summarize the insights from the previous sections. What exactly is the virtue of wonder? The virtue of wonder is the settled disposition to stand in rapt attention and amazement in the presence of something awe-inspiring, mysterious, or novel. We exhibit this virtue when we have the cultivated capability to stand in grateful amazement at what God has made and is remaking. When full of wonder we never lose our childlike ability to appreciate and be amazed by features of the world often invisible to others.

Most virtues have two vices—a vice of deficiency and a vice of excess. For example, the vices that correspond with the virtue of courage are cowardice and rashness. The vices that go with frugality are greed and stinginess. Some virtues, however, have only one vice. There is no excess, only deficiency. Justice and love are the two most well-known examples. There cannot be too much justice or too much love. The virtue of wonder is another such virtue. Like justice and love, there is only one vice corresponding to the virtue of wonder.

This vice is hard to name, but we know it when we see it. It is the inability to perceive and be amazed by what is truly wonder-full. It is the disposition to be indifferent to the wonders of the world and the amazing grace of God. Aristotle describes something similar when he speaks of the vice of deficiency with respect to the virtue of self-control: "People who fall short with regard to pleasures and delight in them less than they should are hardly found, for such insensibility is not human."[51] Taking Aristotle's cue, I call this vice *insensibility*. This names the settled disposition to be deaf to the wonders of the world—to lack sensibility or responsiveness to what naturally evokes wonder.

Another form of this vice involves not lack of responsiveness to the wonders of the world but misplaced wonder: fawning over celebrities, admiring astonishment at the latest military weapon, awestruck veneration of the new shopping mall. In these cases, awe is misplaced and astonishment is misdirected. Our awestruck response to what we take to be awe-inspiring falsifies true wonder. Wonder is warped.

The virtue of *ecological wonder* is the settled disposition to stand in rapt attention and enthralled amazement in the presence of the awe-inspiring natural world. This ecological virtue names the capability of grateful amazement at the world of wonders God has made, sustains, and is remaking. Formed by this virtue, we have the ability to see, appreciate, and be amazed by features of the natural world: the astounding vastness of the Grand Canyon and the quiet closeness of a dense forest trail, the breathtaking beauty of a giant sequoia and the remarkable biochemistry of a pitcher plant, the biomechanics of a ruby-throated hummingbird hovering on the feeder outside the kitchen window, and the tender care of your beloved dog nursing young pups in the backyard.

For Ronald Sandler, wonder is an ecological virtue because it is one of the habitual dispositions required for human excellence and flourishing. Following the human-excellence approach of generating ecological virtues, Sandler lists wonder as one of his "virtues of communion with nature."[52] The other eco-virtues in that category are openness, aesthetic sensibility, attentiveness, and love. With reference to Rachel Carson, Sandler argues that "wonder is a gateway to love, gratitude, appreciation, and care for that which is found wonderful"; thus wonder is "environmentally informed, environmentally responsive, and environmentally productive."[53]

Philip Cafaro employs the human-exemplar approach to generate his list of ecological virtues.[54] He looks to, among others, Henry David Thoreau and Rachel Carson to find the dispositions needed to enable us to care for the world. And one of the virtues he finds in these moral exemplars is wonder. They embody many of the traits associated with wonder, such as curiosity, imagination, alertness, and sensibility to beauty.

The vice corresponding to ecological wonder is *ecological insensibility*. This names the inability to be amazed by the wonders of the world. No night sky, however beautiful, can move us to slack-jawed wonder. No orchid display, no dancing sandhill crane, no acrobatic dusky dolphin can bring us to marvel and be amazed. To the ecologically insensible, the natural world is flat, uniform, monochrome. The acids of modernity or the suspicions of postmodernity have drained the ability to wonder from those who exhibit this vice.

Our insensibility to what is truly amazing may explain some of our misdirected wonder. If we are not responsive to the real wonders of the natural world, then we are more apt to be taken in by pretenders: veneration of those who believe that whoever dies with the most toys wins, adulation of those who think that technology will save us, adoration of those who argue that we can and will control nature. Insensitivity to God's world of wonders can breed misplaced amazement.

Turning now to humility, the virtue of humility is the settled disposition to estimate our abilities or capacities properly. It thus implies self-knowledge and especially knowing the limits of our knowledge. It includes the acknowledgment that we are finite. But we are not just finite; we are faulted. The brokenness we know in ourselves (and the effects we see all around us) is something we acknowledge with regret and seek with God's grace to overcome. In short, finitude and fallenness give us more than ample reason to be humble—to have a proper sense of who we are and what we know. Aware of our ignorance, we do not pretend to know more than we really know. Aware of our sins, we do not pretend to be perfect.

The vice of deficiency is hubris or overweening pride. Hubris is the failure to acknowledge our own limits and brokenness. When full of pride, we overestimate our abilities and are vain and boastful. Thinking ourselves in control, we make foolish decisions that wreak havoc for ourselves and for others. "Pride goeth before the fall," proclaims the old aphorism—no less true for being old.

The vice of excess is self-deprecation. Aristotle speaks of those who belittle their authentic accomplishments as exhibiting undue humility or mock modesty. If bedeviled by this vice, we play down our abilities and speak disparagingly of our legitimate achievements. We are unable to acknowledge our actual gifts and abilities, or we refuse to assess our genuine strengths properly.

What then of *ecological humility*? The virtue of ecological humility is the settled disposition to act in such a way that we know our place and fit harmoniously into it—whether our local community, our bioregion, or our home planet. If ecologically humble, we acknowledge that we are finite and fallen and thus have an honest and accurate estimation of our abilities and capacities (for good and ill). This requires not only self-knowledge and knowledge of the world in which we live but also awareness of the limits of our knowledge. We frankly acknowledge our limited ability to know the future consequences of our actions, and we have an honest awareness of our penchant for self-deception. Before making decisions, we survey as many consequences as possible. We explore alternatives, seek out blind spots, consider worst-case scenarios. If ecologically humble, we act cautiously.

Sandler also includes humility on his list of ecological virtues—in the category of "virtues of sustainability."[55] Indeed, ecological humility is crucial for Sandler, especially given what he calls the modern Western penchant to control and dominate, found, for example, in the use of genetically modified crops. Sandler argues that "humility in our environmental and agricultural practices is justified because it is more conducive to promoting and preserving goods necessary for and conducive to human and environmental flourishing."[56] Humility, in other words, counters our inclination to assume that we are divine.

Cafaro also highlights humility as an ecological virtue, especially when examining the life of Rachel Carson. Indeed, Cafaro argues that humility is one of the most central ecological virtues, since it inspires the cultivation of other ecological virtues.[57] A properly humble understanding of our place in the world—individually and collectively as humans—necessarily precludes greed, wastefulness, and many other vices stemming from hubris. Put positively, ecological humility sets us on a path toward cultivating other virtues such as frugality, simplicity, and wisdom—virtues that are essential for becoming responsible earthkeepers.

The vices corresponding to ecological humility are ecological arrogance and ecological self-deprecation. *Ecological arrogance* puts us, cocky and confident, at the center of the universe. And so, thinking we know everything, we cut corners with the wildlife conservation program. Despite the manifest evidence of both unforeseen and unintended consequences and our own ignorance, we go too fast on the water-reclamation project. Assuming the only value of some animal, plant, or place is its usefulness for us, we put a price tag on "environmental resources" according to their "economic utility." Because of our individual and collective arrogance, the natural world, of which we humans are an integral part, suffers.

Ecological self-deprecation diminishes the role of humans as earthkeepers. If captured by this vice, we undervalue the important place of humans as caretakers of creation and responsible agents of change for the good. We sometimes talk as if the world would be better off without us—that we are a virus, a plague, a scourge upon the earth.[58] We fail to see how we humans have a legitimate and significant role to play in caring for the earth.

The virtues of ecological wonder and ecological humility require an honest recognition of our important yet limited place in the world. These virtues, in other words, require that we have an accurate sense that we are creatures. But this implies an acknowledgment of some sort of Creator.[59] It also implies some basic knowledge of the world of wonders in which we live and which sustains us and all things.[60] In sum, we must have knowledge of humanity, God, and the world.

Wonder and Humility Embodied

He had been walking for weeks. He walked almost two hundred miles from San Francisco to the Yosemite Valley. Prior to that, he had walked a thousand miles from Indiana to Florida and then taken a boat to Cuba, New York City, Panama, and finally up the Pacific coast to San Francisco, arriving at the end of March. It is now May of 1868, and our young man, age thirty, is herding sheep in the foothills of the Sierra Nevada. By July, he is in the Yosemite high country reveling in the rocks, flowers, trees, birds, and animals of what is fast becoming his much-loved home. His wonder knows no bounds, and whatever he learns only makes him more humble. So begins John Muir's first summer in the Sierra.

Muir's explorations and exploits seemingly knew no end. On purpose, he rides out a violent storm one hundred feet up in a Douglas fir tree, commenting that "never before did I enjoy so noble an exhilaration of motion."[61] He nearly falls to his death climbing on Mount Ritter. "With arms outspread, clinging close to the face of the rock, unable to move hand or foot either up or down," he realizes that his "doom is fixed" and "he must fall." Yet "this terrible eclipse lasted only a moment when life blazed forth again with preternatural clearness," and "I seemed suddenly to become possessed of a new sense" so that "my trembling muscles became firm again, every rift and flaw in the rock was seen as through a microscope, and my limbs moved with a positiveness and precision with which I seemed to have nothing at all to do."[62] In his attempt to gain a closer view of Yosemite Falls, hundreds of feet above the ground, he climbs barefoot down to a three-inch-wide shelf and then shuffles horizontally twenty to thirty feet "until close to the outplunging current" in order to obtain "a perfectly free view down into the heart of the snowy, chanting throng of comet-like streamers." While admitting that "hereafter I'll try to keep from such extravagant nerve-straining places," he nevertheless exclaims, "I had a glorious time."[63] In the words of biographer Donald Worster, "He bounded over rocks and up mountain sides, hung over the edge of terrifying precipices, his face drenched in the spray of waterfalls, waded through meadows deep in lilies, laughed at the exuberant antics of grasshoppers and chipmunks, stroked the bark of towering incense cedars and sugar pines, and slept each night on an aromatic mattress of spruce boughs."[64] A glorious time indeed.

Muir's wonder also seemingly knew no end. His writings are full of animated descriptions of the natural world that show his amazement and astonishment.

> How fiercely, devoutly wild is Nature in the midst of her beauty-loving tenderness!—painting lilies, watering them, caressing them with gentle hand, going from flower to flower like a gardener while building rock mountains and cloud mountains full of lightning and rain. Gladly we run for shelter beneath an overhanging cliff and examine the reassuring ferns and mosses, gentle love tokens growing in cracks and chinks. . . . The birds are out singing on the edges

of the groves. The west is flaming in gold and purple, ready of the ceremony of sunset, and back I go to my camp with notes and pictures, the best of them printed in my mind as dreams. A fruitful day, without measured beginning or ending. A terrestrial eternity. A gift of good God.[65]

But not all his descriptions concern the majestic. Of the grasshopper Muir writes:

> Up and down a dozen times or so he danced and sang, then alighted to rest, then up and at it again. The curves he described in the air in diving and rattling resembled those made by cords hanging loosely and attached at the same height at the ends, the loops nearly covering each other. Braver, heartier, keener, carefree enjoyment of life I have never seen or heard in any creature, great or small. The life of this comic red-legs, the mountain's merriest child, seems to be made up of pure, condensed gayety. The Douglas squirrel is the only living creature that I can compare him with in exuberant, rollicking, irrepressible jollity.[66]

John Muir embodies like few others the virtue of wonder.

But it is also clear that, for Muir, humility is hitched to wonder. Where wonder goes, humility follows, or perhaps it is the other way around. For example, Muir remarks, "Perched like a fly on this Yosemite dome, I gaze and sketch and bask, oftentimes settling down into dumb admiration without definite hope of ever learning much, yet with the longing, unresting effort that lies at the door of hope, humbly prostrate before the vast display of God's power."[67] Or looking out on the lower end of the Yosemite Valley, "with its wonderful cliffs and groves, a grand page of mountain manuscript that I would gladly give my life to be able to read," Muir avows, "how vast it seems, how short human life when we happen to think of it, and how little we may learn, however hard we try! Yet why bewail our poor inevitable ignorance? Some of the external beauty is always in sight, enough to keep every fibre of us tingling, and this we are able to gloriously enjoy though the methods of its creation may lie beyond our ken."[68] There is much to learn, yet much remains beyond our ability to know.

In one of his most frequently quoted texts, Muir proclaims, "When we try to pick out anything by itself, we find it hitched to everything else in the universe. One fancies a heart like our own must be beating in every crystal and cell, and we feel like stopping to speak to the plants and animals as friendly fellow mountaineers. Nature as a poet, an enthusiastic workingman, becomes more and more visible the farther and higher we go; for the mountains are fountains—beginning places, however related to sources beyond our mortal ken."[69] We can and do learn much about the natural world, Muir insists, but we must be humble, for there is much that we do not and cannot know. As biographer Frederick Turner puts it, "Drifting through mountains and valleys and along the courses of rivers, he found magic in everything he encountered, from the carcass of a dead bear to a microscopic landscape he discovered in a dewdrop."[70] Magic in everything he encountered. Amazement tethered to humility.

A Nature-Rich World

In a chapter titled "Knowing Our Place" in her book *Small Wonder*, Barbara Kingsolver reflects on the human exodus from mostly rural to mostly urban dwellings in the last century.

> With all due respect for the wondrous ways people have invented to amuse themselves and one another on paved surfaces, I find this exodus from the land makes me unspeakably sad. I think of the children who will never know, intuitively, that a flower is a plant's way of making love, or what *silence* sounds like, or that trees breathe out what we breathe in. . . . I wonder how they [children] will imagine the infinite when they have never seen how the stars fill a dark sky. I wonder how I can explain why a wood-thrush song makes my chest hurt to a populace for whom wood is a construction material and thrush is a tongue disease.[71]

Kingsolver laments what is being lost with this exodus. How will our children imagine the infinite if they have never seen the Milky Way? How will they imagine sonorous beauty without hearing firsthand the loveliness of birdsong? What happens to our ability to wonder in an age in which opportunities to experience the natural world firsthand are few and far between? Kingsolver's lament highlights the need for wonder to be cultivated.

Richard Louv has a name for what Kingsolver laments: nature-deficit disorder. It is one of the maladies of children in America today, he maintains. As he persuasively argues in his award-winning book *Last Child in the Woods*, "Within the space of a few decades, the way children understand and experience nature has changed radically. . . . Today, kids are aware of the global threats to the environment—but their physical contact, their intimacy with nature, is fading."[72] Louv documents this phenomenon in its various manifestations and provides evidence from both the natural and the social sciences for why all people—adults as well as children—need nature to remain physically, emotionally, and spiritually healthy. Indeed, in a chapter titled "A Life of the Senses: Nature vs. the Know-It-All State of Mind," Louv argues that a nature-rich life fosters both wonder and humility.[73] The last two parts of *Last Child in the Woods*—titled "Wonder Land" and "To Be Amazed"—provide creative ideas to cultivate wonder and its cousin, humility. His subsequent books are chock-full of practical ideas that foster wonder and humility.[74]

In an age dubbed "the Anthropocene"—the age of the human—how can we be reminded that we are not the center of the universe? When so easily coaxed into believing that we humans are far superior to all other creatures, what can we do to remind ourselves, as Muir puts it, that "we all travel the Milky Way together, trees and men"?[75] How do we honestly acknowledge our proper place in God's scheme of things—humble humans from the humus, made in God's image, called to serve and protect God's good earth? More opportunities that evoke wonder and humility would deliver us from the conceit of thinking the world revolves around us.

I have forgotten much about that memorable first trip to the Boundary Waters decades ago. I do not remember the names or faces of all the high schoolers who went on that trip. I cannot recall exactly the route we took. But I do vividly remember that pitch-black starry night and the glistening, tremulous northern lights. And I still remember the wonder and the humility evoked by those events. I hope my companions do too.

3

Living with Strength of Mind and Discernment

Self-Control and Wisdom

The secret weapon of environmental change and of social justice must be this—living with simple elegance is more pleasurable than living caught in the middle of our consumer culture.

Bill McKibben[1]

The fear of the LORD is the beginning of wisdom.

Psalm 111:10 (cf. Job 28:28; Proverbs 1:7)

The Nest Egg[2]

Trees were everywhere. Oak and hickory, beech and birch, red maple and yellow poplar, elm and ash and cottonwood, even some loblolly and short-leaf pine scattered hither and yon. Some of the mature beech trees were three feet wide at chest height, and some mature oaks and maples were a neck-craning hundred feet high. The green canopy in the summer allowed only a few glints of sunlight to filter in to the ground below, full of lichens and mosses and ferns. Birdsong filled the dawn and bats cruised at dusk. It was the finest stand of trees in all of Kentucky, about seventy-five acres of mature forest, protected by its owner, Athey Keith. He called it "The Nest Egg." He logged it only for firewood—discerningly and knowledgeably—and so the forest was healthy. If cared for wisely, this beautiful forest could flourish for a long time.

Athey and his wife, Della, farmed five hundred acres of land near the Kentucky River. They raised tobacco and corn, followed by wheat or barley, and then clover and grass. They had cattle and sheep and hogs, and mules to do much of the work. Everything on the place was well kept and looked good, for Athey would have it no other way.

Athey and Della had one daughter, Mattie. She was a handsome girl and hardworking and understanding. She knew farm work and loved the family farm. At the age of twenty-one, Mattie married Troy Chatham. Troy was attractive and smart and energetic. But he was also full of himself and overly ambitious and more than a little ignorant. And he had great aspirations. He would farm more land and make more money than any other farmer in north central Kentucky. He would become a famous all-star farmer.

As Athey grew older, Troy took over more and more of Athey's farm. Troy borrowed money to buy a new tractor, which allowed him to work more land. He soon was working at night planting corn on land rented on a neighboring farm. He bought ever-more-powerful machinery and sank deeper into debt. While Athey used his land conservatively, striving to leave it better than he found it, Troy pushed to use more land in order to produce more corn. While Athey was always studying his fields—the soil, the drainage, the fertility— Troy was busy writing business plans and paying consultants to figure out how to get more out of the fields. While Athey thought he existed to cultivate the farm and serve his local community, Troy thought the farm existed to serve and enlarge him.

After Athey's death, the farm, though legally passed on to Mattie, came under Troy's complete control. Over time, the trees flanking the fields were bulldozed, and one half-acre field was filled with old and worn-out machines. Every bit of plowable land was sown in soybeans or corn. Hogs came to be the only livestock and were kept in a large barn. Other farm buildings were abandoned. To quote Jayber Crow, the town barber, "It did not look like a place where anybody had ever wanted to be."[3] And despite years of bigger machines, additional land, and endless effort, Troy was ever deeper in debt.

One morning on a midsummer day, near his modest cabin down by the river, Jayber heard a strange noise while setting his fishing lines. Anxious to find out what was causing all the commotion, he set off on foot in the direction of the racket. As he approached The Nest Egg, a dull and dark realization slowly crystallized in his mind, and his skin broke out in a cold, clammy sweat. He rounded a rise and saw what he feared: bulldozers clearing the land. Enormous logs, like beached whales, were stacked side by side. Every tree big enough to make two-by-fours was being cut to the ground.

Chainsaws were humming as workers cut the logs. The beloved Nest Egg was being destroyed.

In large part to pay off his debt, but also because of his need to be proud, Troy Chatham had sold the last rainy-day fund available to him and the old-growth forest dear to Athey Keith's heart. It was no coincidence that Troy's wife, Mattie, was in the hospital and unable to observe this egregious act, and perhaps stop it. Jayber saw Troy standing among the big logs, smiling and looking about. Admiring the power of the machines and astonished by the size of the trees, which he was now seeing for the very first time, Troy was proud as a peacock.

Jayber saw things quite differently. He saw Troy for what he truly was. A beaten man who was trying too hard not to admit it. A man who had made his last play in what he sometimes called "the game of farming." A man who had been given everything and did not know it and now had lost it all and struggled to acknowledge it. Jayber heard in his mind the voices of many members of his community of Port William. Together with one voice they shouted, "The damned fool!"[4]

Ruminations about Self-Control

In contemporary American culture, self-control has a bad rap. Let go, get it all out, give up control—that seems to be the motto of our day. Self-restraint, moderation, temperance—this virtue goes by many names—seem so old-fashioned, remnants of an antiquated Victorian culture thankfully long past. But talk to any schoolteacher or sports team coach, music instructor or work boss, and they will insist on the importance of self-control. Indeed, any functioning group—class at school, team at work, family at home—requires a modicum of self-control from its members for it to function. Without some semblance of self-control, needs are not met, feelings are overlooked, and frustration rules the roost.

In ancient Greece, self-control was one of the four cardinal virtues, along with courage, wisdom, and justice. It was impossible to flourish as an individual without self-control. For example, Plato argues that self-control (*sōphrosynē*) is essential for a person to live the good life. You can achieve happiness (*eudaimonia*) only if you are able to obtain "mastery of certain kinds of pleasures and desires."[5] Plato, furthermore, argues that self-control is necessary for a society to flourish, since the multitude of common people need to be able to control their desires—just as soldiers need courage, kings need wisdom, and justice is needed to keep everything and everyone in proper order.[6]

Aristotle echoes his teacher Plato. Self-control is one of the four central virtues needed to live the good life.[7] In particular, self-control is concerned with the bodily pleasures of touch and taste, such as eating, drinking, and sex. Self-control is the mean between the vices of self-indulgence and insensitivity. The self-indulgent person "craves for all pleasant things or those most pleasant, and is led by his appetite to choose these at the cost of everything else," while insensitive people delight in bodily pleasures "less than they should."[8] As J. O. Urmson puts it, while "Aristotle feels a special contempt for self-indulgence," he is not an ascetic, since the temperate or self-controlled person "will enjoy his food and other bodily pleasures so far as they are needful, fitting, and within his means."[9]

In the Christian tradition, the virtue of self-control morphed into the virtue of temperance. Moderation is sometimes used as a synonym, but it does not capture the essence of temperance, since moderation "is dangerously close to fear of any exuberance" and "signifies too exclusively restriction, curtailment, curbing, bridling, repression."[10] Unlike moderation, temperance does not mean always taking a middle-of-the-road path nor does it necessarily imply repression of desire.[11] For Christians during the Middle Ages, temperance meant having the ability to control one's passions and appetites. For example, Thomas Aquinas speaks of temperance as "rectitude of appetite."[12] Temperance is a kind of control over one's inner life—thoughts, desires, emotions—that results in control over one's outer life of action and behavior.

This control requires attending to our inner life—what we today call the self. Josef Pieper notes that there are two modes of turning toward the self: the selfless and the selfish. In the former, what he calls "selfless self-preservation," one turns inward but without fixating on oneself. The focus remains on God. In the latter, the inward turn focuses exclusively on the self and results in anxiety and self-destruction.[13] Lewis Smedes makes a similar observation when he states that while "self-control is about being in charge of the direction our lives are taking," the paradox is that "we get control of our lives, ultimately, not by willpower but by surrender." The final secret, Smedes avers, "lies in amazing grace."[14] He gives as an example his own story of seeking and finding forgiveness in his family of origin—made possible only by surrendering to the God who loves us with no strings attached.

In early American culture, the spirit of the virtue of temperance was captured by Henry David Thoreau: "Most of the luxuries, and many of the so-called comforts of life, are not only not indispensable, but positive hindrances to the elevation of mankind."[15] Articulating what seems now to be a long-lost appreciation for simplicity and frugality, Thoreau strenuously insists that we must distinguish genuine needs from mere wants by recognizing that many so-called comforts actually get in the way of our flourishing. And beyond merely making such distinctions, we must cultivate the virtues of self-control and wisdom in order to "live according to its [wisdom's] dictates, a life of simplicity, independence, magnanimity, and trust."[16]

This venerable tradition of temperance and simplicity runs counter to the materialistic culture of today. Large sums of money are spent to convince us that we really need that new gadget, article of clothing, or electronic device to be happy (and keep up with our peers). As William Cavanaugh observes, "The average person is exposed to thousands of advertising images every week. Virtually everywhere we look or listen—television, radio, websites, newspapers, magazines, billboards, junk mail, movies, videos, T-shirts, buses, hats, cups, pens and pencils, gas-pump handles, walls of public restrooms—is saturated with advertising."[17] We live in a world of "globalized desire" where "everything is available, but nothing matters."[18] As one countercultural maxim puts it, American culture today wants us to "spend money we don't have on crap we don't need."

There is ample evidence that the supposed connection between more stuff and happiness is an illusion. My Hope College colleague (and next-door neighbor), social psychologist David Myers, captures well the conclusions of much social-science research from the last few decades: "*Our becoming much better-off over the last thirty years has not been accompanied by one iota of increased happiness and life satisfaction.* It's shocking, because it contradicts our society's materialistic assumptions, but how can we ignore the hard truth: *Once beyond poverty, further economic growth does not appreciatively improve human morale.*"[19] We think making more money and having more stuff will make us happier, but we are deluded. Once a person or family rises above the poverty line, there is no correlation between happiness and wealth. More stuff does not lead to more satisfaction. "The good life" is not "the goods life." From this research, Myers draws this conclusion: "Realizing that well-being is something other than being well-off is liberating. It liberates us from spending on eighteen-hundred-dollar dresses, on stockpiles of unplayed CDs, on luxury cars, on seagoing luxury homes—all purchased in a vain quest for an elusive joy. It liberates us from envying the life-styles of the rich and famous. It liberates us to invest ourselves in developing traits, attitudes, relationships, activities, environments, and spiritual resources that *will* promote our own, and others', well-being."[20] Giving up the illusion that happiness is found in owning more stuff is liberating. It frees us from believing our well-being is dependent on our possessions.

In his encyclical *Laudato Si'*, Pope Francis captures the heart of the Christian understanding of the virtue of self-control:

> Christian spirituality proposes a growth marked by moderation and the capacity to be happy with little. It is a return to that simplicity which allows us to stop and appreciate the small things, to be grateful for the opportunities which life affords us, to be spiritually detached from what we possess, and not to succumb to sadness for what we lack. This implies avoiding the dynamic of dominion and the mere accumulation of pleasures.
>
> Such sobriety, when lived freely and consciously, is liberating. It is not a lesser life or one lived with less intensity. On the contrary, it is a way of living life to the full.[21]

Contentment leads to liberation. Gratitude produces freedom. Simplicity opens our eyes to the gifts all around us. Self-control frees us to live an abundant life—a life full of what truly matters. And as the pope notes, the virtue of self-control—with its cousins frugality and honesty, insight and contentment—is never more needed than now.

Pope Francis's reference to gratitude is important, for it highlights the fact that temperance is fundamentally fueled not by a desire to control but by an appreciation for what is given—being thankful for the provisions that meet our needs. Gratitude involves feelings—feelings of thankfulness and often also relief and gladness, wonder and joy. But beyond the feelings, gratitude is a disposition, a virtue. Diana Butler Bass captures this distinction: "It cannot be overstated that gratitude is an emotion, a complex set of feelings involving appreciation, humility, wonder, and interdependence. Gratitude is, however, more than just an emotion. It is also a disposition that can be chosen and cultivated, an outlook on life that manifests itself in actions."[22] This habitual disposition, Bass rightly notes, rejects the pervasive supposition that underlies our culture today: *quid pro quo* (literally "this for that"), or "I do this for you; you do that for me." Gratitude dances to the beat of a different drummer—what Bass calls *pro bono* or for the good. When we are truly grateful, we do not act because we are repaying some debt or fulfilling some obligation; rather we respond with gratitude because it is for the good, expecting nothing in return. This is "the right kind of reciprocity, one that is not payback, one that is, instead, the sharing of gifts and care pro bono."[23]

In sum, contrary to its negative reputation in contemporary culture, self-control is a means of freeing us from a kind of bondage. The virtue of self-control is a cultivated strength of mind or will—a character trait that allows us, with the help of other virtues such as wisdom, to perceive what is truly good and to restrain some desires and nurture other desires in such a way as to attain that which is truly good and right.

Ponderings on Wisdom

What is wisdom? We can gain greater understanding of what wisdom is by distinguishing it from three of its near cousins. First, wisdom is not sheer intelligence or smarts or brainpower. These are good things. It's good to be intelligent, but intelligence is not the same as wisdom, for very intelligent people can be fools. Having a high IQ does not necessarily prevent foolish behavior. Second, wisdom is not erudition or accumulated knowledge or book learning. These, too, are good things. Being erudite is, other things being equal, better than not being erudite. One can learn much from good books (just ask any university professor), but such knowledge is not identical to wisdom, for well-read people can be fools. Scholars sometimes act foolishly. Third, wisdom is not merely technical knowledge or skill or know-how. Know-how is a good thing. It's good to know how to change your tire when you get a flat. It's good to know how to make a cake on your child's birthday. But having such skills is still not the same as wisdom, for technically proficient people can be fools. Three good things these are, but none are wisdom.

What is wisdom, then, if not intelligence, erudition, or skill? Wisdom is a kind of sound practical judgment, what Aristotle calls practical knowledge (*phronēsis*), as distinct from theoretical knowledge (*sophia*). This sound practical judgment is sound precisely because it is informed by the collective experience of the community and guided by a keen discernment of what is good and right and true. The wise person, Aristotle writes, exhibits the "capacity to act with regard to human goods."[24] In other words, the wise person knows what the truly good life is and how to achieve it.

Wisdom, therefore, has two dimensions: a knowing what and a knowing how. The wise person is sagacious about the *summum bonum*. She knows from among all the candidates competing for our attention as the greatest good which are counterfeit and which are the real deal. She knows what truly makes for the flourishing of all things. The wise person also has the practical knowledge needed to attain that greatest good, to secure the goal of the good life by living rightly.

This sound practical judgment relies on the cultivated memory and collective experience of the community. In other words, wisdom depends heavily on what we have learned from the past and what is passed on to us by our parents, our family, and the larger community. In short, wisdom means learning from our ancestors.

The virtue of wisdom, then, is the settled disposition to make sound practical judgments, informed by the accumulated experience of the community, and aimed at what is truly good. The wise person is disposed to make insightful and discerning judgments. The virtue of wisdom is shot through with an abiding awareness of life's precariousness, an understanding and prizing of the excellences of life, and an unwavering sense of thanksgiving for the sheer gift of life. As I recall, a student once wrote in a paper, "I realize now how fragile and delicate life really is, and that has helped me to appreciate it more. I also know that there are many things I cannot take for granted anymore." Awareness, appreciation, gratitude—such is the grammar of wisdom.

In this regard, Nicholas Wolterstorff remarks, quoting John Calvin, that "the deepest reason for Christians to worship God is not that they are commanded to worship but that they break forth into worship out of gratitude." This gratitude "will find its manifestation in the appreciative use of the things around us, in joyful delight and delighted joy."[25] We Christians ought to be people who praise God and serve our neighbors not out of duty but out of heartfelt gratitude.

David Orr provides additional insight into wisdom, especially as it pertains to matters ecological. Orr contrasts cleverness with intelligence, though what he calls intelligence I would describe as wisdom. Orr makes several observations. First, "people acting or thinking with intelligence are good at separating cause from effect."[26] These people are able to identify questions about big causes and large consequences and to sort out which is which. This is a kind of insightful discernment—a feature of wisdom.

Second, "intelligence is the ability to separate 'know how' from 'know why.'"[27] Knowing how to make an atomic bomb is one thing; knowing why one should or should not use it is another. This capacity, too, is a feature of wisdom: setting technical knowledge within a larger moral perspective that asks, "Should we do this?"

Third, Orr argues that an intelligent person takes into account the "good order or harmoniousness of his or her surroundings." Following Wendell Berry here, Orr ties what he calls intelligence to the pursuit and preservation of harmony in one's community. This means having a sense of limits as well as respect for unpredictable consequences that could be catastrophic. These are the attributes or abilities of a wise person. On this score, Orr notes, we have not done well, given the reality of "overflowing landfills, befouled skies, eroded soils, polluted rivers, acidic rain, and radioactive waste."[28] We have not lived up to our name *Homo sapiens* (wise human). We are, if we are honest, often an exceedingly foolish species.

Fourth and last, intelligent action "does not violate the bounds of morality." More precisely, it does not demand "the violation of life, community, or decency" in the name of some supposedly greater good but rather "is consonant with moderation, loyalty, justice, compassion, and truthfulness."[29] All of these are virtues that describe a wise person.

Orr's list of advice to educators about how to foster what he calls "real intelligence" only confirms my contention that what he is actually describing is practical wisdom. For example, employing those who have "applied ecological intelligence"—such as farmers, foresters, restoration ecologists, landscape planners, and citizen activists—as mentors and role models is a move to nurture wisdom. Attempting to teach "the things that one might imagine the earth would teach us: silence, humility, holiness, connectedness, courtesy, beauty, celebration, giving, restoration, obligation, and wildness" is a program designed to foster wisdom.[30] Indeed, what Orr describes is a program in virtue cultivation. While the terminology may differ, Orr provides insight into ecological wisdom.

Biblical Insight on Self-Control and Wisdom

The Genesis creation narratives emphasize that the earth is finite. Despite the descriptions of manyness—many individual creatures, many kinds of creatures—Genesis 1–2 does not suggest that the panoply of God's creatures or the earth itself is unlimited. Creation has definite limits. Photographs from space confirm what the Bible portrays: the blue-green sphere on which we live is finite.

Moreover, God's word to humans to be fruitful and multiply (Gen. 1:28) does not suggest, as some maintain, that the earth has an unlimited supply of "resources" for an ever-growing human population. For example, it is often overlooked that this call by God is also given to all living creatures (v. 22). The sea monsters, the fish, and the birds—indeed, every living creature of every kind is given this permissive command. The call to reproduce is no special privilege unique to humans. We must live in such a way that all creatures are able to flourish, which implies the ability to control our desires.

In addition, the call to be fruitful and multiply is actually not a command at all but a blessing by God on the swarms of living creatures brought forth by God's creative word. As Susan Bratton states, God's blessing "is not an ethical imperative, nor is it a way to please God by reaching to excess." Rather, God's

blessing conveys a reproductive power intended to contribute to the flourishing of all creatures on a finite planet. Hence as Bratton concludes, "Human
population growth has no mandate to damage or desecrate the cosmos."[31]
Creation is finite, and we humans have no biblical warrant to act as if it is
infinite. We must exercise self-control if all are to flourish.

Self-control in the context of finitude is emphasized in other biblical texts.
For example, after the Israelites escaped from Egypt, they wandered in the wilderness on the way to the promised land. As narrated in Exodus 16, God provided bread and meat—manna and quail—for them to eat, but only enough
for one day at a time, lest the Israelites forget their dependence on the God
who delivered them. The portions were sufficient for the day. The resources
were not unlimited; hence self-control (as well as trust) was required.

Jesus calls to mind this experience in the wilderness when he teaches his
followers how to pray. After three petitions concerning God's glory, Jesus
asks God to meet human needs. He first prays, "Give us this day our daily
bread" (Matt. 6:11). In other words, in the Lord's Prayer we ask the provision-
ing God of the exodus to give us the nourishment we need for today. Just as
the Israelites received their daily bread, we are to ask for and with gratitude
receive food sufficient for the day. The Lord's Prayer reiterates the theme of
finitude and sufficiency, as well as the virtues of gratitude and self-control.

The apostle Paul mentions self-control (*enkrateia*) in his famous list of the
fruit of the Spirit in Galatians 5:22–23. Along with love, joy, peace, patience,
kindness, goodness, faithfulness, and gentleness is (last but not least) self-
control. In contrast to the "desires of the flesh," these virtues are marks of
the Holy Spirit. The same word (*enkrateia*) shows up in a list of virtues in
2 Peter 1:5–7. Cheek by jowl with goodness, knowledge, endurance, godliness,
mutual affection, and love is self-control. These virtues, the text insists, "keep
you from being ineffective and unfruitful in the knowledge of our Lord Jesus
Christ" (v. 8). Without them we are "nearsighted and blind" (v. 9). In short,
self-control is a pivotal virtue for knowing Christ and following in his way.

While there are similarities between the meaning of self-control in the Bible
and its meaning in ancient and contemporary culture, we need to be clear
that what self-control means in Scripture is not exactly the same as what is
meant by the ancient Greek writers or by writers today. As Philip Kenneson
points out, "Rather than see self-control (understood as self-mastery) in the
way that many of his contemporaries did—as the foundation for all other virtue—Paul's reconfiguration suggests that 'the self' no longer occupies center
stage. . . . In sum, the desires of the self are most determinatively ordered not
when we strive most diligently to bring the self under control but when we use
our freedom in the Spirit to become servants of God and our neighbors."[32]

In contrast to how Plato or Aristotle focuses on the self, when Paul describes the virtue of self-control, he focuses on God and others. Likewise, there are differences between Paul's concept of self-control and what the term means in common parlance today. As Kenneson argues, "Whatever the New Testament writers may have meant when they employed the concept of *enkrateia*, we should not too quickly assume they meant 'self-control,' which in our day means something akin to control *of* the self, *by* the self, *for the sake of* the self."[33] This contemporary understanding of self-control is not what the apostle Paul means by self-control when he lists it as one of the fruit of the Spirit, for each fruit of the Spirit is other-directed. Paul's use of the term *self-control* does not focus on the self but on God and neighbor.

In addition, the biblical understanding of self-control does not refer to some sort of balance or moderation. Kenneson rightly disputes the frequent assumption (from ancient Greek culture) that self-control means "moderation in all things." Christians are not called "simply to moderate the tyrannical demands of the self; rather Jesus calls us to a cross, where our old self is called to die."[34] The life of a disciple of Christ is not some middle path in which one is never committed to any one thing or person. Speaking like a Hebrew prophet, Kenneson declares:

> The tragedy is that our lives are often marked by excess with respect to those things about which we are called to continence, while we are quick to moderate (or be lukewarm about) those things about which we should be passionate. For example, if I want to orient my entire life around my favorite college football or basketball team, adjusting my schedule to attend all home and away games, spending my days memorizing statistics and talking strategy with fellow "fans" (a word from the same root as *fanatic*), some people may consider me slightly eccentric, but most will admire my devotion. . . . If, however, I choose to orient my life around a two-thousand-year-old community brought into existence by a Jewish carpenter, I am likely to be regarded as a "religious fanatic."[35]

Self-control is not "moderation in all things." It is, rather, the right ordering of desire, which means desiring some things—God and God's good future of shalom—with great devotion and passion.

In sum, these texts remind us of finitude—ours and that of the earth on which we live and of which we are a part. The only seemingly limitless physical resource is the energy from our star the sun—a provision fundamental to all life on earth. All else is limited. An acknowledgment of these limits implies the need for virtues such as self-control by which we are enabled to restrain certain desires and cultivate those desires that honor the limits built into our existence. If there is to be enough for all (where "all" includes our nonhuman neighbors), then we need to acknowledge that the basic needs of others take precedence over our (often greedy) wants. Hence we need to be people of self-control. Failure to be so portends much future hardship, for there are limits we transgress only at our own and the earth's peril.

The Bible has much to say about wisdom.[36] Indeed, one of the main sections of the Old Testament is called the Wisdom literature (Psalms, Proverbs, Song of Songs, Job, and Ecclesiastes). From a biblical point of view, wisdom is rooted in the proper worship of God—"the fear of the LORD"—and hence shaped by God's glorious vision of universal flourishing, not our own half-baked schemes and dreams. Wisdom is, in other words, theocentric. The good, the right, and the true are defined in terms of God and God's way with the world. So the biblical sage knows that God is at the center of things and in his mysterious wisdom sends water to places where no people dwell (Job 38:26). The biblical sage knows that the destiny of the world is that all creatures sing praise to God (Ps. 148). The biblical sage knows that those who oppress the poor insult God, while those who are kind to the needy honor God (Prov. 14:31).

Wisdom is also a major theme in other parts of the Bible. In one of the most famous passages in the Hebrew Prophets, speaking of the messianic age and a coming king, Isaiah sings (11:1–9):

> A shoot shall come out from the stump of Jesse,
>   and a branch shall grow out of his roots.
> The spirit of the LORD shall rest on him,
>   the spirit of wisdom and understanding,
>   the spirit of counsel and might,
>   the spirit of knowledge and the fear of the LORD.
> His delight shall be in the fear of the LORD.
>
> He shall not judge by what his eyes see,
>   or decide by what his ears hear;
> but with righteousness he shall judge the poor,
>   and decide with equity for the meek of the earth;
> he shall strike the earth with the rod of his mouth,
>   and with the breath of his lips he shall kill the wicked.
> Righteousness shall be the belt around his waist,
>   and faithfulness the belt around his loins.
>
> The wolf shall live with the lamb,
>   the leopard shall lie down with the kid,
> the calf and the lion and the fatling together,
>   and a little child shall lead them.

> The cow and the bear shall graze,
>> their young shall lie down together;
>> and the lion shall eat straw like the ox.
> The nursing child shall play over the hole of the asp,
>> and the weaned child shall put its hand on the adder's den.
> They will not hurt or destroy
>> on all my holy mountain;
> for the earth will be full of the knowledge of the LORD
>> as the waters cover the sea.

Notice especially in this text how central a place wisdom plays. The spirit of the Lord that rests on this ruler is the spirit of wisdom (*hokmah*) and understanding (*binah*), counsel and might, knowledge and fear of the Lord. Such wisdom and knowledge give the king insight to judge not by what his eyes see or ears hear but with righteousness (*tsedeq*) and justice (*mishpat*), especially concerning the plight of the poor and the meek. Then and now appearances easily deceive. To gain the truth, one must see behind what first appears, perceive beyond what seems to be the case. We need discernment. We need insight. We need understanding. In short, we need wisdom.

And when this messianic king rules as God intended Adam to rule, all creatures will flourish. Imbued with authentic wisdom and true understanding, empowered and directed by the spirit of Yahweh, this Davidic king will rule with righteousness and justice. Because of such Spirit-inspired rule, a peaceable kingdom will come to be—a place in which violence and destruction are no more. Shalom will reign.

The New Testament also speaks of wisdom.[37] For example, Luke notes that, like the king foretold by the prophet Isaiah, Jesus is from the house of David (Luke 1:69). Luke emphasizes that as a child, Jesus was "filled with wisdom, and the favor of God was upon him" (2:40) and that as he grew older, "Jesus increased in wisdom" (v. 52). Matthew records that when Jesus returned to his hometown of Nazareth and taught in the synagogue, the people "were astounded and said, 'Where did this man get this wisdom and these deeds of power?'" (Matt. 13:54). Luke tells us that when in the early church community there was a need to look after widows who were not receiving enough food, seven men of good standing, "full of the Spirit and of wisdom," were appointed (Acts 6:3). Hence the first deacons came to be, who not only saw to it that food was equitably distributed (vv. 1–3) but also functioned as elders by teaching (vv. 9–10).

The apostle Paul speaks often of wisdom. Astonished at the amazing grace of God in bringing together both Jew and Gentile, in doxological language

Paul exclaims, "O the depth of the riches and wisdom and knowledge of God! How unsearchable are his judgments and how inscrutable his ways!" (Rom. 11:33). The wisdom of God is beyond all human comprehension, for the God who made multiple covenants with the Jews has also included non-Jews. To use Paul's metaphor, the wild olive branch that is the gentiles has been grafted onto the tree that is the Jews. This text reminds us, as the old hymn puts it, "There's a wideness in God's mercy like the wideness of the sea." God's mercy extends to all, even if we cannot fathom it.

Contrasting the so-called wisdom of this age with the wisdom of God, in his first letter to the church in Corinth, Paul writes that "among the mature we do speak wisdom, though it is not a wisdom of this age or of the rulers of this age, who are doomed to perish" but rather "we speak God's wisdom, secret and hidden, which God decreed before the ages for our glory" (1 Cor. 2:6–7). God's wisdom is everlasting while the wisdom of this age (*aiōn* not *kosmos*) is perishable. God's wisdom is hidden but has been revealed in Christ, God incarnate, crucified and risen—knowledge revealed only by the power of the Holy Spirit. While many claim to be wise, Paul contends that "the wisdom of this world is foolishness with God" (3:19). Wisdom has many counterfeits. What passes as wisdom in our contemporary culture is not genuine wisdom. Authentic wisdom can be found in the mystery of God in human flesh, dying and rising for the redemption of the world.

With tenderness and love for the church at Ephesus, Paul prays that God "may give you a spirit of wisdom and revelation as you come to know him, so that, with the eyes of your heart enlightened, you may know what is the hope to which he has called you, what are the riches of his glorious inheritance among the saints, and what is the immeasurable power for us who believe, according to the working of his great power" (Eph. 1:17–19). Wisdom is a gift from God, found in coming to know the risen Christ. With this wisdom, we are able to have hope—that confident expectation of God's good future of righteousness and reconciliation made real for all creation. With this wisdom, we come to know our holy inheritance as sons and daughters "in Christ." With this wisdom, we learn what authentic power truly is—the power of love to conquer death and sin (Eph. 2:4–10).

And after a plea that the Colossians clothe themselves "with compassion, kindness, humility, meekness, and patience" and "forgive each other; just as the Lord has forgiven you," Paul exhorts his friends to "let the word of Christ dwell in you richly; teach and admonish one another in all wisdom; and with gratitude in your hearts sing psalms, hymns, and spiritual songs to God" (Col. 3:12–13, 16). This text explodes with virtues: compassion, kindness, humility, meekness, patience, forbearance, gratitude, and wisdom. And most of all, love (*agapē*). Tucked in the middle is the appeal that we teach and admonish one another in wisdom. In order to grow in faith, we need the wisdom made possible by the indwelling of Christ.

In all these texts, wisdom is a cherished possession—a kind of knowing rooted in the worship of God that enables us to live well and all creation to flourish. Wisdom is a trait of character that runs against the grain of our culture's fetish with mere knowledge but with the grain of God's creation as it bends toward shalom. Wisdom is ultimately a gift of the Holy Spirit that helps us comprehend what we can of the mystery of Jesus Christ and forms us to live as servants of Christ—with humility, gratitude, and love.

Ecological Self-Control and Wisdom

Let's summarize what we have learned from the previous sections. The virtue of self-control is the strength of mind or will to regulate desires. The extinction of all desire (as if that were possible) is not the goal. The aim, rather, is disciplined desire. The old-fashioned word *temperance* gets at the core meaning: habitual control of one's appetites in order to have the right desire for the right things.

The vice of deficiency that runs contrary to self-control is self-indulgence. Self-indulgent people lack the necessary self-control. They lack the strength of mind or will sufficient to control certain desires. As Aristotle notes, "These people are called belly-gods, this implying that they fill their belly beyond what is right."[38] Our desire for food is normal, but we need the ability to control what and how much we eat. This vice takes many forms, depending on the object of one's desire: food, alcohol, money, power, sex, stuff. In each case, self-indulgence names the inability to control one's desires.

The vice of excess, in which there is too much self-control, is austerity. Austerity is self-control gone stern and severe. If overly self-controlled, we mistake masochism for moderation and assume the passions are inherently evil. Desire per se is dangerous. Pleasure of any sort is banned or frowned on. This, too, has multiple forms—for example, taking no pleasure in home-cooked food or fine wine or meaningful work. Kathryn Blanchard and Kevin O'Brien succinctly describe self-control and its two vices: "Christians are called to be conscious and deliberate about our consumption, always guarding against mindless self-indulgence at one extreme and joyless abstinence at the other."[39]

The virtue of *ecological self-control* names the habitual disposition to control our desires when it comes to caring for the natural world. When we exhibit this virtue, we have in mind a clear-eyed appraisal of what we have and what we truly need, and we do an honest assessment of what others (human and nonhuman) need. We know what our local place and our home planet are capable of providing, and we are disposed or inclined to control our desires in order to foster the flourishing of others. We say, with gratitude and joy, "I am content; I have enough; I don't need more."

Self-control or temperance shows up often in the writings of those who advocate an ecological virtue ethic. For example, when describing the virtues of moral role models, Philip Cafaro observes that for Henry David Thoreau "virtues crucial for the construction of an environmental virtue ethics include temperance, integrity, sensibility to beauty, and perhaps most important, simplicity."[40] Cafaro also comes at the identification of essential ecological virtues by listing the most damaging vices. In addition to arrogance, greed, and apathy, he lists gluttony as one of the four major ecological vices. While gluttony usually refers to overindulgence with respect to food, it comes in many kinds—for example, excess in drink and sex. In all these cases, Cafaro observes that "traditionally the virtue opposed to gluttony was *temperance* or *moderate use*"; he astutely lists "*gratitude* as a complementary virtue."[41] Temperance and gratitude are two of the character traits necessary to foster not just human well-being but the flourishing of all things.

Ronald Sandler also includes temperance in his discussion of ecological virtues. More exactly, Sandler lists temperance as one of his "virtues of sustainability," along with frugality, farsightedness, attunement, and humility.[42] These virtues dispose people to promote the goods of the natural world around them. Given the influence of materialism in contemporary culture, these virtues are crucial. In Sandler's words, "Consumptive dispositions are bad for people. Greed, intemperance, profligacy, and envy are vices. They tend to be detrimental to their possessor's well-being, and they favor practices that compromise the environment's ability to provide environmental goods. Moderation, self-control, simplicity, frugality, and other character traits that oppose materialism and consumerism are environmental virtues, inasmuch as they favor practices and lifestyles that promote the availability of environmental goods."[43] Peter Wenz echoes Sandler when he argues that frugality and temperance are two of the virtues needed to combat consumerism. "When people have a sense of what is enough," Wenz avers, they "know when to stop eating, when they have enough clothing, and when a fancy wine is just too expensive."[44]

Michael Northcott argues that "temperance is an essential ecological virtue, for it involves the right ordering of human appetites so that these do not lead either to abuse of one's person, or other people, or to abuse and excess consumption in relation to the non-human world." Without temperance, Northcott insists, "we cannot distinguish between a genuine need for food or material security and comfort, and an ecologically harmful quest for luxury and excess."[45] Self-control is an indispensable ecological virtue.

In contrast, the vice of deficiency is self-indulgence. The ecologically self-indulgent consume the earth beyond what they truly need or what the earth can properly bear. Ignorant about the earth and its many inhabitants, they see only themselves and their own desires. Or indifferent with respect to our nonhuman neighbors and the worldwide web of relationships of which we all are a part, the self-indulgent simply don't care enough to preserve what is valuable or restore what is in need of repair. Whether because of obliviousness or apathy, the self-indulgent perpetuate the ruination of the earth.

The vice of excess is austerity. For the ecologically austere, all delight in creation's goodness is squeezed out of life and all joy found in the fitting use of God's good gifts is squelched. There is no pleasure taken in smelling a rose, caressing a cat, beholding a night sky. There is no sabbath delight—no relishing of God's good gift of a world full of wonders. Self-control devolves to a rigid list of dos and don'ts or a somber litany of legalistic requirements. Desire per se becomes the target, not disordered desire. Dour abstinence masquerades as a virtue.

As indicated above, a virtue closely related to ecological self-control is frugality. Frugality is from the Latin *frugalis*, from *frux* (fruit). It is similar to the verb *frui* (to enjoy). Frugality is economy in the use of resources or efficient use, given the limits of the goods available. To be frugal is to use something in such a way that you enjoy it and are able to continue using and enjoying it in the future. It is the proper use of finite goods. Thus, frugality is characterized not by a parsimonious wish to hold in or keep back but rather by a desire to use sparingly that which God has provided, in order that others (human and nonhuman) may live and flourish. Rightly understood, therefore, frugality represents a form of hospitality.

The vice of deficiency that corresponds to frugality is greed—the disposition to excessively acquire, especially beyond one's need. *Avarice* is perhaps a more accurate term, for it denotes a craving to acquire that is blinded to the limits inherent in creation. Driven by acquisitiveness, the greedy person lacks any sense of the finitude of the world. The vice of excess is stinginess, or thrift as an end in itself. Sparing to the point of being mean, the stingy exhibit no generosity. Fearful of whether there will be enough, the tightfisted hold in and keep back. Economy for economy's sake is their motto. In the case of each vice, there is no enjoyment of that which God has provided.

James Nash argues that frugality is a "subversive virtue" much needed today because it "resists the temptations of consumer promotionalism—particularly the ubiquitous advertising that pressures us through sophisticated techniques to want more, bigger, better, faster, newer, more attractive, or 'state of the art'"; it also "struggles against various psychological and sociological dynamics, beyond market promotionalism, that stimulate overconsumption."[46] Frugality is self-control's kissing cousin—that kindred disposition that enables us to feel content with what we have and thus empowers us to respect the rights and meet the needs of our neighbors, human and nonhuman.

In sum, because the earth is finite, we need to care for our home planet, and all God provides for us, by gratefully living within our means. This requires that we cultivate the ecological virtue of self-control, thereby discouraging the currently fashionable vice of self-indulgence while also avoiding the vice of austerity.

What then of the virtue of wisdom? To recap, the virtue of wisdom is the settled disposition to make sound practical judgments. Informed by the time-tested knowledge of the local community and attuned to how God has wisely ordered creation, the wise person is able to recognize what the greatest good really is and has the practical knowledge needed to attain it. So wisdom enables us to ferret out fake ends and discern unfair and/or unloving means of attaining them. If we are wise, we are able to make insightful decisions about the equitable distribution of medical care. We are able to distinguish cause from effect when analyzing why so many homeless folk are on the street. We are able to understand why the tap water is not safe to drink and make discerning judgments about what to do next. Wisdom is the virtue that allows us to live well by praising God and serving our neighbors.

There is only one vice contrary to wisdom—namely, foolishness or the propensity to act unwisely. Foolishness is the habitual absence of sound judgment. If foolish, we lack good sense. We show no discernment. We eschew learning from the past, shower scorn on our elders, and thus make the same mistakes again and again. We perpetually run off after the latest deal, only to be scammed and lose our shirt. We think cleverness is the same as wisdom. If foolish, we confuse "the goods life" for the good life.

The virtue of *ecological wisdom* is the disposition to make insightful and discerning judgments about our common home, the earth. If ecologically wise, we take seriously the cycles and scales of the natural world. We take the long view—we think in terms of decades and centuries—and thus plan (far) ahead. And we expand our range with regard not only to time but also to space. We see everything connected to everything else and so adopt the canoe camper's version of the Golden Rule: treat those downstream as you would have those upstream treat you. Humbly aware of the limits of our knowledge, especially about the natural world, we exercise restraint since there are often unintended and unforeseen consequences to our actions. We adopt the Precautionary Principle and thus go slowly when there are high levels of uncertainty or risk. If ecologically wise, we remind a culture infatuated with the "World Wide Web" that the most important (and original) worldwide web is biodiversity.

Following the lead of Aldo Leopold, Bill Shaw emphasizes the importance of ecological wisdom in his discussion of what he calls "the land virtues": respect for biotic communities, prudence, and practical wisdom. The first refers to the respect we humans show for the intrinsic value of not just nonhuman organisms but also communities and ecosystems. Prudence means being thoughtful and having the habit of "not rushing to judgment" when making decisions about matters ecological. Practical wisdom names an acquired sensitivity to ecological communities and the ability to sort out "the rival claims and interests within and among communities."[47]

Michael Northcott states that prudence (along with love, justice, temperance, fidelity, courage, hope, and peaceableness) "is also of profound ecological significance, for the waste and pollution of non-renewable or pristine natural resources is clearly imprudent, if not in terms of our own welfare, then in terms of the welfare of our children and grandchildren." In addition, Northcott affirms, prudence "would encourage us to be cautious about mobilizing technologies whose hazards are not fully understood and accounted for."[48] For the love of our children and because of the inherent risks of our technology, we ought to be prudent or wise.

Ecological wisdom appears often in discussions of current ecological problems. For example, applying ecological virtue ethics to climate change, Ronald Sandler argues that "because global warming accelerates the rate of change and exacerbates the information deficit and uncertainty about the ecological future, it makes biological and cultural adaptation to ecological changes more difficult, for both us and other species"; hence there is a pressing need for virtues such as humility and patience, self-restraint and practical wisdom.[49] In a warming world, we need more eco-wisdom. Not surprisingly, Philip Cafaro agrees with his friend and occasional coauthor in listing wisdom, along with humility, as one of the two "overarching virtues."[50]

Anders Melin highlights ecological virtue ethics in his discussion of endangered species, and he brings a thoughtful Christian perspective to bear on the virtue of ecological wisdom or prudence. He argues that in addition to respect, reverence, justice, temperance, and courage, "prudence is of obvious relevance in the context of species protection," since "well-considered decisions concerning the protection of species require that we, first of all, determine which values should be realized and how they should be weighed against each other."[51] Melin insists that "prudence is important in connection with environmental decision-making because we need sound judgment and foresight."[52] Sound judgment and foresight—precisely what ecological wisdom provides.

Blanchard and O'Brien also pair the virtue of prudence with the pressing challenge of protecting endangered species. They affirm that "prudence is not about being a judgmental prig or miserly bore, but about intelligence, sagacity, and discretion." They contend that "it is time for the revival of this most basic virtue," for "without prudence none of the other virtues could accomplish anything."[53] Blanchard and O'Brien insist that while "there are many self-interested reasons to care about the diverse species with which human beings share the world," prudence "is not merely about serving self-interest," since in the final analysis Christians "are called to care for the world because . . . it belongs to God."[54] Whether striving to protect the (widely) famous snail darter or the (relatively) unknown burying beetle, we need to embody ecological wisdom.

The vice of *ecological foolishness* is the disposition to act as if the earth is endlessly exploitable and expendable. Because we are enslaved to this vice, ecological services such as the natural purification of water are invisible to us, and we view ecological costs such as air and water pollution as "externalities." Valuing only short-term consequences, we act as if the future—for both our human descendants and the earth's nonhuman creatures—does not matter. Focusing only on three-month economic returns or four-year election cycles, we are blind to the longer life cycles of muskrats and marshes and maple trees. We do not see our home planet as the holy mystery it is, and thus cannot see what goes by the name of "prosperity" for what it truly is—namely, the long-term despoliation of God's good earth.[55]

In sum, ecological wisdom nurtures shalom. If we are to foster the flourishing of all creatures, as well as live the truly good life for ourselves, then we must be people of wisdom. If we are to avoid the ecological foolishness that haunts our age, then we must linger long at the fount of wisdom. If we are to live as God intends, we must worship God and love all our neighbors by acting with discernment and insight.

Self-Control and Wisdom Embodied

Susan Drake Emmerich teaches at a liberal arts college and runs an environmental consulting firm.[56] A former US State Department negotiator, she brings the skills of diplomacy to her work. And because she is a Christian, she also brings her faith to her work. The combination of these two, along with other intangibles of upbringing and experience, means that she is a person of uncommon wisdom. She needed all the self-control and wisdom she could muster when working with the watermen of Tangier Island in the Chesapeake Bay and the environmentalists with whom they clashed, but she pulled off nothing less than a miracle.

The year was 1998 and Susan was on Tangier Island doing research for her doctoral degree from the University of Wisconsin–Madison. She was living among a community of fishermen called the Tangier watermen. Because of pollution, disease, and overharvesting, only one fishery was left—the blue crab. Consequently, the people of Tangier Island were being pressured by a group of environmentalists, the Chesapeake Bay Foundation (CBF), to change their fishing habits. The watermen, meanwhile, worried about their economic well-being and the intrusion of outsiders into their way of life.

Tempers flared and emotions ran high on both sides. Some staff from the CBF were condescending toward the people of Tangier Island and acted in ways that showered disdain on the islanders. Feeling powerless to reverse the decline of their fishery, the watermen showed little respect for those who used the abstract language of environmental science, who were clueless about matters of faith, and whose actions might seriously affect their business bottom line. They were suspicious of the CBF, and for good reason. The impasse seemed inescapable.

Susan immersed herself in the island culture. She lived at the same economic level as the majority of the islanders. She dressed according to the island's conservative standards. She attended worship services and taught Sunday school at the local Methodist church. She helped the women process crabs. Susan genuinely cared about the people and showed respect for their way of life, and thus quickly won the trust and garnered the love of many of the island people.

But it was not easy. Susan was ostracized by certain members of the island community. She even received death threats. And after the circulation of falsehoods about an outside speaker, the whole process of forging a stewardship covenant came perilously close to blowing up in her face. But in the end her efforts paid off, for Susan helped launch a faith-based stewardship initiative, led by the people of Tangier Island, resulting in a cleaner island and a healthier fishery. Realizing that all sides desired a healthy Chesapeake Bay fishery, Susan helped the CBF staff appreciate the watermen's faith-based cultural values, and she helped the watermen appreciate the goals of the CBF and other secular environmentalists. She also enabled the watermen to live into the biblical faith they already professed. Where the Chesapeake Bay Foundation had failed, Susan succeeded beyond anyone's wildest imaginings.

The success of Susan Drake Emmerich on Tangier Island was due to many things: her unique combination of communication skills, her personal integrity, her ability to tap into the already existing biblical ethic of stewardship that the watermen possessed. But her success was also due in large measure to her exceptional strength of mind and uncommon discernment. Susan embodies the virtues of self-control and wisdom.

The Coulters[57]

It was a run-down farm. The old Cuthbert place fronted on Sand Ripple Road just south of Shade Branch Creek. A few rock fences had survived years of neglect. Most of the buildings were dilapidated. Nothing had been painted or repaired in quite some time. The house, shaded by beautiful old sugar maples, was in need of some tender loving care. Once a healthy and productive farm, now, in the spring of 1948, it was almost abandoned. And it was for sale. Nathan Coulter, fresh back from fighting in World War II, was looking to settle down in his hometown of Port William, Kentucky. The Cuthbert place wasn't much, but it was what Nathan could afford. So he bought it.

With his new bride, Hannah—whose first husband, Virgil Feltner, had died in the war—Nathan began the arduous task of restoring the old run-down farm to new life. Nathan and Hannah scraped away the loose wallpaper, washed all the windows, and bought a new stove and refrigerator. They raided their friends' attics for furniture. They got dishes from their grandparents. Nathan mowed the yard, mended a fence, and repaired two stalls in the feed barn. Hannah planted daylilies, put up new curtains, and cleaned everything in sight. Before long, a Jersey cow was grazing with the two mules, and the cow's milk and cream were on the kitchen table. A friend gave them some hens, and soon enough they were eating the eggs from the henhouse. Nathan and Hannah were making a home.

They laid their land out in three levels, in terms of steepness. On the top level, the most gently sloping land, they raised their crops and made their hay. Nathan's rules were steadfast: never plow too much in one year, never grow more grain than you need, and never have too much livestock. Trees were left for shade, and ponds were dug for irrigation water when needed. Where the slopes were steeper but not too steep to mow, they made permanent pastures and kept the cattle off when the ground got soggy in order to prevent erosion.

On the bottom level, where the slopes were the steepest, they let the trees grow and put up fences to keep the cattle out.

On this farm—repaired and on the way to being restored—Nathan and Hannah raised their three children. Here they made a life. Looking back five decades later, Hannah remembers the pattern of their life and comes to realize that with Nathan's death and her growing inability to work, the history of their place is fading away. Nonetheless, she is also aware that all their work and sweat is evident. "Our place," she was proud to say, "shows everywhere the signs of careful use." To those with the eyes to see, she once remarked to Jayber Crow, the town barber, "A lifetime's knowledge shimmers on the face of the land."[58] While not immune from the tragedies that befall us all, Nathan and Hannah lived a good life, not least in wisely caring for their place and all those—human and nonhuman—who were members of it.

While Troy Chatham exuded ecological foolishness, Nathan and Hannah Coulter epitomize ecological wisdom as imaginative embodiments of Wendell Berry's agrarian vision of a flourishing world. The contrast is stunning. Oh, that we today, each in our own place, would strive with God's grace to exemplify the much-needed dispositions displayed by the Coulters—strength of mind and discernment.

4

Living with Respect and Care

Justice and Love

Intergenerational solidarity is not optional, but rather a basic question of justice, since the world we have received also belongs to those who will follow us.

Pope Francis[1]

I still believe that love is the most durable power in the universe.

Martin Luther King Jr.[2]

Love of Trees, Mountains, and Earth

In a section of Aldo Leopold's classic work *A Sand County Almanac*, the pioneering twentieth-century conservationist writes about his preferences when cutting trees.

I find it disconcerting to analyze, *ex post facto*, the reasons behind my own axe-in-hand decisions. I find, first of all, that not all trees are created free and equal. Where a white pine and a red birch are crowding each other, I have an *a priori* bias; I always cut the birch to favor the pine. Why?

Well, first of all, I planted the pine with my shovel, whereas the birch crawled in under the fence and planted itself. My bias is thus to some extent paternal, but this cannot be the whole story, for if the pine were a natural seeding like the birch, I would value it even more. So I must dig deeper for the logic, if any, behind my bias.

The birch is an abundant tree in my township and becoming more so, whereas the pine is scarce and becoming scarcer; perhaps my bias is for the underdog.

But what would I do if my farm were further north, where pine is abundant and red birch scarce? I confess I don't know. My farm is here.

The pine will live for a century, the birch for half that; do I fear that my signature will fade? My neighbors have planted no pines but all have many birches; am I snobbish about having a woodlot of distinction? The pine stays green all winter, the birch punches the clock in October; do I favor the tree that, like myself, braves the winter wind?

So I try again, and here perhaps is something; under this pine will ultimately grow a trailing arbutus, an Indian pipe, a pyrola, or a twin flower, whereas under the birch a bottle gentian is about the best to be hoped for. In this pine a pileated woodpecker will ultimately chisel out a nest; in the birch a hairy [woodpecker] will have to suffice. In this pine the wind will sing for me in April, at which time the birch is only rattling naked twigs. These possible reasons for my bias carry weight, but why? Does the pine stimulate my imagination and my hopes more deeply than the birch does? If so, is the difference in the trees, or in me?

The only conclusion I have ever reached is that I love all trees, but I am in love with pines.[3]

"I love all trees, but I am in love with pines." With these simple words, Leopold expresses his unadorned affection for a family of trees common to his part of the world.

On August 14, 1869, an unknown Scottish immigrant, who had recently arrived in San Francisco and walked 150 miles east to the mountains, wrote in his journal:

On the way back to our Toulumne camp, I enjoyed the scenery if possible more than when it first came to view. Every feature already seems familiar as if I had lived here always. I never weary of gazing at the wonderful Cathedral. It has more individual character than any other rock or mountain I ever saw, excepting perhaps the Yosemite South Dome. The forests, too, seem kindly familiar, and the lakes and meadows and glad singing streams. I should like to dwell with them forever. Here with bread and water I should be content. Even if not allowed to roam and climb, tethered to a stake or tree in some meadow or grove, even then I should be content forever. Bathed in such beauty, watching the expressions ever varying on the faces of the mountains, watching the stars, which here have a glory that the lowlander never dreams of, watching the circling seasons, listening to the songs of the waters and winds and birds, would be endless pleasure. And what glorious cloudlands I should see, storms and calms—a new heaven and a new earth every day, aye and new inhabitants. . . . One would be at an endless Godful play, and what speeches and music and acting and scenery and lights!—sun, moon, stars, auroras. Creation just beginning, the morning stars "Still singing together and all the sons of God shouting for joy."[4]

The writer is John Muir, and these reflections arise from Muir's first summer in the Sierra Nevada of California. After four decades of wanderlust, Muir had, at long last, found his home. He would ramble and roam and explore (and write about) these mountains for the next four decades of his life—until his death in 1914.

Muir's love was all-inclusive—embracing unmoving rocks and frolicking water, enormous trees and tiny flowers, swimming birds and secretive bears. Muir writes of his affection for individual creatures—the silver fir, the water ouzel, the Douglas squirrel—and his wonder at the geologic forces and processes of nature such as glaciers, weather, forest succession. Most of all, he writes in lucid and rapturous prose of his love of this special place: the Sierra Nevada. The Range of Light, as he called it, was his cathedral, and he was never more at home than when he was gamboling about in it. Such love is infectious. In reading Muir, many have caught the bug.

A third voice. Near the end of her award-winning book *Pilgrim at Tinker Creek*, Annie Dillard gives perhaps the most profound description of love of the natural world. After an astonishingly illuminating survey of creatures strange and marvelous, she comments:

> I am a frayed and nibbled survivor in a fallen world, and I am getting along. I am aging and eaten and have done my share of eating too. I am not washed and beautiful, in control of a shining world in which everything fits, but instead am wandering awed about on a splintered wreck I've come to care for, whose gnawed trees breathe a delicate air, whose bloodied and scarred creatures are my dearest companions, and whose beauty beats and shines not in its imperfections but overwhelmingly in spite of them, under the wind-rent clouds, upstream and down.[5]

As Dillard makes abundantly clear, she holds no romanticist view of nature, devoid of all bites, stings, or death. In Dillard's world, what I call the three Ps—parasites, predators, and pathogens—are very much in detailed existence. Nevertheless, this world is "a splintered wreck I've come to care for." Shaped by wonder at both its beauty and its tragedy, Dillard expresses her love for this earth.

What does one make of these expressions of love for plant, place, and planet earth? Are these affirmations of affection explainable in the typical terms and categories we use in ethics? More exactly, what does the virtue of love look like when viewed through an ecological lens? Is the settled disposition to care for beloved animals and precious plants and special places simply another version of the generic virtue of love? And what of justice? What does an ecological take on justice look like?

Examinations of (In)Justice

In the late 1970s, an evangelical Christian pastor founded La Ciudad Cristiana—Christian City—a housing project in Humacao, Puerto Rico. His desire was to build a place free from drugs, alcohol, gambling, and other evils of urban life. Its low-cost housing received financing through Puerto Rico's development agency. The pastor, Ray Figueroa, hoped to provide the residents of Christian City with a concrete expression of their new life in Christ. But shortly after moving into this settlement, some residents became mysteriously ill. Terrible headaches, rashes, dizziness, loss of hair, miscarriages, and other afflictions spread like the plague.

At first the doctors could find no conclusive causes for these illnesses. Then it was discovered that the fish swimming in the creek by Christian City were contaminated with mercury. Tests showed surprisingly high levels of mercury on the banks of the creek and in the soil on which low-cost housing for low-income people was built.[6] Mercury levels there were seventeen to thirty times higher than the average in the United States. Two out of every three residents had higher than normal levels of mercury, with many suffering from intoxication. Why all the mercury? It turns out that during the 1970s industries located upstream from the site of Christian City had regularly dumped their waste into the creek. At least one of them, which manufactured medical equipment, produced mercury—an irony not lost on the stricken residents.

In 1985, all twelve hundred residents of Christian City were evacuated. Because other people incorrectly believed they were carrying a contagious disease, the former Christian City residents were often shunned and ostracized, like lepers. Elizabeth Alagrin, a former resident, described her agonizing five years of life in Christian City this way: "Not even in the Bible is there a hell as bad as this."[7]

Was this just a coincidence? Or is there a connection between where poor people live and where toxic waste is found? Is exploitation of the earth more prevalent in poor communities? Is there not only a correlation but also a causal connection between socioeconomic class and ecological degradation?

Environmental injustice with respect to class is but one manifestation of environmental injustice. Ecological degradation is also linked to race. In 1987, Reverend Benjamin Chavis, then executive director of the United Church of Christ's Commission on Racial Justice, and Charles Lee, also of the United Church of Christ, coauthored a report titled *Toxic Waste and Race in the United States: A National Report on the Racial and Socio-Economic Characteristics of Communities Surrounding Hazardous Waste Sites*.[8] This milestone study examined the locations of hazardous waste facilities and then, controlling for different variables, looked for positive correlations between the locations of those hazardous waste sites and factors like class, sex, and race. The results were striking. The study revealed that although socioeconomic status plays an important role in the location of commercial hazardous waste facilities, race is the leading factor. Three out of the five largest commercial hazardous waste landfills in the United States are located in mostly African American or Hispanic communities. Three out of five African Americans and Hispanics live in communities with one or more uncontrolled toxic waste sites. Cities with large African American populations—such as St. Louis, Cleveland, Chicago, Atlanta, and Memphis—have the largest numbers of uncontrolled toxic waste sites. About half of all Asian/Pacific Islanders and Indigenous peoples live in communities with uncontrolled waste sites.[9]

The overarching conclusion of this groundbreaking study is that race is the best predictor in identifying communities most likely to have toxic waste sites. Charles Lee provides a succinct and clear summary: "The racial composition of a community is the single variable best able to explain the existence or non-existence of commercial hazardous waste facilities in that area. Racial minorities, primarily African-Americans and Hispanics, are strikingly over-represented in communities with such facilities."[10] As a result of this and subsequent studies, a new term was coined—*environmental racism*—to name this particular conjunction of environmental degradation and social injustice.[11]

The links from environmental degradation to socioeconomic class and race represent only two forms of environmental injustice. There are also connections between the degradation of the earth and the oppression of women. When women in a sexist culture are symbolically linked to the earth, then the earth will be abused just as women are. Rosemary Radford Ruether, for example, argues that "we cannot criticize the hierarchy of male over female without ultimately criticizing and overcoming the hierarchy of humans over nature."[12] In other words, the domination of the natural world by humans is linked to the domination of women by men; thus, proper care for the earth must go hand in glove with the liberation of women.[13] *Eco-feminism* is one name for the movement that aims to confront this form of injustice.[14]

What, then, is environmental justice? The Environmental Protection Agency (EPA) offers this comprehensive though ponderous definition:

Environmental justice is the fair treatment and meaningful involvement of all people regardless of race, color, national origin, or income with respect to the development, implementation, and enforcement of environmental laws, regulations, and policies. Fair treatment means that no group of people, including racial, ethnic, or socioeconomic group, should bear a disproportionate share of the negative environmental consequences resulting from industrial, municipal, and commercial operations or the execution of federal, state, local, and tribal programs and policies. Meaningful involvement means that: (1) potentially affected community residents have an appropriate opportunity to participate in decisions about a proposed activity that will affect their environment and/or health; (2) the public's contribution can influence the regulatory agency's decision; (3) the concerns of all participants involved will be considered in the decision making process; and (4) the decision makers seek out and facilitate the involvement of those potentially affected.[15]

Simply stated, environmental justice is fairness for all people. It is evenhandedness in bearing the costs of environmental degradation and impartiality when participating in the decision-making process, regardless of race, sex, or class.[16]

So it shouldn't matter whether you are white or black or brown or any other skin color when it comes to finding an environmentally safe place to rent an apartment or own a house. It shouldn't matter whether you are female or male when it comes to paying your fair share of the cleanup costs for the old foundry. It shouldn't matter whether you are rich or poor when it comes to having a voice in the decision about where to put the new natural gas power plant. Environmental justice requires that we all bear the costs equitably and that we all have a fair say in the process of making decisions about environmental issues in our community.

Justice (not just the environmental kind) has to do with fairness. And fairness has to do with equitably sharing the burdens and the benefits of our common life, without regard to the various identity markers that define us as humans.

Meditations on Love

In his fascinating book *Topophilia*, geographer Yi-Fu Tuan explores the idea of love of place. The word *topophilia* is from two Greek words: *topos* (place) and *philia* (one of the four Greek words for love, in this case, friendship). Tuan defines topophilia as "the affective bond between people and place or setting," or alternately, "all of the human being's affective ties with the material environment."[17] Tuan notes that this affection for place takes many forms and varies in intensity—from simple delight in the feel of air, touch of water, or smell of earth to a profound longing for home as a locus of memories and belonging and hope.

Indeed, Tuan catalogs different aspects or dimensions of topophilia. Physical contact is one such feature. He notices that for farmers the world over, attachment to the land is deep.[18] The smell of hay. The feel of soil. The warmth of a horse or cow or goat. Tactile sensations and physical contact inform knowledge of and love for place. Familiarity is another feature of topophilia. Affection is rooted in a long history in a particular place and a keen awareness of its past. For example, Tuan observes how Australian Aborigines venerate ancestral home sites and see recorded in the landscape the ancient story of their people and culture.[19] Keith Basso makes similar observations about the importance of place to the Navajo in the American Southwest.[20] Local patriotism, notes Tuan, is another aspect of topophilia. Local patriotism is the love of one's *terra patria* or natal land and "rests on the intimate experience of place, and on a sense of the fragility of goodness: that which we love has no guarantee to endure."[21] There is much more to Tuan's analysis, but for our purposes the main point is clear: affection for place is very real, and while topophilia has many facets, love lies at its center.

Other writers speak in similar ways about love of place. Wes Jackson, founder of the Land Institute, speaks of the need to become native to one's place—to learn about and come to love the place in which we live, rather than constantly pining away for some other place. So he argues that universities should offer a "homecoming major" in which students would learn the knowledge and skills necessary to know, love, and care for their home places.[22] There can be no home without love of place.

Perhaps more well known is Wendell Berry, who describes what Tuan calls topophilia in almost everything he writes. An award-winning author of fiction, creative nonfiction, and poetry, Berry writes of the profound need for us today to come to know and love our particular places and of the devastating consequences of our failure to do so.[23] In one of his more recent addresses, Berry argues that "it all turns on affection."[24] Whether we live well, in the end, depends on the depth of our affection for the world—human and nonhuman—and especially for our local community. All of human life is contingent on our knowledge of and love for our home places.[25] In short, Berry and others give ample evidence for what Tuan calls topophilia.

Topophilia, or love of place, is only one kind of love for the natural world. E. O. Wilson describes another basic human love—namely, *biophilia* or the love (*philia*) of living things (*bios*). More exactly, Wilson defines biophilia as "the innate tendency to focus on life and lifelike processes."[26] We have an innate urge to affiliate with other forms of life. While the evidence for biophilia is "not strong in a formal scientific sense," since it has not yet been studied in a rigorous scientific manner, Wilson insists that "the biophilic tendency is nevertheless so clearly evinced in daily life and widely distributed as to deserve serious attention." For example, biophilia "unfolds in the predictable fantasies and responses of individuals from early childhood onward"; it "cascades into repetitive patterns of culture across most or all societies."[27] Furthermore, Wilson observes that "people react more quickly and fully to organisms than to machines. They will walk into nature, to explore, hunt, and garden, if given the chance. They prefer entities that are complicated, growing, and sufficiently unpredictable to be interesting."[28] In short, we have an emotional attachment to other living things.

These reflections describe love as affection for a place and for other living (nonhuman) organisms. But in common parlance the word *love* usually refers to a bond between people. And when speaking of love between people, we sometimes distinguish between benevolence and love.[29] Benevolence is the willingness to promote the well-being of another. Benevolent people have a good (*bene*) will (*volent*); a good will usually produces good works. Benevolence leads to beneficence. Furthermore, such acts are willed even if bonds of affection are absent. It is in this sense that Jesus commands us to love one another (Matt. 22:34–40; Mark 12:28–34; Luke 10:25–28), for while our affections cannot be commanded, our wills can. As both Jesus (Matt. 5:43–48) and Paul (Rom. 12:19–20) remind us, we should will the good, even to our enemies—even to those for whom we have no affection. So also, some argue, we should will the good not only to people but also to animals domestic and wild, ecosystems near and far.

The contrary of benevolence is malevolence. Malevolence or malice is the intention to do evil or cause harm. It is the culpable breaking of shalom. While often fueled by envy and resentment of particular people, it can also be driven by a desire to inflict suffering on victims with no known connection, as, for example, the terrorist whose evil actions are perpetrated against a random group of people. Acts of malice also describe the willful destruction of some creature or part of the natural world: torturing animals, vandalizing habitats, disrupting biotic systems.

How, then, does love differ from benevolence? Love is affection that moves us to care for another person. It is concern for the good of someone you care about. Such bonds of affection usually arise out of personal relationships, such as kinship or friendship. Hence love stands in contrast to benevolence, for which no such affection is required. Expanding beyond the realm of humans, love can also denote care for the house (*oikos*) and its inhabitants. Love includes not only people but also beloved animals (family pets) and favorite plants (aged trees) and special places (calming forests). Love names the affection for and care given to the pine tree, the mountain meadow, the splintered wreck of an earth we call home.

Given this concept of love, the contrary to love is apathy. Not to love is to lack feeling (*a-pathos*) and thus not to care. Hence the opposite of love is not hatred, as many think, but indifference. Apathy is the absence of any affection (and thus care) for creatures, human or nonhuman. Apathetic folk are unconcerned about the havoc wreaked on the earth. They do not understand Aldo Leopold when he laments, "One of the penalties of an ecological education is that one lives alone in a world of wounds."[30] Given these reflections on love, now what can we learn from Scripture?

Biblical Insights on Justice and Love

Justice is a key theme in the Bible. In the Old Testament, God requires of his people righteousness (*tsedeq*) and justice (*mishpat*). Indeed, they are integral to shalom—the grand vision of the flourishing of all things that permeates the Bible like the aroma of fresh-baked bread in Grandma's kitchen. For example, the last half of the Decalogue declares justice to be a central feature of human flourishing (Exod. 20:12–17). Stealing and bearing false witness are violations of justice. They are thefts of goods—material possessions and reputation, respectively—that rightly belong to someone else. The covenant stipulations in Leviticus and Deuteronomy often include requirements to do justice—especially for widows, orphans, and aliens (Lev. 19:15, 33; Deut. 10:18)—precisely because such acts accord with God's character.

Likewise, the prophets regularly thunder that God's justice be done. Amos proclaims, "Let justice roll down like waters, and righteousness like an ever-flowing stream" (5:24). Micah summarizes the requirements of right living with these words: "To do justice, and to love kindness, and to walk humbly with your God" (6:8). And Jeremiah's bones burn with the message of justice, calling on the people of Israel to amend their ways and act justly with one another—especially to make sure the alien, the orphan, and the widow are not oppressed (7:1–7).

We also find this concern for justice eloquently and passionately articulated in the Wisdom literature. For example, hear this prayer for God's blessing on the king.

> Give the king your justice, O God,
>   and your righteousness to a king's son.
> May he judge your people with righteousness,
>   and your poor with justice.
> May the mountains yield prosperity for the people,
>   and the hills, in righteousness.

> May he defend the cause of the poor of the people,
>   give deliverance to the needy,
>   and crush the oppressor. (Ps. 72:1–4)

> For he delivers the needy when they call,
>   the poor and those who have no helper.
> He has pity on the weak and the needy,
>   and saves the lives of the needy.
> From oppression and violence he redeems their life;
>   and precious is their blood in his sight. (vv. 12–14)

Here in Psalm 72 we read of justice. Justice is what allows the king to rule rightly, for rich and poor alike. Justice is what sensitizes the king to those who are weak and needy and thus especially vulnerable to being taken advantage of. Justice is what empowers the king to redeem the enslaved from oppression. And as in many other texts (e.g., Isa. 24), here in this psalm, justice among people is intimately tied to the health and fruitfulness of the land. Social justice and ecological health are bound together. Righteousness and justice, liberation and deliverance, compassion and care, especially for the poor, the needy, the defenseless. The prosperity of a country is rooted in justice, especially for those on the margins. In this robust description of the good king, we catch sight of justice as an integral part of God's good future of shalom.

Of all the elements of shalom in the biblical vision, justice is perhaps the most pervasive.[31] Shalom is absent whenever fundamental rights are flouted, whenever basic needs go unmet, whenever legitimate goods are not enjoyed. Thus liberation from injustice and freedom from oppression are at the very core of shalom. And of special concern in Scripture are the rights of those most vulnerable—the widows, the orphans, and the aliens or sojourners. These three groups show up often in Old Testament discussions of justice. As Nicholas Wolterstorff observes, "What is striking in the Old Testament declarations about justice is the passionate insistence that all members of the community are entitled to a full and secure place in the life of the community. Hence the clanging repetitive reference to orphans, widows, and sojourners. Over and over when justice is spoken of, that trinity is brought into view. For these were the marginal ones in ancient Israeli society. Justice arrives only when the marginal ones are no longer marginal."[32]

As indicated above, justice is an integral component of the larger biblical vision of shalom. There are (at least) three features of this vision. First, shalom names a vision of a flourishing human community. Shalom is not a descriptor for a single individual; rather, it aims to describe a community of people. Second, shalom describes humans at peace in all relationships: with

God, oneself, other people, and the natural world. Shalom is both communal and multirelational. And third, this vision of human flourishing includes more than humans; it has to do with all kinds of creatures living in right relationships. Shalom is as wide as creation itself. As Neal Plantinga puts it,

> The webbing together of God, humans, and all creation in justice, fulfillment, and delight is what the Hebrew prophets call *shalom*. We call it peace, but it means far more than mere peace of mind or a cease-fire between enemies. In the Bible shalom means *universal flourishing, wholeness, and delight*—a rich state of affairs in which natural needs are satisfied and natural gifts are fruitfully employed, a state of affairs that inspires joyful wonder as its Creator and Savior opens doors and welcomes the creatures in whom he delights. Shalom, in other words, is the way things ought to be.[33]

Fulfillment, wholeness, delight. The way things ought to be. God's will done on earth as it is in heaven.

In the New Testament, righteousness and justice are central to the words and deeds of Jesus and the message of the apostle Paul. Jesus redefines for the people of his day what true righteousness is all about. For example, in the Sermon on the Mount (Matt. 5–7), Jesus emphasizes, often in arresting antitheses, that true piety is a matter of the heart. True righteousness is not a matter of external ritual but of purity of heart and hunger for justice. Jesus encourages his followers to "seek first the kingdom of God and God's righteousness [*dikaiosynē*]" (6:33 RSV alt.), and in so doing they will receive the nourishment and bodily provisions they need. In his inaugural address (Luke 4), Jesus defines his mission, in part, as bringing justice to the oppressed. The new age dawning, of which Jesus speaks and to which he bears witness, is all about justice. No amount of interpretive gymnastics can drive Jesus's concern for social justice out of the Gospels.

Turning to the apostle Paul, some say that righteousness (*dikaiosynē*) is at the center of his understanding of the gospel.[34] It is the righteousness or justice of God that is most central for Paul—righteousness that we cannot attain on our own but that Jesus through his death has achieved for us (Rom. 4; Gal. 3; Phil. 3). But while this idea of righteousness as grace or divine favor is central, for Paul it has an inextricable social dimension. It is justice between people, especially Jews and gentiles, that most concerns Paul. As James Dunn puts it, "The Christian doctrine of justification by faith begins as Paul's protest not as an individual sinner against a Jewish legalism, but as Paul's protest on behalf of Gentiles against Jewish exclusivism."[35] It was the way Jews separated themselves from non-Jews, creating an us-versus-them mentality, that drew Paul's ire. Hence, justification "cannot be reduced to the experience of individual salvation as though that was all there is to it"; justification by faith, rather, "is Paul's fundamental objection to the idea that God has limited his saving goodness to a particular people."[36]

The Christian gospel is about reconciliation—with God, with other people, and with the earth. So classism, racism, and sexism (and other isms) have no place in the church and ultimately no place on earth. As Paul reminds us in often-quoted words from Galatians 3:25–28, "Now that faith has come, we are no longer subject to a disciplinarian, for in Christ Jesus you are all children of God through faith. As many of you as were baptized into Christ have clothed yourselves with Christ. There is no longer Jew or Greek, there is no longer slave or free, there is no longer male and female; for all of you are one in Christ Jesus." Paul's message is not that "in Christ" every aspect of our human identity becomes irrelevant. Paul is still very much aware of himself as a Jewish Christian, for example, and he is aware that some people are slaves and others are free. His point is that all these identity markers are irrelevant when it comes to our status in Christ. Water is stronger than blood. Christian baptism trumps race and ethnicity. Our fundamental identity is that we are children of God, one in Christ Jesus, Abraham's offspring. So in Christ there is no place for classism or racism or sexism. Injustice in any form is out of place when all things are reconciled in Christ.

In sum, these texts (and many others) emphasize the centrality of justice. Because the God of the Bible is just, those who worship God should be just. Of particular concern are those most likely to be treated unjustly—namely, the voiceless, the powerless, the homeless. And while this concern is most often focused on humans, it also includes those nonhuman creatures whose voices remain silent to human ears.

If justice is a central motif in Scripture, what then to make of love? A study of all the terms for and references to love in the Bible would require another book. So we must be selective. Let's begin at the beginning.

In the history of the interpretation of Genesis, most of the attention has been given to Genesis 1:26–28. There we read that humans were given dominion over the fish and the birds and the cattle and the wild animals and the creeping things. For many, this means that humans have license to exploit the nonhuman creatures of the earth. That is to say, dominion is understood as domination. However, this reading is clearly wrong, not to mention self-serving. Dominion does not mean domination but responsible care. Genesis 1:28 must be placed alongside Genesis 2:15, where we are told that God put the human in the garden "to till it and keep it." To till (*'abad*) means to serve the earth for its own sake, and to keep (*shamar*) means to protect the earth as one carefully guards something valuable. In Aaron's benedictory blessing, in which God is called on to "bless and keep" his people (Num. 6:22–26), we catch sight of what it means to be a keeper. As God keeps us—with care and concern—we are to keep the earth. In summing up the message of this text, Calvin DeWitt puts it well:

> When we invoke God's blessings to keep the assembled people, we are not praying merely that God would keep them in a kind of preserved, inactive, uninteresting state, like one might keep a museum piece, a preserved specimen, or pickles in a jar, but rather that God would keep them in all their energy and beauty. . . . This is also the thrust of Genesis 2:15. When we act on God's will and charge to keep the garden, we make sure that the creatures under our care are maintained with all the proper connections with members of the same species, with the many other species with which they interact, and with the soil and air and water upon which they depend.[37]

In short, we are called to care for what we keep.

It is no surprise that love shows up in one of the most beautiful descriptions of the flourishing of all things, found in Psalm 85. In a group prayer for deliverance from national adversity, the psalmist pleads:

> Let me hear what God the LORD will speak,
>   for he will speak peace to his people,
>   to his faithful, to those who turn to him in their hearts.
> Surely his salvation is at hand for those who fear him,
>   that his glory may dwell in our land.
>
> Steadfast love and faithfulness will meet;
>   righteousness and peace will kiss each other.
> Faithfulness will spring up from the ground,
>   and righteousness will look down from the sky. (vv. 8–11)

Salvation for those who fear Yahweh is at hand. And what does that salvation look like? Steadfast love (*hesed*) and faithfulness (*'emunah*) will embrace; righteousness (*tsedaqah*) and peace (*shalom*) will kiss. Four more potent words in the Bible could not be found, especially in such close proximity. Faithfulness (*'emunah*) depicts a God who is as reliable and trustworthy as a rock (Ps. 95). Righteousness (*tsedeq*) describes a God who desires rightness in all relationships and who enjoys the delight of boys and girls playing in the street (Zech. 8:3–8). And peace (*shalom*) is that pregnant Hebrew term that strives to name the ideal of this world flourishing in all things and praising God in all ways. All are also crucial marks of God's people and the world God desires.[38]

Of special note here is the Hebrew word *hesed*. Usually translated "steadfast love" or "covenant love," the term indicates the love of God deep and wide. *Hesed* refers to the kind of love—God's love—that endures forever (Pss. 100:5; 103:17). *Hesed* names the everlasting love and compassion that God has for us (Isa. 54:8). The God who hears the groaning of his chosen people suffering in Egypt, remembers his covenant, and acts to relieve their suffering and liberate his people from exile (Exod. 6:2–8) is the God of *hesed* (though the precise term is not used here). So we are admonished to "hold fast to love [*hesed*] and justice [*mishpat*]" (Hosea 12:6). In sum, God's love does not end, will not fail, never gives up.

Turning to the New Testament, we find a great many texts that speak of love. For example, in the Sermon on the Plain (Luke 6:17–49), Jesus instructs his followers on what it means to follow him. He exhorts his followers to love their enemies, do good to those who hate them, pray for those who abuse them. Jesus then states:

> If you love those who love you, what credit is that to you? For even sinners love those who love them. If you do good to those who do good to you, what credit is that to you? For even sinners do the same. If you lend to those from whom you hope to receive, what credit is that to you? Even sinners lend to sinners, to receive as much again. But love your enemies, do good, and lend, expecting nothing in return. Your reward will be great, and you will be children of the Most High; for he is kind to the ungrateful and the wicked. Be merciful, just as your Father is merciful. (vv. 32–36)

Be merciful (*oiktirmōn*), just as God is merciful. God is compassionate, so we also should be compassionate. This is one of the main themes in Luke's Gospel: Jesus is the compassionate savior of all. Hence those who follow him are called to show mercy and compassion.[39]

Compassion, as its etymology suggests, means to bear or suffer (*pati*) with (*com*) another. It is one person feeling the pain of another and reaching out to relieve that pain if possible. As Paul encourages us in Romans 12:15, we are to "rejoice with those who rejoice and weep with those who weep." He exhorts his readers in Colossians 3:12, to "clothe yourselves with compassion [*splanchna oiktirmou*]"—literally "guts of compassion"—or, more colloquially, "have a heart of mercy." Compassion is, as Neal Plantinga succinctly puts it, "the empathetic pity that wants to spare, relieve, or nurture somebody who is suffering."[40] Allen Verhey offers a similar definition: "Compassion is a visceral response to the suffering of another" that "moves us to want to do something in response to another's suffering."[41]

The compassionate person does five things: she perceives the suffering, empathizes with the sufferer, feels sorrow over her suffering, wants to relieve her suffering, and will, if possible, relieve her suffering.[42] This requires, among other things, paying attention. There can be no compassion unless we perceive the suffering of another. Compassion also requires a supple imagination. Feeling the pain of another, when the experience may be foreign to you, implies the imaginative ability to walk a mile in another person's shoes. Compassion also requires the strength of will to act for the good of the sufferer. So a compassionate person cares for the suffering one by virtue of empathizing with that person, and such care is for the sake of those suffering; that is, both the motive and the goal of compassion are directed to the one in need. In short, compassion is the disposition to care, rooted in sympathy for the suffering. It is the kind of *agapē* displayed by Jesus.

It is this feeling-with the suffering of another that marks the fundamental difference between compassion and benevolence. As stated previously, benevolence is the willingness to promote the good of another. Benevolent people are disposed to act kindly. And such good acts are willed even if affection is absent. It is in this sense that Jesus commands us to love one another (Matt. 22:36–40), for while our affections cannot be commanded, our wills can. We can and should will the good, even to our enemies (5:44; Rom. 12:19–20), for whom we have no good feelings. Benevolence is a good thing. It is not to be disparaged. If more of us more often willed the good, even in the absence of any feeling for the sufferer, our world would be a better place. Even better, however, is compassion. Even better is suffering-with. Even better is care for others rooted in sympathy for the suffering.

While the greatest commandment (Matt. 22:36–40; Mark 12:28–31; Luke 10:25–28) is often mentioned as the heart of Jesus's teaching on love, a better candidate is the "new commandment" Jesus gives and the way he himself lived it out. The norm for love is Jesus in word and deed.[43] After enacting his love by washing his disciples' feet and enjoining his followers to do as he did by washing one another's feet (John 13:1–20), Jesus declares, "I give you a new commandment, that you love one another. Just as I have loved you, you also should love one another. By this everyone will know that you are my disciples, if you have love for one another" (vv. 34–35). Love, says Jesus, as I love. Love by serving one another. Love to the point of a cross. And if you love one another the way I love you, people will know you are my followers.[44] After the seventh and last of Jesus's "I ams" ("I am the vine, you are the branches"; 15:5), Jesus repeats this "new commandment" (v. 12): "This is my commandment, that you love one another as I have loved you." In word and in deed, Christ is the exemplar of *agapē*.

A note on terminology. The term *love* in English has come to mean almost everything and thus virtually nothing. In recent times, "love" has been reduced to denote either a romantic feeling or the erotic, which itself has been reduced to sex. By contrast, in ancient Greece, *erōs* meant desire of whatever kind, including but not reducible to sexual desire.[45] And in Scripture, love is commanded, indicating that it is more than merely a feeling. The finer distinctions need not detain us here. It will suffice to distinguish between what C. S. Lewis calls "need-love" (*erōs*) and "gift-love" (*agapē*).[46] Lewis Smedes puts it well: need-love is "the power that drives us to satisfy our own deepest needs"; gift-love is "the power that moves us to satisfy the needs of another."[47] Love for our own sake and love for the sake of the other. We need them both, though they are different, and shalom includes them both.[48] It is gift-love, however, that is of special interest here, for that is the love that plays such a prominent role in the Bible. This is true especially when we examine the words and deeds of Jesus. But what exactly is this kind of love?

Smedes nicely summarizes this kind of agapic love when he speaks of Jesus as "love's living model." In response to the question "How did Jesus love us?" Smedes makes four claims.[49] First, love moved Jesus to help people. He not only had feelings of love; Jesus acted lovingly. Helping "was his life-style and his death-style." Second, love moved Jesus to help all people. Jesus was indiscriminate in his loving. He excluded none and often went out of his way to embrace those most needy. Jesus's love was all-inclusive. Third, love moved Jesus to help all people for their sake. It is extremely difficult to ascribe self-seeking motives to Jesus. Jesus was, to quote Dietrich Bonhoeffer's famous line, "the man for others."[50] Fourth, love moved Jesus to help all people for their sakes without regard for cost. The Gospels do not show Jesus doing a cost-benefit analysis. His was not a calculating love. The price of love was high, but he paid it, ultimately, with his life. In sum, concludes Smedes, "these four pencil strokes in the infinite portrait of divine love suffice to remind us that the love which moved almighty God into our need-zone was very different from the good feelings one has in the presence of an attractive person."[51] *Agapē*, or gift-love, is this kind of love. It means being moved to help others for their sake without regard for cost.

This kind of love is often the topic of conversation in the writings of the apostle Paul. Many passages come to mind. In Romans 12–13, Paul offers his own sort of Sermon on the Mount, instructing us to bless those who persecute us and not repay evil with evil. Indeed, Paul asserts that the Ten Commandments are "summed up in this word: 'Love your neighbor as yourself'" (13:9). In 1 Corinthians 13, love brings up the rear as the most important of the three virtues, for only love in the end will abide. In Ephesians 3, after a profound exposition on grace, faith, and reconciliation, Paul prays that "Christ may dwell in your hearts through faith, as you are being rooted and grounded in love" (v. 17)—a love that surpasses knowledge in its breadth and length and height and depth. In all these texts, the operative word is *agapē*.

This laser focus on love is not limited to the Gospels or the Letters of Paul. The author of Hebrews encourages us to "let mutual love continue," especially in showing hospitality to strangers (13:1–2). Peter echoes Paul's words about not repaying evil for evil and Jesus's command to love one another (1 Pet. 3:8–12). The Epistles of John are filled with encouragements to love (1 John 4:7–21; 2 John 5–6; 3 John 5–6). And, last but not least, the concluding chapters of Revelation describe a mind-bending vision of God's good future—a future of unending love.

In sum, justice and love are central to the Bible and at the core of the Christian faith. Justice is a sine qua non of the biblical vision of shalom. In God's good future, all wrongs are put to right and justice reigns supreme. And the biblical vision of shalom cannot be described except by reference to love. Steadfast love runs like a refrain throughout the Old Testament, and gift-love, Jesus tells us, is the summary of the Law and the Prophets—a love that he embodied in his own life. These words from Scripture reverberate with the affirmations of Martin Luther King Jr.: "There is something in the universe that unfolds for justice," and "Love is the most durable power in the world."[52]

Ecological Justice and Love

Let's recap what we have learned about justice. Justice is about fairness. In whatever form, justice concerns equity.[53] More exactly, as Nicholas Wolterstorff argues, justice is what due respect for the worth of someone requires.[54] It is treating someone as befits her or his worth and, as such, involves respecting the rights of that person.[55] Justice, at its core then, is about respect. Justice is proper respect for the rights of others. For example, distributive justice has to do not only with the allocation of goods based on legitimate claims to those goods but also with the equitable allotment of goods. Justice is done, we say, when we render to each that to which they have a right. So a just society is one in which everyone's sustenance rights are respected—when the basic goods of food and water and shelter are adequately provided and enjoyed by all. Justice, in sum, is fairness fueled by respect.

What, then, is the virtue of justice? The virtue of justice is the habitual disposition to treat others fairly. The just person is inclined to treat others equitably. She treats equals equally and unequals differentially, for equity is not the same as equality. Equality implies sameness: one treats all, regardless of circumstances, the same. Equity implies different treatment depending on circumstances, precisely in order to be fair. As parents know, to be equitable, we treat similar children in similar circumstances the same, but treat children in dissimilar situations differently. All children have chores, but the fifteen-year-old is given more work than the ten-year-old. Differential treatment, not equal treatment, denotes equity.

The fairness at the heart of the virtue of justice is fueled by respect. Respect is an understanding of and proper regard for the integrity and well-being of another. It is looking back—a re-specting—that acknowledges God-given value or worth. If respectful, you show both esteem for and deference to another person because of the value of that person. A respectful person neither overlooks you nor looks you over. You are neither part of the scenery nor an object of conquest. The just person respects your rights.[56]

So the virtue of justice is the disposition to act equitably. It is habitual fairness rooted in respect. Given that it requires the ability to discern when to treat equals equally and unequals differentially, the virtue of justice requires a kind of practical wisdom. In other words, the virtue of justice assumes an ability to discern when circumstances warrant differential treatment and when people, despite differences, should be treated the same. In this regard, Aristotle's exposition on practical wisdom (*phronēsis*) is instructive.[57] Practical wisdom, he argues, involves a number of other intellectual abilities such as deliberation, understanding, and judgment—the latter of which he calls "the right discrimination of the equitable." So the just person not only respects peoples' rights but also knows how rightly to respect one person's rights when faced with the competing rights (and needs) of others. In short, the virtue of justice requires wisdom.

In contrast to most other virtues, the virtue of justice is not a mean. Hence it has only one vice—namely, injustice. Injustice is the propensity to be partial. We play favorites for no good reason or, more perversely, for personal gain. If we are unjust, we are not inclined to be evenhanded, impartial, or fair-minded. We fail to give people their due and thus continually violate their rights. We fail to show respect for others. The parent who always favors, for no good reason, the oldest son over the youngest daughter exhibits the vice of injustice. The city council that continually looks the other way regarding racist housing practices exhibits the vice of injustice. The country that steadfastly refuses to acknowledge the legitimate rights of its native peoples exhibits the vice of injustice. In all these cases, there is no fairness because there is little or no respect.

The virtue of *ecological justice* names the settled disposition to act fairly when faced with the recognized rights or legitimate claims of creatures both human and nonhuman. If we exhibit this virtue, then we not only respect the rights of humans—women and men, racial and ethnic minorities, citizens and immigrants—but also show respect for the value of domestic animals and wild plants, endangered species and damaged ecosystems. We render with equity to human and nonhuman alike that which their worth requires.

Kathryn Blanchard and Kevin O'Brien also emphasize the virtue of justice, though their view on what counts morally seems limited to humans. For them, the virtue of justice is "the ability to treat all people fairly, to include all people in community decisions, and to work toward God's vision of an integrated and equal future for the human race."[58] In their application of the cardinal Christian virtues to various contemporary ecological issues, they pair justice with discussions about pollution and toxic waste. Echoing the two-pronged definition from the EPA, they highlight how environmental justice has to do with "how hazards such as nuclear waste are distributed across the human community" and also "who gets to participate in making decisions about such waste."[59] Whether fighting for healthy neighborhoods in cities or safe working conditions in farm fields, we need "the habit of seeing others as God's children regardless of their differences from ourselves or their distance from our positions."[60] I heartily agree, but respect for the value of other creatures need not be limited to humans.

Among other writers on environmental virtue ethics, Ronald Sandler lists justice as one of his "virtues of stewardship." These virtues include the disposition not only to appreciate environmental goods and maintain them as public goods but also "to see that the goods are justly distributed."[61] In other words, Sandler's notion of eco-justice seems to focus on distributive justice—how we most equitably allocate scarce goods to others.

The vice contrary to ecological justice is *ecological injustice*. This vice names the disposition to violate the rights of others or to fail to respect the worth of others, including nonhuman creatures.[62] So this vice comes in two forms. For nonhuman creatures that have rights, ecological injustice is our failure as moral agents to respect those rights. For example, we violate the rights of domestic animals such as dogs and cats when we fail to care properly for them. Their rights to live and flourish imply duties or moral obligations for us as moral agents. Indeed, these moral obligations are codified by laws against the inhumane treatment of certain animals. Our failure to respect their rights is an act of ecological injustice. To act habitually in such a way is to exhibit the vice of ecological injustice.

For nonhuman creatures without recognized rights but whose intrinsic value generates duties for us as moral agents, ecological injustice names our failure to honor the worth of those creatures or places.[63] For example, while we do not grant giant sequoias rights, we (or at least many people) acknowledge their worth or value. Cutting down such trees in the late nineteenth century was an injustice—not because we violated their rights but because we failed to honor their worth. When we habitually fail to honor properly the value of the natural world and its nonhuman creatures, we also exhibit the vice of ecological injustice. In either case, we treat other creatures—human and nonhuman—unjustly.

What, then, of the virtue of love? There are a number of helpful typologies of love,[64] and while this is not the place to delve into an in-depth discussion of the various types, we do need to make some distinctions. As indicated earlier, benevolence is the promotion of the good of someone as an end in itself, without necessarily feeling moved to and without justice requiring it. In other words, benevolence is the willingness to promote the well-being of another as an end in itself, even if the bonds of affection are absent and even if no one's rights demand it. It is willing the good regardless of affection.

Agapic love (from the Greek *agapē*) is promoting the good of someone as an end in itself simply because that someone is your neighbor. As Wolterstorff puts it, "Agapic love is that form of benevolent love which is bestowed on someone just because she is a neighbor."[65] This is what C. S. Lewis and Smedes call gift-love. This kind of love can coexist with other forms of love such as attraction-love and attachment-love. Indeed, most of the time agapic love is accompanied by these other kinds of love. Bonds of affection and attachment usually arise out of personal relationships that produce a love that promotes the well-being of the beloved for its own sake. But agapic love may also exist by itself. It may, for example, "seek to promote as an end in itself the flourishing of someone to whom I am neither attached nor attracted, someone whose company I don't like."[66]

Love as care, borrowing terminology from Wolterstorff, is that form of agapic love that seeks to promote another person's good. But unlike benevolence, which promotes someone else's good as an end in itself provided justice does not require it, love as care seeks to promote someone's good while also ensuring that the person is treated justly. Love as care "combines seeking to enhance someone's flourishing with seeking to secure their just treatment."[67] In this way, doing justice is an example of love. Justice and love are not contraries, as often thought, but there is justice in love.[68] Love as care names a kind of love that includes justice. In the words of Óscar Romero: "It is a caricature of love to try to cover over with alms what is lacking in justice, to patch over with an appearance of benevolence when social justice is missing. True love begins by demanding what is just in the relations of those who love."[69] Love includes justice.

The virtue of love, then, is the habitual disposition to care for the needs of another person. Often but not always rooted in affection, it is the steady inclination to promote someone's good and secure their rights—not as a means to some other end but as ends in themselves.[70] It is similar to benevolence, for which there need not be feelings of affection, but unlike benevolence the habitual disposition of love includes securing the rights of the one you love. The virtue of love, in this sense, fosters care regardless of what you feel and thus can dispose you to love even your enemies.

The virtue of love is not a mean between extremes. There is no excess but only deficiency, and hence there is only one vice. The vice contrary to the virtue of love is care-less-ness. This is the habitual inclination not to promote someone's good and secure their rights as ends in themselves. It is the failure to seek the flourishing of another person as an end in itself. There are at least two forms: malevolence and apathy. Motivated by ill will, the malevolent actively seek to harm others. Filled with indifference, the apathetic by their neglect allow harm to come to others. In either case, the goods of others go unrealized and their rights are flouted.

The virtue of *ecological love*, as its etymology suggests, names the settled disposition to care about our house (*oikos*) and its inhabitants—to promote the flourishing of all creatures. It is the care we have not only for people but also for animals and plants and special places. Volunteers at the local humane society, workers at the city zoo, children on the family farm or at home with a beloved pet—all these display the disposition of love, a disposition rooted in sympathetic understanding and evident in actions of care. And such love can also be directed to places—forest and mountain, river and desert, park and garden and farm. These places of the heart evoke loyalty, affection, and care. As the writings of Wes Jackson, Wendell Berry, and Terry Tempest Williams demonstrate, we sometimes come to love a place so much that we grieve its violation or its loss.[71]

So who are our neighbors? We Christians are called to love our neighbors, but how expansive is that group? Do we consider the nonhuman inhabitants in our part of God's good earth to be our neighbors? As discussed, Scripture teaches that we are kin with all creatures. We humans are creatures, even if we don't want to admit it. Furthermore, all creation is created and infused by the love of God. So it should not be surprising that we who claim to follow this God of love expand the scope of our love to include more than humans. Our love includes the whole *oikos*.

The vice contrary to ecological love comes in two forms: *ecological malevolence* and *ecological apathy*. In neither form is there care or concern for the *oikos*. Ecological malevolence is the habitual disposition to destroy other creatures and places. The ecologically malevolent intentionally wreak havoc on the earth. They engage in the willful destruction of the nonhuman world. Torturing animals. Vandalizing habitats. Disrupting biotic systems.

Ecological apathy is the absence of care for other creatures and places. The ecologically apathetic are oblivious to and unconcerned about the havoc wreaked on the earth. They do not lament the loss of the giant catalpa tree. They do not grieve the destruction of the old meadow. They do not weep when the water is no longer drinkable. The ecologically apathetic do not mourn the loss of anything natural.

When creatures and places are well known and thus evoke affection, care usually comes easily. But people who embody the virtue of ecological love promote the flourishing of nonhuman creatures and places even when affection is absent. Geoffrey Frasz speaks of this when he describes benevolence as an environmental virtue.[72] This virtue is the active and consistent care for the flourishing of more than humans. Frasz expands the concept of community to include the nonhuman, both living and nonliving. This expansion of the sphere of moral concern to include all things—species and ecosystems and watersheds—is what for Frasz distinguishes benevolence as such from benevolence as an environmental virtue. The environmental virtue of benevolence, he also argues, implies the related virtues of proper humility, patience, and perseverance, as well as the character traits of imagination and attentiveness.

Frasz is not the only one to emphasize love-as-care as an ecological virtue. Philip Cafaro also includes care among the other environmental virtues he lists (patience, persistence, self-control, humility, respect, and self-restraint).[73] He defines care as "respect for non-human beings" and describes it as "one key environmental virtue that natural history study strongly promotes."[74] Cafaro also comes at the ecological virtue of love by exploring the environmental vices of gluttony, arrogance, greed, and apathy.[75] Apathy, he argues, is lack of care for others, including nonhuman others, and thus is the contrary of love, supporting my claim that apathy (not hatred) is the vice contrary to the virtue of love.

Louke van Wensveen develops a set of ecological virtues she calls "virtues of care." These include humility, friendship, attentiveness, benevolence, and love.[76] She, too, distinguishes between benevolence and love and argues that care and benevolence are among those virtues that would most likely be considered the most important virtues.[77] These cardinal environmental virtues sensitize us to the needs of all creatures, human and nonhuman, and thus are crucial dispositions if we are to properly care for the world in which we live.

Justice and Love Embodied

What does ecological justice look like embodied? Many names come to mind, but there are few more celebrated than Wangari Maathai, founder of the Green Belt Movement and cofounder of the Nobel Women's Initiative; recipient of the Nobel Peace Prize and the Indira Gandhi Prize for Peace, Disarmament, and Development; receiver of the Conservation Scientist Award from Columbia University and the World Citizenship Award from the Girl Scouts. Her list of awards and honors seems endless.

Born in a rural Kenyan village in 1940, Wangari Muta Maathai was educated by Catholic missionaries and later received bachelor's and master's degrees in biology in the United States. She went on to earn a doctoral degree in veterinary anatomy in Germany. She died in 2011.

A celebrated advocate of environmental restoration and women's rights, Maathai is best known for her work planting trees as part of the Green Belt Movement. She founded the Green Belt Movement in 1977 as a grassroots nongovernmental organization (NGO) based in Nairobi, Kenya. On June 5 in Kamukunji Park on the outskirts of Nairobi, Maathai and others from the National Council of Women of Kenya planted seven trees in honor of community leaders. This was the first "Green Belt." Many more were to follow. Maathai encouraged women to plant trees and develop tree nurseries all over Kenya, using seeds from trees native to the area and paying the women a small stipend for each seedling that was later planted. Her goal was to help women by providing fuel for cooking and to stop deforestation and soil erosion. This was not just a program in ecological restoration but also a way to empower women and fight poverty. It was (and still is) a rich example of how people can work together for both environmental conservation and social justice.

Since the Green Belt Movement started, over 51 million trees have been planted, and over 30,000 women have been trained in forestry, beekeeping, food processing, and other trades that help them earn income while preserving their land. This NGO uses planting trees and facilitating community education to change the system of oppression that prevents women in rural Kenya from accessing education, resources, and land. The Green Belt Movement also provides resources to communities that strive to hold national leaders accountable.

Wangari Maathai's humble beginning planting trees in Kenya has grown to become the Green Belt Movement International. By providing education, access to water, and social equity, among other things, this global organization empowers people—most of them poor and most of them women—to improve their lives. By planting trees and facilitating community education to change the current systems of oppression that prevent women from getting the education and resources they need to flourish, the kind of work for ecological justice first begun in Kenya is being replicated around the world.

Maathai was a living portrait of the virtue of ecological justice. In her own words:

> Although I was a highly educated woman, it did not seem odd to me to work with my hands, often with my knees on the ground, alongside rural woman. Some politicians and others in the 1980s and 1990s ridiculed me for doing so. But I had no problem with it, and the rural women both accepted and appreciated that I was working with them to improve their lives and the environment. After all, I was a child of the same soil. Education, if it means anything, should not take people away from land, but instill in them, even more, respect for it, because educated people are in a position to understand what is being lost. The future of the planet concerns all of us, and we should do what we can to protect it. As I told the foresters, and the women, you don't need a diploma to plant a tree.[78]

The statement announcing her as the 2004 recipient of the Nobel Peace Prize is perhaps the most succinct summary of her life: "Maathai stood up courageously against the former oppressive regime in Kenya. Her unique forms of action have contributed to drawing attention to political oppression—nationally and internationally. She has served as inspiration for many in the fight for democratic rights and has especially encouraged women to better their situation."[79] Ecological justice embodied.

What does ecological love look like in action? Listen to these wise words from a longtime lover of the land: "In a lifetime of trying to preserve wilderness, I have seen love's impact and known its power. . . . I think back to my own early experience in the Quetico-Superior country, when our first battles were fought by a handful of men who, because of their feeling for the canoe country, dedicated themselves to its preservation. They did not fight because of any interest in the material values of the area's resources, but for their love of something they had found beyond price."[80] Such are the reflections, late in life, of Sigurd Olson (1899–1982)—one of the greatest environmentalists of the twentieth century.[81]

Olson dedicated his life to the preservation of wild places, not only those he knew but also those he didn't know. He is most famous for his unwavering efforts over four decades to bring into existence in 1978 the Boundary Waters Canoe Area Wilderness—one million acres of wilderness in Superior National Forest in northeastern Minnesota, contiguous along a 120-mile border with another million acres of wilderness in Ontario's Quetico

Provincial Park. Olson also helped establish Voyageurs National Park in northern Minnesota, Alaska's Arctic National Wildlife Refuge, and Point Reyes National Seashore in California. If that were not enough, Olson had a strong hand in drafting and passing the Wilderness Act of 1964. He also served as president of the Wilderness Society and president of the National Parks Association.

A bestselling author and well-known activist, Olson is the only person to receive the highest honors from all four of the most prominent wilderness organizations: the Sierra Club, the National Wildlife Federation, the Izaak Walton League, and the Wilderness Society. Also, in 1974 he received the John Burroughs Medal, the highest award in nature writing. And in 1972 Northland College, nestled along the south shore of Lake Superior in Ashland, Wisconsin, opened the Sigurd Olson Institute to commemorate his work and continue his legacy of wilderness conservation.

Olson worked his entire adult life to ensure that the Quetico-Superior remain forever wild. Why? Because of his love for that place. In the succinct words of biographer David Backes, "Love was the most important element in Olson's environmentalism."[82] In Olson's own words, "There can be no real lasting land ethic without love."[83] Using the language of Aldo Leopold, Olson acknowledges that no effort at land conservation will persevere without care for the land. Love of place is crucial. As Olson affirms:

> Without love of the land, conservation lacks meaning or purpose, for only in a deep and inherent feeling for the land can there be dedication in preserving it. Love has many meanings, and it is harder to speak of with respect to environment than of one's attachment to another person. However it is interpreted, love is the lodestone that makes possible the sacrifice of time, energy, and money required to carry on any effort to save a portion of the natural scene or the earth itself from the impact of man's manipulations.[84]

This kind of love, Olson admits, is hard to describe, but it is, nevertheless, very real. And it takes many forms and has many objects. "Love involves sensitivity, a sense of stewardship and concern. One can love a flower for its beauty, a rock for its permanence and stability, or a tree for its meaning in the kaleidoscope of vegetational change. One can love an animal and cherish the return of its affection; love has to do with associations over the years, some particular place where a person has known happiness with others."[85] Sigurd Olson is an example of a person who embodied over a lifetime the ecological virtue of love.

Thinking like a Mountain

In the mid-1920s, a young US Forest Service ranger, newly assigned to the Gila National Forest in New Mexico, was on patrol with his coworkers. Eating lunch high up on the edge of a river valley, they spotted what they thought, from a distance, was a female deer fording the river down below. When the animal emerged on the other side, they realized it was not a doe but a wolf. Our friend writes, "A half-dozen others, evidently grown pups, sprang from the willows and all joined in a welcoming melee of wagging tails and playful maulings. What was literally a pile of wolves writhed and tumbled in the center of an open flat at the foot of our rimrock." He continues, "In those days we had never heard of passing up a chance to kill a wolf. In a second we were pumping lead into the pack, but with more excitement than accuracy: how to aim a steep downhill shot is always confusing. When our rifles were empty, the old wolf was down, and a pup was dragging a leg into the impassible slide-rocks."[86]

And so begins the story told by Aldo Leopold in the essay "Thinking like a Mountain" from his seminal work *A Sand County Almanac*. As he indicates, wolves were then known as dangerous predators of the deer that hunters prized, and so Leopold and his friends shot at the wolves unthinkingly, hitting one adult and a pup. Impressed with themselves, the group hurried down to the river to examine their target. In now-famous prose, Leopold describes his experience of watching the adult wolf die: "We reached the old wolf in time to watch a fierce green fire dying in her eyes. I realized then, and have known ever since, that there was something new to me in those eyes—something known only to her and to the mountain. I was young then, and full of trigger-itch; I thought that because fewer wolves meant more deer, that no wolves would mean hunters' paradise. But after seeing the green fire die, I sensed that neither the wolf nor the mountain agreed with such a view."[87] Lament and remorse. An expression of grief and a recognition of error. And a resolution that things must change.

As a professor at the University of Wisconsin–Madison, Leopold would go on to write the very first textbook on "game management," found the field of wildlife management, teach and mentor countless students and future leaders, work to change state laws and federal regulations, and begin his own experiment in land restoration at his famous "Shack."[88] Writing some thirty years later in his magnum opus, Leopold reflects on this pivotal experience of shooting and killing the wolf:

> Since then I have lived to see state after state extirpate its wolves. I have watched the face of many a newly wolfless mountain, and seen the south-facing slopes

wrinkle with a maze of new deer trails. I have seen every edible bush and seedling browsed, first to anaemic desuetude, and then to death. I have seen every edible tree defoliated to the height of a saddlehorn. Such a mountain looks as if someone had given God a new pruning shears, and forbidden Him all other exercise. In the end the starved bones of the hoped-for deer herd, dead of its own too-much, bleach with the bones of the dead sage, or molder under the high-lined junipers.

I now suspect that just as a deer herd lived in mortal fear of its wolves, so does a mountain live in mortal fear of its deer. And perhaps with better cause, for while a buck pulled down by wolves can be replaced in two or three years, a range pulled down by too many deer may fail of replacement in as many decades.

So also with cows. The cowman who cleans his range of wolves does not realize that he is taking over the wolf's job of trimming the herd to fit the range. He has not learned to think like a mountain, hence we have dustbowls, and rivers washing the future into the sea.[89]

Leopold learned to "think like a mountain." We today need to learn to think like a mountain—to think ecologically, with greater understanding of how interdependent everything is. And this understanding must be infused with respect for the earth and care for its many creatures. In short, we need to cultivate the ecological virtues of justice and love.

In the famous concluding section of *A Sand County Almanac*, titled "The Land Ethic," Leopold writes, "It is inconceivable to me that an ethical relation to land can exist without love, respect, and admiration for the land and a high regard for its value."[90] If no love, then no ethical relation. Just a few pages earlier, Leopold comments that "we can be ethical only in relation to something we can see, feel, understand, love, or otherwise have faith in."[91] And a few pages earlier yet, Leopold observes that "the land ethic simply enlarges the boundaries of the community to include soils, waters, plants, and animals, or collectively: the land." He then remarks, "This sounds so simple: Do we not already sing our love for and obligation to the land of the free and the home of the brave? Yes, but just what and whom do we love?"[92]

What and whom do we love? The language of love is deeply woven into Leopold's land ethic. That is as it should be, for love in action is the embodiment of his ethic. Love in action is also at the center of the Christian calling to be earthkeepers. But this love, to be love, must include justice. Love as care can be what it is only if it includes respect for what and whom we love. We must understand justice and love as symbiotic partners as we expand our respect and care to include all that has value and stands in need. Ecological justice and love. May each of us find ourselves like Leopold in love with a special tree or like Muir in love with a favorite mountain and thus filled with respect and care for this splintered wreck of an earth on which we live.

5

Living with Fortitude and Expectation

Courage and Hope

I wanted you to see what real courage is, instead of getting the idea that courage is a man with a gun in his hand. It's when you know you're licked before you begin but you begin anyway and you see it through no matter what.

Atticus Finch, in *To Kill a Mockingbird*[1]

"God's reign is already present on our earth in mystery. When the Lord comes, it will be brought to perfection." (quote from Vatican II, *The Church in the Modern World*)

That is the hope that inspires Christians. We know that every effort to better society, especially when injustice and sin are so ingrained, is an effort that God blesses, that God wants, that God demands of us.

Óscar Romero[2]

Susan's Dilemma[3]

Susan Hart's home was nestled in the quietest corner of a hollow in Prestonsville, Kentucky, a place her family had called home for four generations. Tiptoeing the upper boundaries of middle age, Susan lived alone. Her two children had long since moved out of the family home, from which she now operated a daycare service for local families. Each morning she opened her doors to overwhelmed parents who trusted their children to her expert care. She spent each day playing with, cooking for, and cleaning up little boys and girls until midevening, when she opened her door with a knowing smile to the last tired and grateful parent returning from work.

At last Susan could have some calm. Sitting on the steps of her front porch, she took in the peace and stillness of the old hills at dusk. As she beheld acres of land that had been home to her family for nearly one hundred years, Susan was filled with a great sense of belonging. Yet she found herself unable to empty her mind of worry. Left alone with her thoughts, her mind was consumed with the previous evening's telephone conversation.

The night before, the phone rang just as she sat down on the porch steps, giving her a start. Susan stood back up, opened the creaky screen door, and shuffled in her slippers over to where the telephone rested on its cradle. The man on the phone was a legal representative of Omega Energy, Inc., one of the nation's leading extractors of Appalachian coal. After politely introducing himself, the man wasted no time in informing Susan that Omega Energy was interested, very interested, in acquiring her property, since the company was in the process of drawing up plans to strip-mine the adjacent mountain. He was quite direct in his manner of speaking. Omega would pay her fairly for her acreage. He then named the company's price. Moments later, after the man left her with his phone number and a promise to be in touch soon, Susan slowly hung up the phone, silent and bewildered.

Now, with time to think, Susan considered the proposal. Omega had offered a tempting sum of money. With only the income from the daycare to support her, Susan, like so many of her neighbors, was forever financially insecure. With the money from the coal company, she could live comfortably in the present as she never had before, and her fears about the future would be assuaged as well. If she refused to sell, she would likely lose the revenue from her daycare center. What parent in their right mind would deposit their child so close to a mountaintop removal (MTR) site, with its warlike explosions and its hulking coal trucks hustling down the narrow mountain roads?[4] If Susan were to hold her ground, she might lose her business and her livelihood.

Whatever her decision, the community was clearly divided by these recent developments. Of those approached by Omega, some residents said they were choosing to stay while others had decided to take the money. The takers were doing so because of their poverty and perhaps out of fear. In the past, it was not uncommon for holdouts to be harassed. Susan thought of the array of bumper stickers plastered on her neighbors' trucks, sporting phrases such as "I'm a Friend of Coal" and "Don't Like Coal? Sit in the Dark!" Many people in her community were unfalteringly loyal to the industry that had fed their families for generations.[5] To stand her ground and refuse this offer might be taken as a statement of dissent—one that would, at the very least, cause a rift between Susan and the pro-coal members of the community. This was disconcerting to Susan, who was agreeable and generally apolitical by nature. Even the idea of discussing the predicament with her neighbors was unsettling. Despite the strong sense of community in the hollow, residents did not generally discuss decisions like this with one another. To bring this sort of thing up would be perceived as prying, and that just wasn't done.

And yet the prospect of selling her land to the coal company didn't sit well with Susan. According to the Omega lawyer, the company wanted to acquire her property for purposes of strip-mining and would pay her fairly. This all seemed very cut-and-dried—the language of a business transaction. But to Susan, the phrasing was deceivingly abstract. After all, if Omega did "acquire her property," the company would then own and control the hallowed place of nearly a century of her family's history. They would be acquiring the first tree she ever climbed—a dogwood her father helped her scramble up when she was just five years old. They would own the stream in which her children had gleefully splashed only a few years ago.

And surely the mining would permanently disfigure the mountain that had been the backdrop of her life in the hollow.[6] Susan knew that the process the lawyer had referred to as "strip-mining" was also commonly known as mountaintop removal.[7] But what could possibly be a "fair price" for the utter destruction of this land? What could possibly be "just payment" for the loss of her home and the uprooting of her life? And Susan had heard rumors that MTR causes water pollution,[8] poses risks of cardiovascular disease and lung disease,[9] and increases the risk of birth defects and cancer.[10] She didn't want anything to do with those things.

Susan's children argued that the coal industry's preeminence had prevented Appalachia from developing any semblance of a healthy economy. The promise of abundance brought by MTR mining, they contended, was especially unreasonable given that the highly mechanized technique was devised in part as a way to keep costs low by employing fewer workers. But in a culture trapped in a relentless cycle of poverty, any perceived threat to income is taken seriously, especially when those most profiting from coal extraction actively fan the flames of job-loss fear. The result is the vehemently pro-coal stance that grips much of Appalachia, evident in the ubiquitous bumper stickers and billboards that declare "Coal Keeps the Lights On" and more severely in the intimidation and harassment of anti-coal activists.[11] Such behavior gives potential on-the-fence holdouts like Susan reason to fear. In Susan Hart's hollow in Kentucky and throughout Appalachia, people are in search of courage.

It was growing dark. Susan's long day and restless mind had exhausted her. She stood up to go inside, but before she made it through the door, Susan turned around to glance once more at the land in front of her home. A soft pink-yellow glow from the setting sun lingered just over the mountains. A northern cardinal, the state bird, gave its signature call. With a sigh, Susan crossed her threshold and shut the door behind her. Though the hour was late, she dialed the phone number Omega's legal representative had given her. This time she was the one to keep things direct. In a terse voicemail, she informed the lawyer that she would not be parting with her home any time soon.

Contemplations about Courage

A knight in shining armor battling the bad guys. A group of soldiers planting a flag on foreign soil. A Jedi master vanquishing an evil marauder. Our popular idea of courage has long been connected with obvious displays of heroism. While these figures are, in one sense, heroic, does courage consist solely of daring acts of aggression? Naming characters from the popular Harry Potter series as exemplars of courage, Rebecca Konyndyk DeYoung cites Harry's thrilling triumphs against Voldemort and James Potter's dying defense of his family against the same villain as illustrations of this aggressive and daring courage.[12] However, she also contends that this kind of bravery, while admirable, does not provide a complete understanding of courage.

Louke van Wensveen seconds that assertion. "Rambo-like pictures of courage," she argues, are not only incomplete but also dangerous.[13] To think that courage necessarily implies violence is simply false and easily perpetuates a never-ending cycle of violence. Courage comes in more kinds than the ones that traffic in violence. What about the acts of courage shown by Martin Luther King Jr. and his followers in the civil rights movement, who responded to bombings, beatings, and police brutality with nonviolent resistance? What about the palpable courage shown by family and friends who face a diagnosis of cancer with fearlessness and endurance? Courage is not necessarily yoked to violence.

Furthermore, the view of courage as necessarily violent has a decidedly male legacy. It stereotypically defines courage as a virtue available only to men, since males (it is assumed) are by nature aggressive, and courage (it is assumed) has to do with aggression. Hence women are incapable of being courageous, or if they are capable, the courage of women is inferior to that of men. For example, listen to these words from a widely quoted tutor in virtue ethics: "Clearly, then, moral virtue belongs to all of them [men, slaves, women, children]; but the temperance of a man and of a woman, or the courage and justice of a man and of a woman, are not, as Socrates maintained, the same; the courage of a man is shown in commanding, of a woman in obeying."[14] In Aristotle's view, a woman can be courageous only insofar as her subservient nature allows her. Thomas Aquinas, too, doubted women's ability to possess courage, because he believed women to be less rational than men. In his opinion, women are ruled by emotion, rendering them more likely to succumb to fear and thus less likely to display courage.[15] Needless to say, this sexist legacy regarding courage is highly problematic. Such interpretations of courage as necessarily masculine or strictly aggressive do not capture the clear examples of courage that span the range of humans, male and female. What, then, is a better understanding of courage?

DeYoung gets to the heart of the matter when she observes that "the virtue of courage is most often defined by its regulation of fear." As she succinctly puts it, "Courageous people need not be fearless, but they are not overcome by their fear. Rather, they have mastery over it—at least enough to persevere in doing some good or noble deed."[16] So courage names the habitual disposition that allows us to take our fears seriously but not be overwhelmed by them—to persevere when fearful in order to obtain some good. For example, in J. K. Rowling's Harry Potter series, Peter Pettigrew, whose fear leads him to betray those he loves, stands in contrast to Harry Potter, who "shows us how courage is the power to withstand fear for the sake of protecting what is good."[17] Both experience fear: one is overcome by it, while the other exercises control over it. Courage, in short, is a kind of strength in the face of fear.

Fear is a natural and normal emotion that we experience from time to time. There is nothing wrong with being fearful in circumstances that genuinely are dangerous or pose some threat. The moral question has to do with what we do when we feel that emotion. Do we cave in to it, ignore it, or control it? As DeYoung insists, "If fear is the main passion courage moderates, then endurance—bearing with difficulty and standing fast against our fear of danger—must be its paradigmatic act."[18] Courage is a kind of endurance that perseveres in the face of fear. Indeed, endurance is a more comprehensive (and accurate) name for what we often mean by courage. And thus it is no surprise that the Greco-Roman virtue of courage, inherited by Christians and molded by Scripture and church tradition, morphed into the virtue of fortitude.[19]

Thomas Aquinas provides some further insight in his *Treatise on the Virtues*.[20] Following the lead of Aristotle, who describes courage as the mean between cowardice and rashness, Aquinas describes fortitude as the mean between faintheartedness and rashness.[21] The essence of fortitude, as Josef Pieper notes, "lies not in knowing no fear, but in not allowing oneself to be forced into evil by fear, or to be kept by fear from the realization of good."[22] In other words, if we have fortitude we acknowledge our fear but hold it in check in order to attain some good, neither allowing our fear to overwhelm us nor acting impetuously as if there were nothing to fear. Thus, Pieper insists that for Aquinas "endurance is more of the essence of fortitude than attack."[23] In short, fortitude is a kind of enduring strength in the face of adversity.

But fortitude cannot operate alone. Aquinas argues that "the moral virtues cannot exist without the intellectual virtues."[24] In the case of fortitude, the sister virtues of prudence and justice are required. Fortitude presupposes prudence or practical wisdom because without it fortitude is blind. A person of fortitude takes for granted a "correct evaluation of things, of the things that one risks as well as of those which one hopes to preserve or gain by the risk."[25] Without such a sagacious assessment of risks, fortitude cannot exist. But fortitude also requires justice. The doing of justice makes actual the good that fortitude intends to preserve. As Pieper puts it, "Without prudence, without justice, there is no fortitude; only he who is just and prudent can also be brave."[26]

Finally, Aquinas contends that fortitude is not real fortitude without love. While fortitude and the other moral virtues can produce good works, without love (*caritas*) none of the moral virtues can attain their true end. And this love is a gift from God. "But insofar as they [moral virtues of fortitude, temperance, prudence, and justice] are productive of good works in relation to a supernatural last end, and thus truly and perfectly attain the nature of virtue, they cannot be acquired by human acts but are infused by God. Moral virtues of this kind cannot exist without charity."[27] Fortitude does not reach completion or perfection except as shaped by love. Indeed, as Stanley Hauerwas puts it, "No true virtue is possible without charity."[28] And this *caritas* is a gift that surpasses our natural powers to acquire. In these ways, Aquinas's account of fortitude differs from Aristotle's explanation of courage.

Aquinas distinguishes between two different circumstances in which fortitude is required. Sometimes we need fortitude because we cannot avoid a threat. Summarizing Aquinas, DeYoung writes, "Courage is necessary because evil comes from a cause that is stronger than we are and outside of our control. . . . Our helplessness and vulnerability make facing the threat inevitable and escape impossible." We need fortitude to endure an inescapable evil. At other times, we need fortitude because we should not avoid a threat even if we can. In these cases, "to fight back will also compromise the good we love and are trying to protect, or compromise our moral integrity. Even if we do have greater power, or the power to fight back, faithfulness to what we love—not (just) the greater force of what threatens—requires that we lay down our power of aggression and endure what comes."[29] We need fortitude to resist an escapable evil but without the use of violence. What people with these two forms of fortitude have in common is their willingness to risk death for the sake of something they love. In short, at the core of fortitude is love, not power.

This brings us back to the characters from the Harry Potter series. Harry's decision to lay down his life in defense of his friends is seen as the ultimate act of courage. But it is love, not power as we usually think of it (violence or revenge), that moves him. Harry's love for his friends proves greater than his love for his own life.

In the Christian tradition, it is the martyrs who most clearly display courage or fortitude, with Christ as the paradigmatic exemplar. Yet those who courageously endure do not necessarily meet death. Indeed, in the wisdom of the church, one should not seek martyrdom but only be willing to endure suffering for the sake of God's kingdom. In the first three centuries, when the church embraced pacifism, courage and fortitude meant resisting injustice, but nonviolently. While often pilloried as "unrealistic," such courage to endure violence through suffering has proven to be very effective in enacting change. Mahatma Gandhi, Martin Luther King Jr., and Cesar Chavez all led successful social movements by practicing nonviolent resistance, enduring arduous and dangerous conditions for the sake of justice and peace.[30] They were and still are sterling exemplars of courage and fortitude.

This understanding of courage calls to mind what Atticus Finch tells his daughter, Scout, in Harper Lee's classic, *To Kill a Mockingbird*: "I wanted you to see what real courage is, instead of getting the idea that courage is a man with a gun in his hand. It's when you know you're licked before you begin but you begin anyway and you see it through no matter what."[31] This kind of courage as fortitude is quite different from the courage often portrayed in films and television programs in America today. It is not the stuff of Hollywood action films. For Christians, the virtue of fortitude, or courageous endurance, points to the sacrifice of Jesus and thus reminds us of our calling to follow Christ as we strive to bear witness to God's good future of shalom.

Reflections on Hope

A famous poem by Emily Dickinson is a good place to start when it comes to understanding hope:

> "Hope" is the thing with feathers -
> That perches in the soul -
> And sings the tune without the words -
> And never stops - at all.[32]

Like a northern cardinal on a cold spring day, singing despite the frost, hope is something in our soul that keeps us going. Hope is a kind of expectation about the future that buoys our spirit. Hope is a confidence that squelches despair.

Plenty Coups, the last great chief of the Crow nation, knew something about hope. Facing the destruction of his people and their way of life at the end of the nineteenth century, he had a dream—a vision of a radically new future. But this dream meant that he and his people would have to be willing to give up almost everything they understood about the good life. They would have to imagine and believe possible a radically different way of life—what Jonathan Lear calls "a radical hope." Radical hope "anticipates a good for which those who have the hope as yet lack the appropriate concepts with which to understand it."[33] Hope, in short, requires using our imagination to envision some good future, even if it transcends our traditional ways of thinking.

In his study of the Crow nation and its struggle for hope amid cultural collapse, Lear notes that radical hope is different from optimism.[34] Optimism rests on naive beliefs about some possible future, while hope is based on some warranted reason or evidence, even if it offers no proof or certainty. As Lear affirms, true courage and hope are not boldness and bluster, since "bold acts that derive merely from optimism are not themselves courageous. They are at best a simulacrum of courage." People of courage and hope face up to reality—soberly assessing the risks and potential losses—and endure whatever hardships come for the sake of what is good; in contrast, "merely confident persons are so because they just assume they are the strongest and no harm will come to them."[35] Hope is different from optimism because optimism is an inclination to put the most favorable face on actions or events, without adequate warrant or reason, while hope rests in something more secure.

David Orr heartily agrees that optimism and hope are not the same. While "optimism is the recognition that the odds are in your favor," hope is "the faith that things will work out whatever the odds." Optimism, he continues, "leans back, puts its feet up, and wears a confident look, knowing that the deck is stacked," while "hopeful people are actively engaged in defying the odds or changing the odds."[36] Orr proceeds to list the rising odds against a good life in a hotter world: more heat waves and droughts, more and larger storms, bigger hurricanes, rising ocean levels, more tropical diseases in formerly temperate places, more and nastier bugs. It's a long and sobering list. He concludes that "we are playing a global version of Russian roulette." Optimism in these circumstances, he maintains, "is like whistling as one walks past the graveyard at night. There is no good case to be made for it." Hope, however, "requires us to check our optimism at the door and enter the future without illusions. It requires a level of honesty, self-awareness, and sobriety that is difficult to sustain."[37]

Orr also notes the connections between hope and courage. "Authentic hope," he argues, "is made of sterner stuff than optimism. It must be rooted in the truth as best we can see it, knowing that our vision is always partial. Hope requires the courage to reach farther, dig deeper, confront our limits and those of nature, work harder, and dream dreams."[38] In the face of climate change, Orr argues, it is the glaring absence of such courage that renders genuine hope so difficult. How can we imagine a good future if we are unwilling to face the present courageously and clear-sightedly? As long as we refuse to acknowledge that we are playing "climate roulette," we will not make progress on addressing climate change. We need, asserts Orr, to learn from Lincoln or Churchill how to tell the truth courageously in order to offer authentic hope.[39]

While Orr highlights how courage can help the hopeful persist in seeking the truth, Lewis Smedes emphasizes the role of hope in energizing the courageous to act. "Hope gives us the courage to do what we are afraid to do," affirms Smedes. "We fear and hope at the same time." A visit to a doctor illustrates this well. "We are afraid we might be sick, and we are afraid the doctor may tell us that we are very sick. But we have a hope that if we are sick, the doctor can cure us. Fear says, 'Don't go, you may get bad news.' Hope says, 'Go ahead, he may find a way to heal you.' If it is hope that encourages, the loss of hope is the death of courage."[40] Courage is powerless without hope. Without some expectation of future good, we are unlikely to act with bravery or endurance. As Smedes insightfully observes: "People do not revolt against tyranny because they are oppressed; oppressed people revolt when they have hope that freedom is theirs for the taking. Hungry people do not revolt because they do not have enough to eat; hungry people revolt when they have hope that their children can be fed. . . . Hope gives us reason to do the very thing we are afraid to do, because hope is faith in the ultimate triumph of what we struggle for."[41] But, Smedes reminds us, hope is not magic. Not every disease is defeated. Not every good future is realized. Death comes to us all, no matter how much we hope to live.

Smedes further elaborates on hope in his book *Standing on the Promises*.[42] He describes hope as confident expectation of some future good. It requires three things: wishing, imagining, and believing. In his words, "Hope begins to stir in me when I truly wish for things I do not have. It takes on a life of its own when I imagine what it would be like if my wish were granted. And hope arrives ripe and mature when I believe that the dream I want to come true *can* come true."[43] We wish for some good future, we imagine that good future, and we believe that such a good future is possible. Absent from this list but implicit in much else he says about hope is the place of our own action. When hopeful, we not only desire and believe possible some imagined future but also act in such a way as to bring that good future to fruition. We live so as to make real that for which we hope.

Similar to Smedes, William C. Mattison III defines hope as "longing for a good future that is possible yet difficult [to obtain]."[44] But Mattison distinguishes flighty day-to-day wishes from a lifelong yearning for a dream to come true. He observes that "how we hope reveals what we think life is all about," since people describe the object of hope differently. For some people, there is no possible good future and thus no reason for hope. Two famous twentieth-century existentialists, Albert Camus and Jean-Paul Sartre, often serve as examples of people with no reason for hope. For them, life is inescapably meaningless; there is no good future, so despair seems to be the rational response. For most of us, however, hope is real because the future good we yearn for is possible, even if difficult to achieve. While fame and fortune seem to be common objects of hope for many in America today, for most of us the object of our hope is a good marriage, a fulfilling job, a healthy family. Whatever the good future, if we are hope filled, we believe that, with effort and patience, our imagined good future is possible.

So when we hope, we do four things: we wish, we imagine, we believe, and we act. For example, when my friend Anna hopes for a healthier Lake Macatawa, she wishes that our local lake would be a healthier place. She imagines this lake purged of all invasive species and free of harmful bacteria. She believes such a future is actually possible, especially given the good work of a watershed-wide cleanup effort called Project Clarity. And, finally, she acts in such a way that this vision might become a reality—for example, by financially supporting Project Clarity, by not using fertilizer with phosphorus, and by leading canoe trips whose purpose is to pick up garbage.

This last aspect of hope is often overlooked and therefore needs emphasis. As David Orr pithily puts it, "Hope is a verb with its sleeves rolled up." As he insists, "In contrast to optimism or despair, hope requires that one actually do something to improve the world. Authentic hope comes with an imperative to act. There is no such thing as passive hope."[45] So, as the title of Orr's book puts it, hope is an imperative. Hope impels us to action. Desiring and imagining and believing in some good future lead us to do something to make that good future come to life.

Biblical Insight on Courage and Hope

"Be strong and of good courage." Such is one refrain (in the old King James Version) from the Old Testament. For example, Moses, in his farewell speech, says to the people of Israel, "Be strong and bold ['amets]; have no fear or dread of them, because it is the LORD your God who goes with you; he will not fail you or forsake you" (Deut. 31:6). On the cusp of leading the people of Israel into the promised land, Moses repeats these very words to Joshua and adds, "Do not fear or be dismayed" (vv. 7–8). Joshua knows that the God of Abraham and Isaac and Jacob is with him; therefore he need not be afraid. After Moses dies, God speaks directly to Joshua and, in similar language, reaffirms his promise to Moses and repeats his words of encouragement: "As I was with Moses, so I will be with you; I will not fail you or forsake you. Be strong and courageous" (Josh. 1:5–6; see 1:9). Similar language is found throughout the Old Testament, whether in words of assurance when going to battle (2 Sam. 10:12), words of encouragement when building the temple (1 Chron. 22:13; 28:20), or words of comfort in facing the future (Dan. 10:19).

The Greek equivalent (*tharreō*) of the Hebrew "be of good courage" (*'amets*) shows up in 2 Corinthians 5:6–8 as the apostle Paul writes of the confidence Christians have in facing death. We have courage, says Paul, because whether in or away from the body, we are never without the presence of the Lord.

Paul uses a variety of terms to speak of courage elsewhere in his letters. In Philippians 1:20 he writes, "It is my eager expectation and hope that I will not be put to shame in any way, but that by my speaking with all boldness, Christ will be exalted now as always in my body, whether by life or by death." The RSV translates the Greek phrase *en pasē parrēsia* as "with full courage" rather than "speaking with all boldness" (NRSV); courage here is a kind of oratorical boldness. In 1 Thessalonians 2:2 Paul writes that "though we had already suffered and been shamefully mistreated at Philippi, as you know, we had courage in our God to declare to you the gospel of God in spite of great opposition." Courage in this passage (from the verb *parrēsiazomai*) means "to speak openly and fearlessly." Despite suffering and opposition, Paul describes acts of courage in preaching the good news. In Acts 28:15 Luke writes that the apostle Paul and his entourage, after seeing that fellow Christ-followers had journeyed from Rome to meet them at the Forum of Appius—a distance of forty-three miles—thanked God and took courage (*tharsos*). Worried and anxious, Paul and his friends are now encouraged. In the face of exhaustion, they are now fortified and muster the ability to press on.

Beyond the terminology, of course, the Bible is full of stories of courage. Some are familiar: the stories of Moses leading the people of Israel out of Egypt, or of David facing Goliath, or of Shadrach, Meshach, and Abednego in the lions' den. Others are not as well known: the tales of Amos denouncing Israel and its neighbors for trusting in their military might and for trampling the poor, or of Jeremiah condemning (and lamenting) Judah for its worship of other gods, or of Stephen who is "full of grace and power" and does "wonders and signs among the people" before he is stoned to death—a victim of the first persecution of the early church (Acts 6:8–8:3). Not least is the story of Jesus himself—whether challenging the powers that be by turning over the tables in the temple (John 2) or enduring the pain and suffering of the cross (pick your Gospel). The passion narrative is a story of courage and fortitude par excellence. All these (and more) testify to the importance of courage and provide us with examples of courageous living.

What, then, of hope? In the Bible, hope is multifaceted. No fewer than fifteen words or phrases are used in Hebrew and Greek to convey the meaning and nuances of hope. In the Old Testament, there are four main verbs (*qavah*, *yahal*, *hakah*, and *sabar*), each of which means "to long after, to wait, or to wait for (usually for God)." The most common noun is *tiqvah*, mentioned especially in the Wisdom literature (Psalms, Proverbs, Job). The essence of hope is the expectation of some future good. The veracity of one's expectation depends first and foremost on the object of one's trust. For the Jews, confidence in their desired good future of shalom is rooted in a God who is like a reliable rock or a sturdy refuge (Pss. 42:5; 62:5; 71:5)—and thus worthy of trust. For the Hebrew prophets, God is the "hope of Israel" (Jer. 14:8; 17:13; see Isa. 51:5); thus Israel's future is secure in God's loving embrace. In short, Yahweh is the guarantor of Israel's hope. Absent such a reliable guarantor—a covenant-making and promise-keeping God—hope is futile and will come to nothing (Prov. 11:7).

Turning to the New Testament, it is striking that the main words for hope (*elpis*, *elpizō*) are scarce in the Gospels. The verb *elpizō* occurs only five times (Matt. 12:21; Luke 6:34; 23:8; 24:21; John 5:45). This seeming shortage of terms in the Gospels is made up for by Paul, who in his letters to the various churches of the Greco-Roman world speaks often of hope. Perhaps most well known is the triad of faith, hope, and love mentioned in 1 Corinthians 13:13. Tucked into the middle of Paul's discourse on the gifts of the Holy Spirit (chaps. 12–14) and after his famous discussion of love (*agapē*), Paul states, "And now faith, hope, and love abide, these three; and the greatest of these is love." While perhaps overlooked given the preeminence of love, hope nevertheless occupies a pivotal place in Paul's pantheon of virtues. Hope (*elpis*) is an expectation of some future good—confidence that what is envisioned will come to be, based on trust in someone who is both able and willing to bring that good future to fruition. For Paul, what is envisioned is union with Christ and the reconciliation of all things in Christ by the Triune God who was incarnate in Jesus Christ and is ever present in the Holy Spirit.

Elsewhere Paul also speaks in one breath of faith, hope, and love. In his opening words to the church at Colossae, he writes, "In our prayers for you we always thank God, the Father of our Lord Jesus Christ, for we have heard of your faith in Christ Jesus and of the love that you have for all the saints, because of the hope laid up for you in heaven. You have heard of this hope before in the word of the truth, the gospel, that has come to you" (1:3–6). The hope laid up in heaven is that good future secured by the work of God in Christ that has broken into this world but has not yet reached its completion—its consummation in the future.[46]

This triad appears yet again in the opening words of Paul's first letter to the church at Thessalonica. "We always give thanks to God for all of you," writes Paul, emphasizing once again the role of gratitude, "and mention you in our prayers, constantly remembering before our God and Father your work of faith and labor of love and steadfastness of hope in our Lord Jesus Christ" (1 Thess. 1:2–3). Work of faith, labor of love, steadfastness of hope. Paul insists elsewhere (Romans) that faith is not a work, if by "work" we mean something we earn. Faith is a gift of God's grace. But faith does work. And one of the works that faith does is allow us to trust God with the future. Love is something we must work at, if by "love" we means caring for the needs of those around us. And hope clearly is not hope without being steadfast—unwavering, dedicated, persistent.

In sum, hope in the New Testament is marked by three features. First, what we hope for is centered on God, not on us. It goes by many names: the coming of the kingdom of heaven (Matthew), the coming of the kingdom of God (Mark and Luke), eternal life (John), union with Christ (Rom. 6), the resurrection of the body (1 Cor. 15), righteousness (Gal. 5:5), reconciliation (Eph. 2), salvation (1 Thess. 5), a renewed and united heaven and earth (Rev. 21–22). Regardless of the name, the object of our hope (what we hope for) has to do with God and, as the Lord's Prayer teaches us, God's will being done on earth as it is in heaven.

Second, the good future for which we hope rests on the person and work of Jesus Christ, not on our good works. As Paul argues in 1 Corinthians 15, because Christ is risen—"the first fruits of those who have died" (v. 20)—we also shall be raised. As Paul hammers home in Ephesians, "For by grace you have been saved through faith, and this is not your own doing; it is the gift of

God—not the result of works, so that no one may boast" (2:8–9). The good future for which we Christians hope is a gift. We do not (and cannot) earn it. This gift is steadfastly rooted in the crucifixion and resurrection of Christ.

Third, we can therefore be confident that though we now "hope for what we do not see" (Rom. 8:25), someday we will see the fullness of God's good future made complete. One day we will see "face to face" (1 Cor. 13:12). Thus faith (trust in what is not seen) and hope (desire for an as-yet-unrealized future) will one day pass away, as Paul acknowledges, though love will always abide.

In sum, for Christians the expectation of a good future is based on God's promises and God's character as a keeper of promises. We hope for shalom because God keeps covenant with his chosen people. We hope for the reign of God because God raised Jesus from the dead as a sign of the future restoration of all things. Mattison nicely summarizes the radical nature of Christian hope:

> Christians have a distinctive understanding of the ultimate good, a good that is future and possible yet difficult. The source and goal of Christian hope is God. Christians ground their hope in their faith in who God is, what God has done, and what God plans for us. Christians profess a God of love, who made all things out of love and in particular human beings in the *imago Dei* as uniquely capable of love. Despite human sinfulness, which is at root a human rejection of God's loving offer of fullness of life in preference for living on our own terms, God continually reaches out to humanity to reconcile us to himself.[47]

Human hope is rooted in divine grace. This is the gospel—good news indeed.

Ecological Courage and Hope

So what have we have learned from the previous sections? The virtue of courage is moral strength in the face of danger. The courageous are not without fear; they simply are not overcome by their fear. One of the four cardinal virtues for the Greeks, *courage* denotes a firmness of mind and resoluteness of spirit despite the fearful awareness of danger. A virtue particularly sought after by soldiers in the ancient world, courage, in the Christian tradition, was transmuted into fortitude—a kind of steadfastness and courageous endurance. Courage as fortitude is tenacity in the face of opposition—stubborn persistence in the face of adversity. Though tempted by apathy, ignorance, and fear, people of courage and fortitude persevere.

The vice of deficiency is cowardice. The coward is unable to overcome fear. Paralyzed with fear, the coward lacks the ability to act when the situation calls for decisive or swift action. Perceived danger becomes debilitating. Those who lack courageous endurance are overwhelmed by anxiety and/or overcome with fatigue and thus are unable to act.[48] Those without fortitude become fainthearted.

The vice of excess associated with courage is rashness. While courageous people honestly face their fear and persevere despite its potentially paralyzing effects, rash people refuse to acknowledge their fear and thus act hastily or without proper caution. In so doing, they often put themselves and/or others in danger. Often masquerading as (male) bravado, this vice is really a recklessness that foolishly ignores signs of danger. With respect to fortitude, those who pay no attention to fatigue become reckless. It is one thing to show persistence in the face of adversity; it is another to blindly (or pridefully) endure hardship under the guise of being tenacious.

What, then, is *ecological courage*? It is moral strength when fearful about real or potential ecological losses and steadfast endurance in the face of seemingly intractable ecological problems. It is courage with respect to caring for our *oikos*—our common home. This kind of courage expands the scope of what counts morally to include more than humans. We cannot adequately care for our neighborhood garden or local watershed, the endangered trees in the national park, or the undersea coral reefs in the international bio-preserve, without the courage to act and the fortitude to keep going.

In his typology of environmental virtues, Ronald Sandler lists virtues of sustainability, communion with nature, environmental stewardship, and environmental activism. Under the latter category, he includes fortitude and courage, among others, since such character traits are "crucial to achieve and maintain protection of environmental goods."[49] Using the moral-exemplar approach to identify ecological virtues, Philip Cafaro lists patience, physical endurance, and persistence among "the virtues of the naturalist"—virtues he finds evident in the life of Aldo Leopold.[50] Similarly, in his discussion of benevolence as an environmental virtue, Geoffrey Frasz mentions the importance of perseverance and persistence.[51] Courage in some form is a common virtue among those who think and write about ecological virtue ethics.

Kathryn Blanchard and Kevin O'Brien apply the virtues of courage and fortitude (what they call "the courage of staying power") to the pressing issue of energy. In the twenty-first century, many of us have fears about energy: degradation and pollution, political injustice, restriction of freedom, or a global slowdown. Christians, Blanchard and O'Brien rightly insist, "are called to understand such fears and cultivate courage in the face of them."[52] The authors describe (with exemplars) three forms of ecological courage: the courage to use existing energy wisely, the courage to abandon fossil fuels, and the courage to use less. Clearly, courage and its kin are important ecological virtues.

The vice of deficiency is *ecological cowardice or faintheartedness*. This names the inability or unwillingness to act with courage when some environmental good is at risk or some nonhuman creature is in peril. It is the disposition to cave in when courage is needed to confront the perpetrators of the local water crisis. It is the habitual failure to stick with that letter-writing campaign to preserve the local park.

The vice of excess is *ecological recklessness*. When this habitual disposition becomes a character flaw, we charge ahead with our group's favorite "environmental project" without doing the necessary homework or listening to the needs and wants of all those affected. Louke van Wensveen observes that courage can be warped into something sinister when pushed to excess. Extreme "Rambo-like" courage can glorify fearlessness and place pressure on individuals to repress instinctive emotions. In such a context, fear is interpreted as a sign of weakness, and a culture of repression can flourish.[53] So ecological recklessness is a counterfeit, a bogus imitation, of ecological courage.

Turning now to the virtue of hope, let's summarize what we have learned thus far. The virtue of hope is the settled disposition to act with confidence to bring about some imagined good future—graduating from college, getting that dream job, decreasing your carbon footprint. If we embody this virtue, then we imagine and desire this good future and believe it is possible, no matter how improbable, and we are inclined to live in ways that bring this future to fulfillment. The virtue of hope is the inclination to live into an imagined world that is really possible, no matter how improbable it may seem. For Christians, our expectation is of God's good future of shalom, based on God's character as a keeper of promises. We hope because we worship a God who raised Jesus from the dead as a sign of the future restoration of all things. One of the classic theological virtues, along with faith and love, hope is absolutely necessary for life itself.[54]

There are two vices that correspond to the virtue of hope. The vice of deficiency is despair. As its etymology suggests, it is the loss of all hope (*desperare*). Despair is the absence of any expectation of a good future. There is no good future or no reason to believe some imagined better future might actually be possible in this world. Hence despair is cynicism of a profound kind, for it signals a failure or inability to believe or trust. So despair undercuts faith, since faith is, in its essence, entrusting oneself to another and ultimately to God. And despair also undermines action, for there is no good future to work for. Despair is, as Søren Kierkegaard powerfully describes it, the sickness unto death.[55] Indeed, as recent research attests, "the person without hope is the likeliest candidate for suicide."[56] When despairing, we exhibit little or no confidence in the future and thus have precious little to live for.

Some today say that despair is one of the main characteristics of young adults. The suicide rates among young people give credence to this observation.[57] What is it about our culture today that kicks the legs out from under hope? What social, economic, and political factors promote a culture of despair? There are some obvious candidates. Widespread and seemingly intractable ecological degradations. The apparent devolution of democracy and the consequent growing oppression and injustice. A global economy that continues to fuel a growing gap between the richest 1 percent and the other 99 percent. Is it any wonder that many people are caught up in despair?

So in this discussion of despair as a vice, we must take into account our larger cultural context. There are, sadly, good reasons for the rise in despair. As one of my students recently said, "The world is going to hell, so why hope?" Any attempt to build hope must take seriously this apparent epidemic of despair.

The vice of excess with respect to hope is presumptuousness. In contrast to the confident expectation of genuine hope, if overtaken by this kind of false hope, we exude a brashness that takes the good future for granted. We have an unwarranted audacity of belief. We are unjustifiably overconfident about our hoped-for good future. And so we overstep our bounds in believing that we need do nothing to bring the good future to fruition. We sit on our hands believing the politicians or scientists or God will "do it all." We fail to take seriously our need to act on our belief about any good future.

The virtue of *ecological hope* names the settled disposition to yearn for and act to bring about some good future—in Christian terms, God's good future of shalom for all the earth—rooted in confidence that such a future ultimately lies in God's good hands. If we embody this virtue, we remember the rainbow promise made to Noah, we celebrate the resurrection, and we anticipate the New Jerusalem. We imagine our local lake purged of all invasive species and free of water contaminated by harmful bacteria; thus we do whatever we can to make such a future come to be. We act in such a way that God's good future—a thriving neighborhood, a healthy watershed, a flourishing home planet—becomes reality.

Hope and its near cousins are noticeably absent in much of the environmental virtue ethics literature. Much is written of the other virtues mentioned in this book, but little is said about hope or its rough equivalents, such as expectation and confidence. Charles Taliaffero acknowledges that "God wills the consummate fulfillment of creation," but he does not explicitly mention hope as a virtue made possible by such a theological claim.[58] He comments on gratitude and respect but makes no reference to hope. Louke van Wensveen mentions hope in her capacious catalog of virtues but does not elaborate on it.[59] Neither Philip Cafaro nor Ronald Sandler mentions hope in their extensive discussions of ecological virtues.

In contrast (and not surprising given their explicit Christian orientation), Kathryn Blanchard and Kevin O'Brien include an insightful treatment of hope in their discussion of the cardinal Christian virtues. For example, they rightly point out that presumption, the vice at the other end of the spectrum from despair, is "not simply a surplus of appropriate hope" but rather "a misplaced hope."[60] Thinking that "things will just work out" is not an exhibition of genuine hope. After describing what the virtue of hope is and is not, Blanchard and O'Brien turn to the controversial issue of human population and offer a helpful discussion of how to hope in a world in which some fear there are too many people and others fear coercion regarding reproductive rights. In light of both fears, Blanchard and O'Brien argue for a position that "demands both gratitude and stewardship."[61]

The vice of deficiency is *ecological despair*. This vice names hopelessness in the face of our aching earth. Given pervasive ecological degradation, some cannot imagine that any livable future on earth is possible. Aware of intractable ecological problems, some find it hard to believe there is any way forward. Persistently pummeled by climate change data, some abandon belief in any bearable planet. Despair is the relinquishing of belief in the possibility of any good future. Thus it fosters inaction—doing nothing—since there is nothing that could make things better.

The vice of excess is *ecological presumptuousness*. This is a disposition of overconfidence that presumes something will save us and thus we need do nothing. Some scientific breakthrough or newfangled technology will extricate us from the shortage of potable water to drink or the scarcity of clean air to breathe. Some new political leader or educational guru will bring in the future we hope for. It's all on "them." If we fall victim to this vice, we fail to realize that there are pretenders to hope in our anxious world. We may be taken in by prophets of easy credibility or presume that ecological healing will be pain-free or will not demand much from us. In any case, we overconfidently assume all will be well with the world, whether we do anything or not.

Courage and Hope Embodied

Many people come to mind as exemplars of courage and hope. Dietrich Bonhoeffer was a brilliant and caring German pastor who, at the age of thirty-nine, was put to death by the Nazis in 1945 as a result of his involvement in a plot to kill Hitler. Bonhoeffer embodied both great courage and robust hope. Martin Luther King Jr. easily qualifies as a beacon of courage and hope for people still today. Mother Teresa of Calcutta was a shining embodiment of courage and hope. However, for this chapter, with its focus on ecological virtues, Jane Goodall stands out as a sterling example of ecological courage and hope.

Jane's story is well known, but let me briefly rehearse some of the details. Born in London in 1934, Goodall developed an interest in chimps when her father gave her a stuffed chimpanzee instead of a teddy bear when she was a child. She moved to Kenya in 1957, found work as a secretary and, on the advice of a friend, contacted Louis Leakey, the famous archaeologist and paleontologist. Leakey hired Goodall as a secretary but sent her to Olduvai Gorge to do research on chimps. After Goodall spent time in London studying primate behavior, Leakey then sent her to what is now Gombe Stream National Park in Tanzania. After two years of research, Goodall began a doctoral program at Cambridge University, completing a PhD in ethology (animal behavior) in 1965 that focused on her research with chimpanzees. Goodall continued her pioneering work in Africa for the next four decades, during which time she became a tireless activist for the protection of animals and the preservation of their habitats.

In 1977 Goodall established the Jane Goodall Institute, an environmental conservation organization based in Virginia; in 1991 she founded Roots and Shoots, a conservation awareness program for children that is now active in seventy countries. A prolific author, some of her most well-known books are *In the Shadow of Man, The Chimpanzees of Gombe: Patterns of Behavior, Reason for Hope: A Spiritual Journey*, and *Hope for Animals and Their World: How Endangered Species Are Being Rescued from the Brink*. She has also authored eleven children's books, has received (at last count) twenty awards, and is the recipient of a dozen honorary doctoral degrees.

Goodall is famous for her groundbreaking research on the behavior of chimpanzees. She was one of the first scientists to observe and record emotion, intelligence, and family relations among chimps. And even more controversially, she documented chimps' use of tools and aggressive behavior among chimps from the same troop—claims that ran counter to the science of the time. As a result, her research was criticized. Despite such criticism, much of it due to the regnant sexism of the time, she persevered in her research and, as the titles of four of her books explicitly indicate, came to eloquently express and embody hope for animals and those who care about them. Goodall also contravened the scientific conventions of the day by naming the animals she studied and developing close relationships with them, the most famous perhaps being the male chimpanzee David Greybeard.

Goodall is well known as a resolute example of courage and an inspiring beacon of hope for all those who are striving to preserve and protect the nonhuman creatures most endangered and the world in which they and we live. When asked why she is hopeful, she gives four reasons: "(1) the human brain; (2) the resilience of nature; (3) the energy and enthusiasm that is found or can be kindled among young people worldwide; and (4) the indomitable human spirit."[62] In explaining her first reason, she acknowledges the marvels of the human brain, while noting both the wonderful innovations and the disastrous "dark side" of human technology. She cites growing public awareness of environmental problems and many examples of "corporate environmental responsibility" as signs that we may finally be using our brains to "face up to these problems" that confront us.[63]

In addition, Goodall finds hope "in the amazing resilience of nature if we give her a chance—and, if necessary, a helping hand."[64] She cites numerous examples of the natural world's ability to bounce back from degradation— dead rivers now brimming with fish and birds, species brought back from the brink of extinction, forests once cut but now healthy and supporting all manner of humans and other animals. She argues that we must counter "just-meism"—the belief that one person cannot really make a difference—by simply doing the right thing and imagining if everyone did the same.

Third, Goodall finds hope in "the new understanding, commitment and energy of young people around the world."[65] There is, she observes, "a powerful force unleashed when young people resolve to make a change," and she finds many such people in her travels around the world—from precocious five-year-olds who hand her the change they have saved to help protect chimps to high schoolers who take on a local project to pick up trash to college students who choose a course of study because they want to make the world a better place.

This leads to Goodall's fourth and final reason for hope: the resolute and determined human spirit. When asked where she gets her energy, Goodall replies, "Much of it comes from the spiritual power I feel around us. But an awful lot comes from the amazing people I meet."[66] She offers story after story of remarkable people: political leaders who challenged the status quo, spiritual leaders of indigenous peoples who fight to maintain their cultures, musicians and artisans who continue practicing their crafts without fingers, zoo visitors who rescue animals from drowning. With these examples of people "moving toward the ultimate destiny of our species—a state of compassion and love," there is reason for hope.[67]

Susan and Her Friends

"Don't Like Coal? Sit in the Dark!" reads a pro-coal bumper sticker. There is an uncomfortable yet irrefutable truth in this maxim. At least for now, coal does keep the lights on in many communities—not only in Kentucky but also in West Virginia and Pennsylvania and Indiana. If our electricity is generated from a coal-fired power plant, then like it nor not we are contributing to the demand for coal and possibly the demolition of mountains in Appalachia. Put this way, it is easy to feel helpless, become hopeless, and slip into despair.

But then there is Susan Hart. Susan understands that her choices involve risks to her social standing and safety. Yet she endures the fear of being scorned or even harassed for the sake of what she loves: her home and the surrounding mountains. Susan's decision to hold her ground was not easy. It exemplified courage, born of a love that proved greater than fear or want of money.

Susan is not alone. She has many friends and collaborators, only some of whom she knows or who know her. Some are activists in coal communities all over the United States who courageously endure character assassinations, threats of violence, and social exclusion. Some have the courage to withstand assertions that they have no right, by virtue of their non-Appalachian upbringings, to speak out against MTR. Some engage in nonviolent resistance and civil disobedience, like those who temporarily shut down an MTR mine site in Lincoln Country, West Virginia, in 2012 "through a series of coordinated lock downs, tree-sits and banner drops."[68] Twenty activists were arrested and put in jail. Such acts of courageous endurance are pivotal in the fight for the mountains—or our fight for our home planet.

In part because of the work of Susan and her friends, coal-fired power plants are in decline. About one-fifth of the coal-burning plants in the United States are expected to be shut down by 2020, largely because of heightened emissions standards and the competing prices of other fuels (natural gas, wind, solar) that make burning coal less profitable.[69] Grassroots activists nationwide are rightly demanding that their local power plants move away from dirty fossil fuels to cleaner alternatives. In my own community of Holland, Michigan, the seventy-five-year-old coal plant was shut down in April of 2016. In Michigan, in large part because of the renewable portfolio standards (RPS) adopted in 2008 and renewed in 2016, an increasing percentage of energy (10 percent by 2015, 15 percent by 2021, 35 percent by 2025) is coming from renewable sources.[70] Indeed, energy from renewables is gaining traction not only in the United States but all over the world.[71] These are visible reasons to continue to be courageous and have hope.

I am guessing that Susan Hart has never met Desmond Tutu, but it seems to me they are cut from the same cloth, for both embody the virtues of courage and hope. In the case of Tutu, we have his words to illuminate his deeds. His reasons for being courageous and hope filled, not surprisingly, originate in his Christian faith. He is, he avows, no optimist, for "optimism relies on appearances and very quickly turns into pessimism when the appearances change." He calls himself "a realist," since "the vision of hope [he wants] to offer you is based on reality." While Tutu acknowledges that "there is considerable evil in the world" and insists that "we mustn't be starry-eyed and pretend it isn't so," he emphasizes that the reality of evil "isn't the last word; that isn't even the most important part of the picture in God's world."[72]

The most important part of the picture for Desmond Tutu is that "this is a *moral* universe, which means that, despite all the evidence that seems to be to the contrary, there is no way that evil and injustice and oppression and lies can have the last word." And his reason for believing this is that "God is a God who cares about right and wrong. God cares about justice and injustice. God is in charge." And thus, "in the end good will prevail." Tutu observes that it was precisely this set of beliefs that undergirded the people of South Africa in their struggle to free themselves from the oppression of apartheid. As he recounts, "During the darkest days of apartheid I used to say to P. W. Botha, the president of South Africa, that we had already won, and I invited him and other white South Africans to join the winning side. All the 'objective' facts were against us—the pass laws, the imprisonments, the teargassing, the massacres, the murder of political activists—but my confidence was not in the present circumstances but in the laws of God's universe."[73] One of those laws is that the universe bends in the direction of justice, and it does so because of the God who made it and loves it and redeems it.[74] In the end, good will prevail. In the end, love wins.

The history of Christianity, Tutu reminds us, is filled with examples of this kind of transformation—from the biblical stories of Paul and Peter to the work of the South African Truth and Reconciliation Commission and the 1994 elections in South Africa, which for the first time included all those previously excluded from the polls. Totally improbable events serve as beacons of hope. And that object of hope—that imagined and desired possible good future—is captured in God's dream for us. In Tutu's words, this is God's dream:

> It is a dream of a world whose ugliness and squalor and poverty, its war and hostility, its greed and harsh competitiveness, its alienation and disharmony are changed into their counterparts, where there will be more laughter, joy, and peace, where there will be justice and goodness and compassion and love and

caring and sharing. I have a dream that swords will be beaten into plowshares and spears into pruning hooks, that My children will know that they are members of one family, the human family, God's family, My family.[75]

May we all seek the courage and conjure the hope to make such a world more visible and palpable.

6

Digging In

Becoming a Person of Character

By contrast the fruit of the Spirit is love, joy, peace, patience, kindness, generosity, faithfulness, gentleness, and self-control.

Paul (Gal. 5:22)

Only by cultivating sound virtues will people be able to make a selfless ecological commitment.

Pope Francis[1]

Camp Fowler

"Future world and local leaders in training here." So states a well-placed sign by one of the parking areas near the prayer cabin at Fowler Camp and Retreat Center in upstate New York. Located in the Adirondacks, just south of the little hamlet of Speculator, Camp Fowler is a 285-acre summer camp and year-round retreat center located on beautiful Lake Sacandaga—which means "lake of many stones" in the language of those native to this place. Founded in 1954 by the Reformed Church in America—a small Protestant denomination with roots that go back to 1620—this camp continues to be a vibrant place many decades later.

In certain ways, Camp Fowler is similar to most Christian summer camps. There are many of the usual staples of church camp: morning worship before breakfast, time each day devoted to learning the stories of the Bible, chapel time at night with enthusiastic singing—much of it led by a minister who volunteers as chaplain for the week. There are regular opportunities for swimming and fishing and sailing, as well as weeklong wilderness canoeing and backpacking trips to other parts of the Adirondacks. Camp Fowler's goals are shared by many other Christian camps: to glorify God, to foster growth in Jesus Christ as Lord, to experience life in a Christian community, to encourage people to live as disciples of Christ.

In addition to these features common to Christian summer camps, Camp Fowler is in other ways quite distinctive. You sense things are different the moment you arrive at Camp Fowler. Whether it's the above-mentioned sign or the funky bicycle the staff uses to haul the latest food waste to the compost bins out by the garden or the many log buildings that seamlessly fit their north-woods setting, you sense this camp has been carefully thought through.

Your first impressions are confirmed at the first meal. The campers line up outside Fenimore Dining Hall only to have to answer crazy (and often funny) trivia questions to be admitted to the dining hall. The menu includes organic and vegetarian items seldom found in typical camp fare, including in-season vegetables from the camp's organic garden. After the meal, the campers learn the results of their competition to determine which cabin had the least amount of noncompostable food left over (*ort*, for those of you wondering what the technical term is), with all the compostable leftovers going into the bear-proof compost bins out by the garden. Also following each meal one of the staff leads everyone in a zany song.

None of this is by accident. Because of its Christian identity, Camp Fowler's core values include simplicity, hospitality, and community. Simplicity names the intention to cut the clutter in our lives—stuff, busyness, technology—that distracts us from what is truly important. Hospitality means that anyone and everyone is welcome, regardless of the identity markers—race, class, and religion to name but a few—that typically separate us. Community indicates the commitment to live and work and play as people who acknowledge their interrelatedness and their dependence on the earth and its life-giving systems. And because of these core values, everything is suffused with the theme of caring for creation. An organic garden, composting toilets, multiple arrays of solar panels, a nature center, leave-no-trace camping on all out-trips—all this and more are indicators of how a Christian commitment to earthkeeping is woven into this place and of how life at Camp Fowler is structured in such a way as to foster ecological virtues.

The main reason for this vision and the intentionality with which it has been pursued is the camp director, Kent Busman. In the summer, Kent trains staff, deals with emergencies, and pays the bills. He also tells bedtime stories to the many kids who flock to camp, and when he gets a chance, joins in the evening music by playing his mandolin. The rest of the year he runs retreats, raises money, and promotes the camp among neighbors near and far. In his spare time, he cultivates an organic garden in unforgiving Adirondack soil. The work is seemingly endless, the job never done.

Kent has been at Fowler since 1986, and his imprint over these many years is considerable. Through the years, he has with purpose and creativity shaped the place and its practices to reflect the core values of the gospel, not least of which is the commitment to caring for the earth. But such care is always specific to a particular place. So Kent knows the history of his camp, and while he has learned much from its past, he is not slavishly bound by it. (He has made some mistakes, as he himself will tell you, but he has also learned from them.) Kent also knows this particular place very well—the nonhuman as well as human inhabitants. He observes the pileated woodpeckers and barred owls, tends the tamaracks and the golden birches, and visits folks in the local village as well as his neighbors in the cabins down the shore. This commitment to caring for the earth has informed and inspired efforts to develop a program aimed at fostering certain practices and cultivating certain virtues.

For example, because of his extensive local knowledge, Kent is able to discern the possibilities of this place and is grateful for them. He also knows when enough is enough, and thus resists the pressures to think bigger is better. Consequently, the camp remains relatively small and of a humane scale. Even after decades of living in this place, Kent is still awestruck by the beauty of this land forever wild—aware of both its fragility and its resilience. He is rightly proud of the improvements over the years, largely owing to his leadership, but he is also genuinely humble about what has been achieved, aware that little could have been done by him alone. And he knows the place itself is humbling—weather, soil, landscape. In striving to make the camp more hospitable to others, whether from New York City or Uruguay, Kent embodies a hunger for justice and exhibits a pursuit of love. In all this, he exudes an infectious joy, such that all who come to Fowler—campers, volunteers, staff—catch the spirit of this holy place. In sum, Kent Busman embodies many of the ecological virtues described in this book: wonder and humility, self-control and wisdom, justice and love, courage and hope.

Living as Holy Creatures in a World That Is Holy

In his essay "Christianity and the Survival of Creation," Kentucky farmer, essayist, and poet Wendell Berry argues that the indictment by anti-Christian conservationists that Christianity is culpable in the destruction of the natural world "is in many respects just." As he writes, "Christian organizations, to this day, remain largely indifferent to the rape and plunder of the world and its traditional cultures. It is hardly too much to say that most Christian organizations are as happily indifferent to the ecological, cultural, and religious implications of industrial economics as are most industrial organizations." Nevertheless, in the very next breath, Berry insists that "however just it may be, it [the indictment of Christianity by anti-Christian conservationists] does not come from an adequate understanding of the Bible and the cultural traditions that descend from the Bible." Critics too often dismiss the Bible, usually without ever reading it, Berry observes. He thus concludes, "Our predicament now, I believe, requires us to learn to read and understand the Bible in light of the present fact of Creation."[2]

Never reticent to speak his mind, Berry offers his own short list of basic understandings. First, in the Bible we discover "that we humans do not own the world or any part of it." We are always guests and stewards of God. Second, we find that "God made not only the parts of Creation that we humans understand and approve but all of it," including stinging insects, poisonous weeds, and dangerous beasts. Third, we discover that "God found the world, as He made it, to be good, and that He made it for his pleasure, and that He continues to love it and find it worthy, despite its reduction and corruption by us." Fourth, we find that "Creation is not in any sense independent of the Creator, the result of a primal creative act long over and done with, but is the continuous, constant participation of all creatures in the being of God."[3]

In summary, Berry concludes, "The Bible leaves no doubt at all about the sanctity of the act of world-making, or of the world that was made, or of creaturely or bodily life in this world. We are holy creatures living among other holy creatures in a world that is holy. Some people know this, and some do not. Nobody, of course, knows it all the time." Berry follows his frank conclusion (as usual) with a probing question: "But what keeps it from being far better known than it is? Why is it apparently unknown to millions of professed students of the Bible? How can modern Christianity have so solemnly folded its hands while so much of the work of God was and is being destroyed?"[4]

In an earlier work, Berry puts forward what is perhaps the most succinct summary of his reading of the ecological wisdom of Scripture: "The ecological teaching of the Bible is simply inescapable: God made the world because He wanted it made. He thinks the world is good, and He loves it. It is His world; He has never relinquished title to it. And He has never revoked the conditions, bearing on His gift to us of the use of it, that oblige us to take excellent care if it." And, again, as usual Berry poses a provocative question:

"If God loves the world, then how might any person of faith be excused for not loving it or justified in destroying it?"[5]

From this understanding of what the Bible teaches, Berry comes to this provocative conclusion: "Our destruction of nature is not just bad steward-ship, or stupid economics, or a betrayal of family responsibility; it is the most horrid blasphemy. It is flinging God's gifts into his face as if they were of no worth beyond that assigned to them by our destruction of them." He then draws this inescapable inference: "We have no entitlement from the Bible to exterminate or permanently destroy or hold in contempt anything on the earth or in the heavens above it or in the waters beneath it. We have the right to use the gifts of nature but not to ruin or waste them."[6] Such is a moral maxim appropriate for holy creatures living among other holy creatures in a world that is holy.[7]

Berry is right. Earthkeeping is integral to Christian faith. The Bible begins and ends with rivers and trees. The Bible speaks of humans as earthkeepers. The Bible portrays God's good future as earthly and earthy. In the Lord's Prayer, we pray that God's will be done on earth as it is in heaven. And beyond the Bible, in the Apostles' Creed, we begin with a confession of God as Maker of heaven and earth. In the Doxology, we sing that all creatures here below praise God. Earthkeeping is woven into the warp and weft of our faith—Scrip-ture, creeds, prayers, songs—if only we had the eyes to see and ears to hear. As the prophetic ecological theologian Joseph Sittler puts it, "When we turn the attention of the church to a definition of the Christian relationship with the natural world, we are not stepping away from grave and proper theological ideas; we are stepping right into the middle of them. There is a deeply rooted, genuinely Christian motivation for attention to God's creation."[8]

If all this is true—the insights and arguments of Berry, Sittler, and a host of others—then what kind of people do we need to be? I hope the preceding chapters have helped to answer that question. But now another important question: How do we become the kind of people who embody virtues such as wonder and humility, self-control and wisdom, justice and love, courage and hope? In this final chapter, let's look at some examples of ecological virtue ethics formation. Let's explore some programs and places that cultivate these earthkeeping virtues.

Little Hawks Preschool and STREAM School

"Connecting people, land, and nature." That is the succinct motto of the Out-door Discovery Center Macatawa Greenway (ODCMG), a local nonprofit in

my home community of Holland in southwestern Michigan. Since its founding in 2000, the Outdoor Discovery Center has focused on nature education
for people of all ages on its 155-acre site south of town. The site includes trails
around lakes and marshes and in forests and prairies, a natural play space, and
a catch-and-release fishing pond. Buildings house displays of local flora and
fauna, such as owls and other birds of prey, snakes, and frogs. There is also
dedicated space for biology lab investigations and educational presentations.

The Macatawa Greenway Partnership started as its own nonprofit in 1996.
Its goal was to protect and connect land along the Macatawa River and its
tributaries and construct a greenway path along the river. The Macatawa
Greenway became part of the Outdoor Discovery Center in 2010, as part of
a larger vision for creating a nature-rich community. The ODCMG has since
flourished under the excellent leadership of executive director Travis Williams,
the steady wisdom of a talented board of directors, the generous support
of local donors, and the enthusiastic participation of a growing number of
people from the community. A sampling of recent programs includes "Marvelous Mammals," "Animal Crime Scene Investigation," "Investigating Owl
Puke," and "Wings, Talons, Ears, and Eyes (Birds of Prey Lab)."

In addition to various educational programs, the ODCMG offers conservation services, such as removing phragmites, an invasive perennial grass
that can take over wetlands, and raising *Galerucella* beetles to combat the
spread of purple loosestrife, another non-native invasive species. Through its
Explorer Network, the ODCMG offers nature-based group trips to national
and international destinations—for example, a trip through Alaska's Inside
Passage from Seattle to Juneau, or a trip to Ecuador that includes visits to the
Amazon rain forest, Ecuador's capital city of Quito, and the Galapagos. The
ODCMG has also spearheaded Project Clarity, a regional effort to clean up
our watershed. If that were not enough, the ODCMG also runs two popular
educational programs for children.

The Little Hawks Discovery Preschool is a nature-based preschool program for three- and four-year-olds, located on the ODCMG nature preserve.
It began in 2013 through a partnership between a local school district and
the ODCMG. The children spend time outdoors each day—rain, snow, or
shine—learning through active play and exploration. They go on nature
walks, do scientific investigations, frolic on playgrounds, and listen while
outside during story time. With a staff of fourteen and 175 currently en-
rolled children now enjoying the use of a brand-new building, Little Hawks
is flourishing and thus cultivating more interest in nature-based education.
And the children (and their parents) are over-the-top excited about learning
and going to school.

STREAM School is a special program for sixth through eighth graders run by the Hamilton Community Schools (a Holland-area school district) in partnership with the ODCMG. A play on the acronym STEM (science, technology, engineering, math), STREAM School is an alternative to indoor, classroom-based learning. It pairs two teachers from each of the three grades to work together to provide hands-on project-based learning that connects students to the world in which they live. Currently, sixty students spend three hours a day (afternoons usually) exploring and studying the natural world. For example, students learn math and science (as well as writing and public speaking) by catching and measuring fish in the local rivers and macroinvertebrates in the local creeks, investigating soil composition on family farms and plant succession in local forests, and sampling water in the nearby lakes.

Much more could be said about these programs (e.g., about how successful they have been in promoting student engagement and learning[9]), but my point here is simply this: in each of these creative educational programs, students are not only learning facts and analyzing data; they are being formed to be caretakers of their home place. Earthkeeping dispositions such as wisdom and love are being nurtured. Ecofriendly ways of seeing the natural world are being fostered. The seeds of justice and courage are being sown. In short, ecological virtues are being cultivated. Each of these programs is like a nursery that provides a nourishing habitat for eco-virtues such as wonder and humility and hope. As stated previously, virtues are habits formed over time, and while these students are too young to tell whether their education is actually forming in them the virtues needed to be earthkeepers, I wager that many of these students will become people who care deeply for the world in which we live.

Adirondack May-Term Course

"This course changed how I see the world." So wrote a student in a course evaluation for a college class I teach each May. The student commented that the course was life changing in part because of particular practices and how they cultivated certain habits. Going without cell phones, preparing and eating meals together, paddling a tandem canoe, birding by day and stargazing at night, having daily reflection time—all these and more helped this student see the world differently. Without directly using the language of virtue, my student noted how this course had fostered certain praiseworthy dispositions.[10]

For three decades, I have been teaching a course at Hope College titled Ecological Theology and Ethics. This course is taught over May term, during which students take one course intensively, on or off campus, for four weeks. Originally taught in the Nantahala National Forest in western North Carolina, just south of Great Smoky Mountain National Park, since 1995 this course has been taught in the Adirondacks of upstate New York.[11] The course begins with two days of class (three hours a day) at Hope and ends with four days of class (also three hours a day) at Hope, but the two weeks in the middle are spent white-water rafting, flat-water canoeing and kayaking, and backpacking in the Adirondacks. I teach with three other instructors, so the eleven students are divided into two groups, each with two instructors (one male, one female), with a total of seven or eight people per group.

For the eight-day expedition phase of the course, we travel together by water and by trail and learn basic wilderness camping skills, such as how to paddle and portage a canoe, how to cook food on a backpacking stove, how to keep food safe from bears, how to use a map and compass, and how to identify certain plants and animals and constellations. The course also provides opportunities for students to develop leadership skills, since the students, in pairs, are the "leaders for the day" and thus responsible, among other things, for making sure morning and evening chores get done, deciding when and where to have lunch, navigating and not getting lost. In addition to teaching wilderness skills and cultivating leadership ability, the course is a long conversation about ecological theology and ethics. Needless to say, such a course provides many opportunities for growth and learning, not least with respect to virtues.

Students may take their electronic devices with them to Camp Fowler, our base of operation in the Adirondacks, but once we are on the wilderness canoeing and backpacking portion of the course, they have no electronic gadgets. Many students experience the anxieties of "technology withdrawal," but most later (if not at the time) express amazement that they are able to survive, even flourish, without Facebook and Twitter. Indeed, many students voice their gratitude for the chance to unplug. With faces no longer fixed to mobile phones or computer screens for many hours a day and with an always interesting and astoundingly beautiful world surrounding us, the virtue of ecological attentiveness gets a chance to develop. Geoffrey Frasz describes this kind of attentiveness as "an expansion of the capacity of imaginative dwelling on the condition of the other"—an expansion that requires "sustained nature watching and observation of animals in their wild habitats."[12] Philip Cafaro likewise emphasizes the need for continuous attentiveness, along with persistence and patience, by those who would learn what nature has to teach.[13] Attentiveness is a prerequisite for learning virtually any wilderness skill, whether paddling, birding, or attending to the stove when cooking that delicious dessert in the dark. Ecological attentiveness is that kind of sustained and focused attention that over time gives us the ability to understand the natural world more deeply.[14] By restricting the use of electronic devices, by looking for animal scat and tracks, by identifying trees and birds and explaining the roles they play in their home places (niches and habitats), we instructors intentionally introduce practices that are designed to increase attentiveness.

While there are many opportunities for cultivating ecological attentiveness during this course, one that comes immediately to mind is white-water rafting the Upper Hudson River. We spend a whole day paddling eight-person rafts on a seventeen-mile stretch of class 3–4 white water. For most students, this is something they have never done before, and while they are very excited about this part of the course, they also are more than a little anxious. White-water paddling of any kind (canoe, kayak, raft) is nothing if not one long seminar on attentiveness. Knowing what exactly to attend to (which waves? which current?) is a constant challenge, especially if you are trying to avoid the souse holes and hidden boulders that might flip you and your mates into the roaring water. Keeping your focus on the right things for an extended period of time is no mean feat. In this case, it involves learning how moving water works: how rocks form waves, how water flows around rocks and trees, how water moves in shallow and in deep places and around bends, what waves tell you about what lies beneath the surface, how currents separate and combine—literally how to read a river in order to navigate it safely. For river running, the object of one's attention has more to do with physics than with biology, more to do with fluid dynamics than with ecology. So it may not be quite accurate to call it ecological attentiveness, compared, for example, to how birding offers a similar education in attentiveness. But white-water rafting is very clearly tutelage in attentiveness about an important feature of the natural world.

Along with attentiveness comes its twin sister: patience. Patience is calm forbearance. One of the virtues I associate with the theological motif of sabbath and the ethical principle of rejuvenation,[15] patience is that trait of character that allows us to resist the press of the moment. It is the settled disposition to wait (with good reason) calmly and without complaint. And yet patience also guards against inaction. Patience is not the same as fainthearted-ness or reticence. The patient person knows when to wait and also when to act. Hence impetuousness and timidity are the two vices that correspond to patience—having, respectively, too little or too much patience.

Ecological patience gives us the ability to discern the right time to act in our care for our home planet. On the one hand, ecological patience steels us against the temptation to take the fast track, when what is needed is a longer view. No aged oak springs from an acorn overnight. No wetland is restored in a week. No endangered species recovers in a year. On the other hand, ecological patience does not allow us to procrastinate or do nothing. Oak trees do not live at all if they are never planted. The pond won't clean itself up. An endangered species more likely recovers when we help it along. Given our "We want it hot and now" culture, learning the geology and ecology of any biological community forces us to reset the clock to think in terms of decades and centuries and millennia rather than seconds or hours or days, and thus promotes ecological patience.

The May-term course provides ample opportunities for students (and instructors) to learn good old-fashioned patience. Waiting for supper when famished after a long day of paddling provides an opportunity to learn patience. Hiking at a pace slower than you normally walk builds patience. Waiting out the rain from a thunderstorm develops patience. There are seemingly endless opportunities for cultivating patience on a wilderness trip of whatever sort.

But on this course there are also many opportunities to learn ecological patience. For example, the Adirondack Mountains are very old—much older than the Rockies or the Sierra Nevada—and paddling around and hiking on such aged mountains seeps in. These mountains have existed for millions of years. It is hard not to find one's own sense of time changed after living for a while in this place. The forests, while cut over in the nineteenth and early twentieth centuries, have largely grown back, but on the timescale of decades and centuries. The process of reforestation (both natural and human aided) requires of us a learned patience about the length of time necessary for forests to regain ecosystemic health. As any tree planter knows, trees take time to grow; thus one must be exceedingly patient. And studying acid rain, whose results are evident in the forests we hike through, also fosters a kind of ecological patience, given that the acidity of many lakes and the lack of natural buffering agents in the sediment of the lakes make for a slower than desired recovery time.[16]

I could continue, but I hope the point is clear: this college course is intentionally designed to cultivate in students the formation of ecological virtues such as attentiveness and patience, not to mention faith, hope, and love.

Creation Care Study Program

"I learned so much, and I know I am a better person because of it." So wrote a former student about her time studying in Belize with the Creation Care Study

Program. Belize is a country in Central America tucked between Guatemala, Mexico, and the Caribbean Sea. About the size of New Hampshire, Belize is small, as countries go, and has fewer than four hundred thousand permanent residents—less than many midsize cities in the United States. Indeed, Belize has the lowest population density of any country in Central America. It is also one of the most biologically diverse places in the world, with an abundance of terrestrial and marine species in its many different ecosystems. No surprise that Belize plays a key role in the Mesoamerican Biological Corridor. It is also no surprise that ecotourism has become in recent years one of the leading sources of income.

The Creation Care Study Program (CCSP), a US-based nonprofit educational organization, has been offering college courses in Belize since 1996 and began a similar program in New Zealand in 2002. In Belize, over one semester (fifteen weeks) students take a common set of three courses: Tropical Ecosystems of Belize, Sustainable Community Development, and God and Nature. For their fourth course, students take Environmental Literature or do an internship. In New Zealand, students take the same three core courses (with Ecosystems of New Zealand for the science course) and have the option of studying Maori or doing an internship for the elective course. So all students take integrated courses in the natural sciences, social sciences, and the humanities. Most of these courses are taught as intensive weeklong courses one at a time.

In addition, in both Belize and New Zealand, all the students live together in the same place and share common daily routines and weekly rhythms. For example, when the weeklong classes are in session (except for the field-based excursions), everyone eats meals together (and takes turns doing dishes), does specified housekeeping chores, and/or works in the garden. Every morning there is a brief time of communal prayer. During the week students lead common worship, and on Sunday they attend a local church of their choice. There are also group excursions to important cultural sites, such as Mayan ruins in Belize or Guatemala and Maori communities in New Zealand. During weeklong breaks, students in small groups of four to five explore other places in that part of the world, such as birding sites in Mexico or the fjords and mountains of the South Island of New Zealand.

Since 1998 I have been teaching in this unique program. Whether in Belize or New Zealand, I teach a weeklong intensive course, typically during my spring break in March. The course, God and Nature, introduces students to the biblical roots, theological concepts, and ethical implications of earthkeeping from a Christian point of view. We meet three hours every morning and two to three hours every night for five days, with afternoons free to read and relax. The daily and weekly routine bears more than a little resemblance to that of Benedictine monks. Compared to "normal life" for most of us, life for CCSP students (and faculty) is simple, ordered, and bare-bones, and (many would say) therefore we are focused, content, and joyful. Distractions are few, genuine needs are recognized and met, and the strangeness and wonder of the natural and cultural setting are impossible to ignore.

All the faculty I know who teach for CCSP are experts in their respective fields, very creative teachers, and Christians committed to spreading the good news about the call to care for creation. Perhaps most important, the faculty understand that education—all education but especially this kind of education—is not just about the dissemination of information but about the formation of character.

Needless to say, the CCSP is a case study in virtue formation. As the opening quote from my former student indicates, students themselves often recognize the formative nature of this type of education, and they realize that this is often quite different from the educational patterns and practices they are familiar with in their home colleges and universities. Bird-watching in the rain forest is nothing if not an education in patience. The sounds of birds are everywhere, but the tree canopy is so thick that the birds are hard to see. On one birding expedition, my expert ornithologist friends Dave and Joe had identified a dozen birds by sound before I had seen a single one. "Patience," they counseled and gave me, the novice, advice on where to look and how to see. And with patience came wonder, as I spotted for the first time a keel-billed toucan and a rufous-tailed hummingbird. Living in community nurtures love and wisdom. The monkish daily routines cultivate care for others and discernment about what is best for the whole community. Observing firsthand the grinding poverty in Belize fosters a renewed passion for justice; direct experience with the Maori and their customs in New Zealand prompts respect for a people who have much to teach the rest of us.

Not infrequently students say that CCSP changed their way of seeing the world, something most study-abroad programs aim to accomplish and something many do, in fact, achieve. But the changes prompted by studying with CCSP in Belize or New Zealand, students report, have to do not just with seeing the world differently. They also have to do with changing dispositions to act—with virtues.

Daily Life

All the previous examples have had to do with education of one sort or another—preschool, summer camp, a college course, an undergraduate study-abroad program—but unless we are teachers or students, we are most likely not involved in such activities.[17] All of us, however, live our daily lives. We often don't think much about our quotidian existence, but digging in and becoming the kind of person who embodies ecological virtues begins with how we order our daily lives. So what can we learn from people who have built earthkeeping practices into their daily lives and thus come to embody the virtues mentioned in this book?

In their coauthored book *Caring for Creation in Your Own Backyard*, Loren and Mary Ruth Wilkinson clearly and creatively describe what caring for creation can look like in everyday life.[18] Organizing their book around the four seasons, Loren and Mary Ruth describe literally hundreds of "things to do" and how to do them. For autumn, the suggested actions are arranged around the tripartite refrain of reduce, reuse, and recycle. The winter actions are ordered by the triad of make it, fix it, and share it. The spring actions fall under the triumvirate of planting, eating, and protecting. And for summer, the actions are organized according to the triplet of here, there, and everywhere.[19] Whether with respect to heating and lighting your home, using water and paper, knowing what to recycle and how to compost, sharing tools, planting trees, tending a garden, or traveling on vacation, Loren and Mary Ruth borrow from their own lifelong experience to give many examples of ways to care for creation in your own backyard. Interlaced with family stories, guidelines, bullet lists, recipes, and the like, this practical guide is an easy-to-read treasure trove of virtues embodied.

I have known Loren and Mary Ruth for some time and have visited them at their home on Galiano Island near Vancouver, British Columbia. They live their book. They are people of character who embody the ecological virtues of wonder and humility, self-control and wisdom, justice and love, courage and hope. Other virtues also grace their lives—virtues such as gratitude and frugality and fidelity. These character traits have been honed by a lifetime of commitments and practices.

Practice does not make perfect as the adage alleges, but it does make permanent, for better or for worse. Recall (from chap. 2) that virtues are habitual dispositions to act well. They are good habits formed by practice over time that enable us to act in excellent ways so that eventually these actions become second nature—things we do without much thought since they are woven into our character. By taking up certain practices, such as those described by Loren and Mary Ruth, we cultivate virtues.

Leah Kostamo, her husband, Markku, and their two daughters live on Kingfisher Farm just east of Vancouver, not far from Loren and Mary Ruth Wilkinson. In her book *Planted: A Story of Creation, Calling, and Community*, Leah winsomely (and often humorously) describes homemaking for her family in this A Rocha community in southwestern Canada.[20] A Rocha is an international Christian conservation organization founded in 1983 in Portugal by Peter and Miranda Harris and focused on protecting birds and their habitats. A Rocha now has communities in twenty countries with conservation projects of all sorts—from protecting Asian elephants to making bio-sand filters, from mangrove restoration to reducing micro-plastics in the marine environment.

Leah's reflections on earthkeeping come complete with sketches and drawings and lots of honesty about the challenges of living in community. Most of all, her musings serve as an easy-to-read practical guide to homemaking in the broad sense. I know Leah and Markku and have visited them at their home. I have seen firsthand the fruit (literal and metaphorical) of their labors and can attest that they strive to walk their talk. And in that walk, because of those practices, they have come to embody many of the dispositions I have described in this book: simplicity and humility, patience and love, wisdom and hope.

Closer to home, I know many people in my own community who exhibit the ecological virtues (and their practices) discussed in these pages. Faculty, staff, and students at Hope College through their work on the Green Team (Campus Sustainability Advisory Committee) have made Hope a more sustainable place.[21] That did not happen without perseverance and patience. Friends at local churches have fostered changes in how energy is used (and conserved) and how lawns are cared for. That has not been achieved without wisdom and love. The good folks at Eighth Day Farm, a local CSA (community-supported agriculture), grow and harvest delicious food. That does not happen without courage and hope. The list could go on. In short, there are more people than we often realize who exhibit ecological virtues in their daily lives.[22]

One thing these moral exemplars have in common is knowledge of and love for their home place. This knowledge is of two sorts: knowledge of the natural history and of the inhabitants (both human and nonhuman) of the particular place where we live, and an adequate understanding of our role as human beings in the various biophysical systems of this earth. *Ecological literacy* is one umbrella term for these kinds of knowledge.[23] Let's briefly examine each with an eye to how it fosters virtue formation.

First, a key step in increasing eco-literacy is to develop an adequate understanding of the place where we live. Do we know where our water comes from? Do we know where our garbage goes? Do we know the history of the land on which we live? Do we know the nonhuman neighbors with whom we share our place? Attaining this knowledge can seem an unreachable goal, especially to those who are starting from scratch.[24] But it is not as daunting as it may seem. Rachel Carson counsels parents to introduce their children to the outdoors, even if they themselves have minimal knowledge about the natural world. Simply spending time exploring a place can help both parent and child see the beauty and value of the natural world. This does not necessarily mean wilderness camping trips or multiple-day birding expeditions. The first steps require no particular expertise and can be taken slowly. In Carson's words:

> If you are a parent who feels he has little nature lore at his disposal; there is still much you can do for your child. With him, wherever you are and whatever your resources, you can still look up at the night sky—its dawn and twilight beauties, its moving clouds, its stars by night. You can listen to the wind, whether it blows with majestic voice through a forest or sings a many-voiced chorus around the eaves of your house or the corners of your apartment building, and in the listening, you can gain magical release for your thoughts. You can still feel the rain on your face and think of its long journey, its many transmutations, from sea to air to earth. Even if you are a city dweller, you can find some place, perhaps a park or a golf course, where you can observe the mysterious migrations of the birds and the changing of the seasons.[25]

Increasing ecological literacy can begin with actions as simple as paying greater attention to the nonhuman world immediately surrounding us. The very act of paying attention to flora and fauna, rocks and weather, birds and insects is a step toward recognizing that these things have value—part of Annie Dillard's trying to be there with eyes open. It is a short step to calling these things by name and finding enjoyment in perusing the pages of a bird book or a tree identification guide. Whatever form it takes, a lesson in local eco-literacy is a vital step in overcoming our arrogance by acknowledging that we are not God's only creation.

In addition to knowing our home place, we need to understand our role as human beings in the various biophysical systems of this earth. The aim of this second kind of eco-literacy is, in the words of David Orr, to obtain "a basic comprehension of ecology, human ecology, and the concepts of sustainability, as well as the wherewithal to solve problems."[26] Today it is all too easy to be ignorant of our dependence on the earth. We fill up our cars with gasoline from a pump, forgetful that this resource is finite and was formed within the earth for millions of years before being harvested for our purposes. We turn on our lights with a casual flick of a switch, ignorant as to where that electricity is coming from. We shop in supermarkets, where food mysteriously appears perfectly packaged, oblivious to the long process involving soil, water, sun, and farmers. The result? We have succumbed to what Aldo Leopold referred to as the "two spiritual dangers in not owning a farm"—namely, "supposing that breakfast comes from the grocery" and that "heat comes from the furnace."[27] Most of us are disconnected from the world that sustains us, with little understanding of our dependence on the earth.

This is where knowing our place in the second sense—as creatures inextricably woven into the ecology of the earth—is so crucial. Lisa Gerber aptly describes this aspect of ecological humility as the ability to properly respond to the realities of the world we live in.[28] An ecologically humble person acknowledges the interconnectedness of all things, the dependency of human flourishing on the earth, and the intrinsic value of creation. Her humility allows her to act with restraint, tempering her appetites for more. Acting with restraint can be difficult. It usually requires us to reject the status quo, to choose contentment over the god More Stuff. Ecological humility means eschewing the human arrogance that permeates much of contemporary culture. It means, like Job, remembering our place on God's good earth.

These are some of my examples of people, programs, and places that cultivate the development of ecological virtues. There are many more examples of ecological virtue ethics formation, some hidden in plain sight in your own community. Now it is your turn. Who is on your list? What people exemplify these virtues? What programs work to form the earthkeepers of tomorrow? What places (summer camps, farms, rural nature preserves, urban parks, etc.) are fertile ground for virtue formation? How can you further your own spiritual and moral formation?

Living as Aching Visionaries

We who follow Jesus are called to bear witness to God's good future of shalom. We yearn for the fullness of shalom to come to fruition. As Richard Mouw puts it, "We must share in God's restless yearning for the renewal of the cosmos."[29] So in the Lord's Prayer we pray that God's will be done on earth as it is in heaven. In the Doxology we sing that all creatures here below might praise God. In the Apostles' Creed we confess our faith in the resurrection of the dead and the life everlasting. And we strive in our everyday living to make this vision incarnate. We yearn for the biblical vision of shalom to be made real. We are, in short, visionaries.

But in our world shalom is often in short supply. It is known as much by its absence as by its presence. And so our yearning is tinged with sadness. We mourn the loss of what could have been. We grieve for what should have been. Thus we are not merely visionaries but aching visionaries. We ache because we painfully realize that the time of shalom, in all its glorious fullness, is not yet here. We ache because we mourn with those who suffer. In his moving meditations on the occasion of the untimely death of his son, Nicholas Wolterstorff speaks of Christians in precisely these terms—as aching visionaries. Reflecting on the beatitude "Blessed are those who mourn, for they shall be comforted," he writes:

> Who then are the mourners? The mourners are those who have caught a glimpse of God's new day, who ache with all their being for that day's coming, and who break out into tears when confronted with its absence. They are the ones who realize that in God's realm of peace there is no one blind and who ache whenever they see someone unseeing. They are the ones who realize that in God's realm there is no one hungry and who ache whenever they see someone starving. They are the ones who realize that in God's realm there is no one falsely accused and who ache whenever they see someone imprisoned unjustly. They are the ones who realize that in God's realm there is no one who fails to see God and who ache whenever they see someone unbelieving. They are the ones who realize that in God's realm there is no one who suffers oppression and who ache whenever they see someone beat down. They are the ones who realize that in God's realm there is no one without dignity and who ache whenever they see someone treated with indignity. They are the ones who realize that in God's realm of peace there is neither death nor tears and who ache whenever they see someone crying tears over death. The mourners are aching visionaries.[30]

We followers of Jesus are called to be aching visionaries. Inspired by God's vision of shalom and mindful of how far the world is from realizing that vision, we yearn for that realm of peace and justice and compassion and wisdom of which the Bible speaks. Wolterstorff's powerful reflections remind me of these words from Desmond Tutu: "All over this magnificent world God calls us to extend His Kingdom of shalom—peace and wholeness—of justice, of goodness, of compassion, of caring, of sharing, of laughter, of joy, and of reconciliation. God is transfiguring the world right this very moment *through us* because God *believes in us* and because God *loves us*."[31] God is transfiguring the world right this very moment *through us* because God *believes in us* and because God *loves us*. May God bless you. Indeed, may God bless all of us as we respond to that love by caring for this world of wonders.

Appendix

A Brief Survey of Christian Environmental Virtue Ethics

A number of Christian scholars have made forays into environmental virtue ethics. One of the first was Jay McDaniel, who includes a discussion of ecological virtues in his presentation of a biocentric or life-centered ethic. After speaking of the need for various "biocentric practices," such as not eating meat and protecting endangered species, McDaniel argues that "such practical steps are not enough if Christians are to overcome the anthropocentrism of our past. What is required . . . is a conversion of sensibility and character."[1] In spelling out what he means by character, he mentions three virtues: reverence for life, *ahimsa* or noninjury, and the exercise of active goodwill. In his discussion, it becomes clear that the first virtue is actually respect (not reverence) for all living things, the second is nonmaleficence or the inclination not to inflict pain on other sentient creatures, and the third is benevolence or the disposition to foster opportunities for an animal to realize its interests. Each virtue, McDaniel affirms, is an application of *agapē* or neighbor love to our nonhuman neighbors.

James Nash was another early spokesperson for Christian environmental virtues in his 1991 book, *Loving Nature: Ecological Integrity and Christian Responsibility*. While most of the book focuses on the doctrines of Christian theology, Nash includes a short section on what he calls "ecological virtues." Given the various dimensions of the ecological crisis, he asks, "What attitudes and habits will enable individuals and communities to respond remedially to these problems? Or what are the characteristics and traits that are conducive to the goal of ecological integrity and that, therefore, we ought to cultivate?"[2] He proceeds in three pages to describe nine virtues: sustainability, adaptability, relationality, frugality, equity, solidarity, biodiversity, sufficiency, and humility, claiming that "humility is a guiding norm for all other virtues."[3] Nash provides a creative and suggestive, if brief, discussion of some important virtues.

Michael Northcott's *The Environment and Christian Ethics* was published in 1996. This informed and insightful book set the bar high for subsequent Christian environmental ethicists. After a survey of traditional environmental ethics, Northcott concludes that neither consequentialism nor deontology will suffice in environmental ethics. In contrast, he argues that "the reversal of the environmental crisis . . . will only come about when we recover a deeper sense for the relationality of human life to particular ecosystems and parts of the biosphere, and where communities of place foster those virtues of justice and compassion, of care and respect for life, human and non-human, of temperance and prudence in our appetites and desires."[4] Later in the book, Northcott briefly describes eight virtues that "enable us to become more fulfilled as persons, to live in solidarity with one another, and to live in harmony with the created order."[5] His list of ecological virtues includes love, justice, temperance, prudence, fidelity, courage or fortitude, hope, and peaceableness. Rooted in both a perceptive analysis of modern culture and a rich retrieval of the Christian theological tradition, Northcott's work has much to commend.

In his more recent volume *Place, Ecology, and the Sacred*, Northcott lists virtue ethics as one of the four main approaches to environmental ethics and argues that "virtue ethics has the considerable advantage over the other approaches to environmental ethics of highlighting the importance of face to face relationships of education and nurture, and of small-scale communities of place, in the formation of moral agents."[6] He reiterates the importance of traditional virtues such as love, justice, temperance, prudence, and courage and highlights the role of "exemplary practices that inculcate such virtues"—practices such as recycling used materials, canoeing in wild places, and learning to identify nonhuman species by name.[7]

Willis Jenkins, in his book *Ecologies of Grace: Environmental Ethics and Christian Theology*, adds a distinctive contribution to this discussion. The bulk of the book is an insightful exploration of three ethical strategies—eco-justice, Christian stewardship, and ecological spirituality—and does not directly address environmental virtues, but in one chapter Jenkins mines the work of Thomas Aquinas for resources to illuminate environmental virtues, despite the fact that Aquinas is not often seen as a promising source for environmental ethics.[8]

Jenkins identifies two key virtues: contemplative charity and prudential providence. Contemplative charity (from *caritas*) names that virtue infused by God that disposes us to seek communion with God and love others for the sake of God. It includes "fine awareness, receptive appreciation, and rich responsibility," but unlike other takes on love as a virtue in a world of finitude and competition, this "knowing intimacy comes into harmony with nature's own peace and goodness, for it assumes a cosmos overabundant with divine love."[9] So, argues Jenkins, not only does "love for our human friends give us reason enough to preserve green spaces" and not only does "care for other intellectual creatures" inspire us to want "the resources of creation [to] be made equitably accessible," but, according to Aquinas, "charity also refers to a justice more universal, to active promotion of the goods of creation for itself."[10] So contemplative charity is an environmental virtue insofar as it names the disposition to promote the flourishing of more than merely humans.

Prudential providence is, in essence, the human virtue of wise stewardship. This virtue is a kind of practical wisdom that enables us to know how to promote creation's own integrity, following the pattern of God's providential care for all creation. While acknowledging that Thomistic renditions of dominion have been used to justify exploitation, Jenkins argues that "Thomas' stewardly dominion in fact must operate in attentive respect of creaturely goods and ecological orders."[11] Respecting creaturely goods and ecological orders, Jenkins perceptively notes, "requires savvy ecology: concern for keystone habitats and healthy ecosystems, for the integrity of nature's own self-regulatory and developmental processes."[12] In sum, Jenkins finds insight into environmental virtues in what some take to be an unlikely place—a timely reminder of how valuable the Christian tradition can be.

Nash, Northcott, and Jenkins are established scholars who have much to contribute, but newcomers also offer insight. In his 2011 doctoral dissertation, Seth Bible offers a perceptive analysis of some of the main writers in the field of environmental virtue ethics—namely, Ronald Sandler, Louke van Wensveen, and Philip Cafaro.[13] In addition to his insightful presentations and criticisms of these three thinkers, Bible concludes with some proposals for Christians who espouse environmental virtue ethics. His "list of premises" about "a distinctively *Christian* environmental virtue ethic" includes some sound recommendations—for example, that such an ethic must be theocentric rather than anthropocentric or biocentric or ecocentric, that such an ethic can and should combine deontology with areteology, and that such an ethic should embrace the moral-exemplar approach to defining virtues.

Further evidence for increasing interest in Christian environmental virtue ethics can be found in *Green Discipleship*—an anthology on Catholic theological ethics and the environment. In a chapter devoted to environmental virtue ethics, Nancy Rourke explains the basics of Christian environmental virtue ethics—its goal, the definition of virtue, the role of moral exemplars.[14] She highlights the classic Christian virtues of fortitude, temperance, justice, prudence, faith, hope, and love. Attention to the virtues is also evident in other chapters, such as chapters on Francis of Assisi and Thomas Aquinas. While not breaking any new ground, the inclusion in such a book of an essay explicitly devoted to environmental virtue ethics indicates an increasing acknowledgment of its importance.

While a number of Christian scholars have made forays into environmental virtue ethics, surprisingly little substantive work has been done. One of the more significant ventures into Christian environmental virtue ethics is found in the pioneering work of Louke van Wensveen. In her early essays, she surveys the field of Christian ethics and the growing environmental movement, noting especially the different roles the Bible plays and the various ways biblical texts are retrieved. She states (in 1995) that "the emergence of a Christian ecological virtue ethic" is "still inchoate in shape," but remarks that certain traditional Christian virtues (humility, frugality, temperance, hope) continue to figure prominently.[15] In a paper given at a conference at Harvard in 1998 (published in 2000), she compares emerging ecological virtue ethics with the ethics of Thomas Aquinas. While noting various similarities and differences, she concludes that "the superficial similarities, on closer inspection, dissolve into rather significant differences" and thus "simply retrofitting the Aristotelian-Thomistic virtue tradition for ecological purposes becomes unrealistic." So she proposes that "we follow the man Aquinas, rather than cling to the whole system of his thought, and engage in the creative task of transforming the Christian virtue tradition from the bottom up, looking to ecological praxis to provide new structures and content."[16]

In her subsequent work, van Wensveen follows her own advice. Her most complete statement is found in her book *Dirty Virtues*.[17] After noting the ubiquity of virtue language in the literature on ecological issues, she asks, "If such a rich variety of ecological virtues and vices exist in such a wide range of literature, why is this moral language not better known?"[18] Indeed, in her "catalogue of ecological virtues and vices"—terms that occur in environmental literature since 1970—she includes 189 virtues and 174 vices,[19] so there is no dearth of terms and concepts. To bring some semblance of order to this plethora of terms, van Wensveen explores the work of Murray Bookchin and Thomas Berry as well as the Aristotelian-Thomist tradition.

She also draws on eco-feminism to illuminate the gender-constructed nature of virtue language—all for the purpose of distinguishing genuine virtue (and vice) from their imposters and pretenders. She revisits the seven deadly sins and creatively turns them into ecological vices. She provides an insightful and nuanced case study of courage as an eco-virtue, borrowing from Augustine and Aquinas while also learning from modern psychology and feminist theory. She concludes by constructing a typology of views on nature and ecological ethics.[20] In sum, *Dirty Virtues* represents one of the first truly substantive discussions of Christian environmental virtue ethics.

In a subsequent essay (published in 2005), van Wensveen surveys the field and classifies the smorgasbord of virtues into four groups: virtues of position, virtues of care, virtues of attunement, and virtues of endurance. Virtues of position are "constructive habits of seeing ourselves in a particular place in a relational structure and interacting accordingly."[21] In other words, those who possess these virtues see themselves not in the position of domination over nonhuman creatures, but (in the words of Aldo Leopold) as plain members and citizens of the larger ecological community. She cites as examples humility, self-acceptance, gratitude, and appreciation of the good in others (borrowing from Thomas Hill), as well as respect, prudence, and practical judgment (courtesy of Bill Shaw). Other virtues in this group are wisdom (citing Susan Bratton and Celia Deane-Drummond), "ecological sensibility" (quoting John Rodman), and "the sensitivity of the naturalist" (referring to Holmes Rolston).

Virtues of care are "habits of constructive involvement within the relational structure where we have found our place."[22] That is to say, those who embody these virtues cast their net widely to perceive various kinds of need. They cultivate friendships with the natural world and thus are able to notice and address the needs of those (human and nonhuman) around us. Virtues included in this group (borrowing from, respectively, Lisa Gerber, Jennifer Welchman, and James Nash) are attentiveness, benevolence, and love.

Virtues of attunement are "habits of handling temptations by adjusting ('tuning') our positive, outgoing drives and emotions to match our chosen place and degree of constructive, ecosocial engagement."[23] In other words, people who exhibit these virtues are able and willing to adjust their desires and goals to fit their place, construed in the widest sense. They are attuned to their local community—including the land and its many members—and thus live in ways appropriate to their place. Virtues in this category include James Nash's concept of frugality as well as Philip Cafaro and Lisa Newton's notion of simplicity. These virtues, van Wensveen stresses, are not to be confused with sour self-denial but rather denote the joy of living simply.

Finally, virtues of endurance are "habits of facing dangers and difficulties by handling our negative, protective drives and emotions in such a way that we can sustain our chosen sense of place and degree of constructive ecosocial engagement."[24] Tenacity and loyalty are the two examples of virtue in this category mentioned by van Wensveen, citing Randy Larson and Jennifer Welchman. This brief summary of van Wensveen's work illustrates the fruitfulness of her contribution to this field.

Another significant contribution to Christian environmental virtue ethics is the theologically rich work of Jame Schaefer.[25] Deeply rooted in the Catholic tradition and also aware of pioneering Protestant theologians such as Joseph Sittler, erudite in theology and ethics while also knowledgeable in the natural sciences, Schaefer is exemplary in many ways. No one else has so thoroughly explored the riches of the early and medieval Christian tradition for contemporary ecological virtue ethics. Citing a veritable who's who from the history of the church prior to 1500—Clement of Alexandria, Ephrem of Syria, Athanasius of Alexandria, Basil of Caesarea, John Chrysostom, Augustine, Benedict of Nursia, John Scotus Eriugena, Simeon the New Theologian, Hugh of St. Victor, Bernard of Clairvaux, Hildegard of Bingen, Francis of Assisi, Thomas Aquinas, Bonaventure, Gregory of Palamas—Schaefer shows how environmental ethics in the present can learn much from Christian theology of the past.

While the book is not primarily about virtue ethics, the titles of the first nine chapters indicate the crucial role of virtues: valuing the goodness of creation, appreciating the beauty of creation, reverencing the sacramental universe, respecting creation's praise for God, cooperating within the integrity of creation, acknowledging kinship and practicing companionship, using creation with gratitude and restraint, living virtuously within the earth community, and loving the earth. In each case, Schaefer first develops a particular concept (e.g., the integrity of creation) by mining the Christian tradition (e.g., Augustine on the commonwealth of creatures). Then she shows how this patristic-medieval idea can be reconfigured when informed by a relevant concept from contemporary science (e.g., ecosystem). Next she illustrates how this concept addresses a contemporary problem (e.g., degradation in the Great Lakes). Finally, Schaefer outlines specific behaviors that are implied by this idea (e.g., acknowledging biotic and abiotic contributions to ecosystems, assuring the sustainability of ecosystems, being penitent for jeopardizing ecosystem sustainability). These behaviors look a lot like the habitual dispositions to act excellently otherwise known as virtues.

In a chapter titled "Living Virtuously within the Earth Community," Schaefer describes, with the help of Aquinas, the cardinal virtues of prudence, temperance, justice, and fortitude. While explaining the meaning of these virtues, she shows how temperance includes certain "subvirtues," such as humility, and how justice must be expanded to include more than humans. She also illustrates what living virtuously (prudently, moderately, justly, courageously) would look like in the case of the Great Lakes ecosystem. Much more could be said, but this should suffice to indicate the depth of Schaefer's fine work.

The final contribution to Christian environmental virtue ethics discussed here is the excellent work of Kathryn Blanchard and Kevin O'Brien in their book *An Introduction to Christian Environmentalism: Ecology, Virtue, and Ethics*. Scholarly without being stodgy, in understandable and often winsome prose, and with much biblical insight and knowledge of the Christian tradition, this book presents a compelling case for "the idea that the seven moral and theological virtues passed down through Christian tradition can be vital resources for responding to environmental problems and ordering our environmental lives."[26] Blanchard and O'Brien creatively pair each of the seven main Christian virtues (cardinal and theological) to a different ecological issue: prudence to species extinction, courage to energy use, temperance to food insecurity, justice to toxic waste, faith to climate change, hope to human population, and love to the need for action. In each case they show how that particular virtue addresses that specific ecological issue. So, for example, they show how prudence—foresight, sagacity, discernment—is needed if we are to tackle the problem of increasing species extinction. They illustrate how courage—fortitude, perseverance, determination—is necessary to face the energy fears of the twenty-first century. They explain how faith—belief in the goodness of God, fidelity to fellow creatures, faithfulness to God's purpose—can help us confront the challenges of climate change. Drawing from a diverse range of thinkers—Wendell Berry and Bill McKibben, Dietrich Bonhoeffer and Martin Luther King Jr., Eastern Orthodox Patriarch Bartholomew and Ed Abbey—in addition to the Bible and the Christian tradition, Blanchard and O'Brien persuasively show how "virtue ethics is an important tool for engaging contemporary environmental issues." And they rightly remind us, using the words of Aldo Leopold, that while "the world is full of wounds," we Christians "have been called by a suffering Messiah to pay attention to those wounds."[27] I used many of the insights of these Christian sisters and brothers in this book.

Notes

Introduction: Ecological Ethics Reframed

1. Thomas Hill Jr., "Ideals of Human Excellence and Preserving Natural Environments," in *Environmental Virtue Ethics*, ed. Ronald Sandler and Philip Cafaro (Lanham, MD: Rowman & Littlefield, 2005), 47.

2. David Orr, *Earth in Mind* (Washington, DC: Island Press, 1994), 62.

3. Hill, "Ideals of Human Excellence," in Sandler and Cafaro, *Environmental Virtue Ethics*, 47.

4. Hill, "Ideals of Human Excellence," in Sandler and Cafaro, *Environmental Virtue Ethics*, 50.

5. Of central importance is the work of Alasdair MacIntyre, for example, *After Virtue: A Study in Moral Theology*, 2nd ed. (Notre Dame, IN: University of Notre Dame Press, 1984). See also the classic by Philippa Foot, *Virtues and Vices and Other Essays in Moral Philosophy* (Berkeley: University of California Press, 1978). Collections of helpful essays can be found in Robert Kruschwitz and Robert Roberts, eds., *The Virtues: Contemporary Essays on Moral Character* (Belmont, CA: Wadsworth, 1987); Daniel Statman, ed., *Virtue Ethics: A Critical Reader* (Washington, DC: Georgetown University Press, 1997); and Daniel Russell, ed., *The Cambridge Companion to Virtue Ethics* (Cambridge: Cambridge University Press, 2013).

6. Some of the most helpful books are Michael Austin and R. Douglas Geivett, eds., *Being Good: Christian Virtues for Everyday Life* (Grand Rapids: Eerdmans, 2012); Romanus Cessario, *The Moral Virtues and Theological Ethics* (Notre Dame, IN: University of Notre Dame Press, 1990); Rebecca Konyndyk DeYoung, *Glittering Vices: A New Look at the Seven Deadly Sins and Their Remedies* (Grand Rapids: Brazos, 2009); Benjamin Farley, *In Praise of Virtue: An Exploration of the Biblical Virtues in a Christian Context* (Grand Rapids: Eerdmans, 1995); Stanley Hauerwas, *Character and the Christian Life* (San Antonio: Trinity University Press, 1985); Stanley Hauerwas and Charles Pinches, *Christians among the Virtues* (Notre Dame: University of Notre Dame Press, 1997); Philip Kenneson, *Life on the Vine: Cultivating the Fruit of the Spirit in Christian Community* (Downers Grove, IL: InterVarsity, 1999); Joseph Kotva, *The Christian Case for Virtue Ethics* (Washington, DC: Georgetown University Press, 1996); Jean Porter, *The Recovery of Virtue: The Relevance of Aquinas for Christian Ethics* (Louisville: Westminster John Knox, 1990); Lewis Smedes, *A Pretty Good Person: What It Takes to Live with Courage, Gratitude, and Integrity* (San Francisco: Harper & Row, 1990); Jonathan Wilson, *Gospel Virtues: Practicing Faith, Hope, and Love in Uncertain Times* (Downers Grove, IL: InterVarsity, 1998).

7. See, for example, the pioneering work of Holmes Rolston III, *Environmental Ethics: Duties to and Values in the Natural World* (Philadelphia: Temple University Press, 1988) and his more recent volume *A New Environmental Ethic: The Next Millennium for Life on Earth* (New York: Routledge, 2012). See also the important work of Erazim Kohak, *The Embers and the Stars: A Philosophical Inquiry into the Moral Sense of Nature* (Chicago: University of Chicago Press, 1984), and his more recent book *The Green Halo: A Bird's Eye View of Ecological Ethics* (Chicago: Open Court, 2000). Other important works are Robin Attfield, *The Ethics of Environmental Concern*, 2nd ed. (Athens: University of Georgia Press, 1983); Baird Callicott, *Beyond the Land Ethic: More Essays in Environmental Philosophy* (Albany: State University of New York Press, 1999); Andrew Light and Eric Katz, eds., *Environmental Pragmatism* (London: Routledge, 1986); Christopher Stone, *Earth and Other Ethics: The Case for Moral Pluralism* (New York: Harper & Row, 1987); Paul Taylor, *Respect for Nature: A Theory of Environmental Ethics* (Princeton: Princeton University Press, 1986).

8. The best place to start is Sandler and Cafaro, eds., *Environmental Virtue Ethics*. This anthology includes many of the most important essays. The leading scholars (and their works) in this emerging field of study will be introduced in chap. 1.

9. See, for example, the pioneering book by Louke van Wensveen, *Dirty Virtues: The Emergence of Ecological Virtue Ethics* (Amherst, NY: Humanity Books, 2000), and the very fine work of Seth Bible, "Pursuing Ecological Virtue: A Critical Analysis of the Environmental Virtue Ethics Models of Ronald Sandler, Louke van Wensveen, and Philip Cafaro" (PhD diss., Southeastern Baptist Theological Seminary, 2011). See also the outstanding volume by Kathryn Blanchard and Kevin O'Brien, *An Introduction to Christian Environmentalism: Ecology, Virtue, and Ethics* (Waco: Baylor University Press, 2014).

10. Loren Wilkinson et al., eds., *Earthkeeping: Christian Stewardship of Natural Resources* (Grand Rapids: Eerdmans, 1980), published in a revised second edition as Loren Wilkinson, ed., *Earthkeeping in the Nineties: Stewardship of Creation* (Grand Rapids: Eerdmans, 1991).

11. See the Religions of the World and Ecology book series, ed. Mary Evelyn Tucker and John Grim (Cambridge: Harvard University Press, 1998–2004). The series includes books on Buddhism, Christianity, Confucianism, Daoism, Hinduism, Indigenous traditions, Islam, Jainism, Judaism, and Shinto. For work from various non-Christian religious perspectives that focuses explicitly on virtue ethics, see, for example, John Patterson, "Maori Environmental Virtues," *Environmental Ethics* 16 (Winter 1994): 397–409, and Pragti Sahni, *Environmental Ethics in Buddhism: A Virtues Approach* (London: Routledge, 2008).

12. For one description of this phenomenon of loss of wonder, see Richard Louv, *Last Child in the Woods: Saving Our Children from Nature Deficit Disorder* (Chapel Hill: Algonquin Books, 2006). For a prescription, see Richard Louv, *Vitamin N: The Essential Guide to a Nature-Rich Life* (Chapel Hill: Algonquin Books, 2016).

13. The claim that humans have some "inner divinity, which goes by a number of names, such as God-consciousness or Higher Self" or, more boldly, that "we are gods" is one of the tenets of the "wide-ranging, amorphous movement commonly called New Age." See Steve Wilkens and Mark Sanford, *Hidden Worldviews: Eight Cultural Stories That Shape Our Lives* (Downers Grove, IL: IVP Academic, 2009), 120–23.

14. I am not making this up. These are actual bumper stickers I saw when living in Los Angeles.

15. One of the main challenges to environmental virtues, writes Sandra Jane Fairbanks, is "our materialistic conception of a good life." Indeed, she argues that "our capitalistic culture poses a very serious threat to the successful inculcation of essential environmental virtues." ("Environmental Goodness and the Challenge of American Culture," *Ethics and the Environment* 15 [2010]: 90, 97). One attempt to address the cultural malady of materialism can be found in the diverse collection of readings edited by Michael Schut, *Simpler Living, Compassionate Life: A Christian Perspective* (Denver: Living the Good News, 1999).

16. For one example of perceptive cultural analysis that focuses on how modern technology is shaping us, and often for the worse, see Jaron Lanier, *You Are Not a Gadget* (New York: Knopf, 2010).

17. For both a perceptive cultural analysis of contemporary injustice and insightful biblical and theological reflections on justice, see Bethany Hanke Hoang and Kristen Deede Johnson, *The Justice Calling: Where Passion Meets Perseverance* (Grand Rapids: Brazos, 2016).

18. For a number of years, pollsters have tracked American attitudes regarding various environmental issues, for example, climate change and species extinction. While the results show some positive change (for example, from 2016 to 2017 there was an increase from 37 percent to 45 percent of Americans who say they "worry a great deal" about climate change), the level of apathy remains quite high. For more details, see Lydia Saad, "Global Warming Concern at Three-Decade High in U.S.," Gallup, March 14, 2017, http://www.gallup.com/poll/206030/glo bal-warming-concern-three-decade-high.aspx. For one attempt to combat this indifference, see James Hansen, *Storms of My Grandchildren: The Truth about the Coming Climate Catastrophe and Our Last Chance to Save Humanity* (New York: Bloomsbury, 2009).

19. For more on fear (and denial) with respect to environmental degradation, as well as courage and hope as remedies, see Mary Pipher, *The Green Boat: Reviving Ourselves in Our Capsized Culture* (New York: Riverhead Books, 2013).

20. For a perceptive analysis of this aspect of contemporary culture, with a robust hope-filled prescription for what ails us, see Bob Goudzwaard and Craig Bartholomew, *Beyond the Modern Age: An Archaeology of Contemporary Culture* (Downers Grove, IL: IVP Academic, 2017).

21. "If these matters and the virtues, and also friendship and pleasure, have been dealt with sufficiently in outline, are we to suppose that our programme has reached its end? Surely, as the saying goes, where there are things to be done the end is not to survey and recognize the various things, but rather to do them; with regard to virtue then, it is not enough to know, but we must try to have and use it, or try any way there may be of becoming good." Aristotle, *Nicomachean Ethics*, in *The Basic Works of Aristotle*, ed. Richard McKeon (New York: Random House, 1941), book 10, chapter 9.

Chapter 1: Mapping the Territory

1. Aristotle, *Nicomachean Ethics*, in *The Basic Works of Aristotle*, ed. Richard McKeon (New York: Random House, 1941), book 2, chapter 5.

2. C. S. Lewis, *The Magician's Nephew* (New York: Macmillan, 1978), 125.

3. Made (in)famous by Nixon-era Secretary of Agriculture Earl L. Butz.

4. Wendell Berry, "The Clearing Rests in Song and Shade," in *This Day: Collected and New Sabbath Poems* (Berkeley: Counterpoint, 2013), 44.

5. For a brilliant treatment of these basic issues, see Lewis Smedes, *Choices: Making Right Decisions in a Complex World* (San Francisco: Harper & Row, 1986), chap. 1.

6. David Cunningham, *Christian Ethics: The End of the Law* (New York: Routledge, 2008), 26.

7. For example, Peter Singer argues that the range of what counts morally includes all sentient beings—that is, those creatures capable of experiencing pleasure and pain, and not just human beings. See Peter Singer, *Animal Liberation: A New Ethics for Our Treatment of Animals* (New York: New York Review, 1975).

8. Bob Goudzwaard and Craig Bartholomew, *Beyond the Modern Age: An Archaeology of Contemporary Culture* (Downers Grove, IL: IVP Academic, 2017). See also Steve Wilkens and Mark Sanford, *Hidden Worldviews: Eight Cultural Stories That Shape Our Lives* (Downers Grove, IL: IVP Academic, 2009).

9. Clive Barnett, Philip Cafaro, and Terry Newholm, "Philosophy and Ethical Consumption," in *The Ethical Consumer*, ed. Rob Harrison, Terry Newholm, and Deirdre Shaw (London: Sage, 2005), 13.

10. For a lively and insightful discussion of the role of emotions, personality traits, and social norms in the formation of character and ethical decision making, see David Brooks, *The Social Animal: The Hidden Sources of Love, Character, and Achievement* (New York: Random House, 2011). For a scholarly treatment of the role of emotions in our intellectual life and a compelling argument for taking emotional intelligence seriously in ethics, see Martha Nussbaum, *Upheavals of Thought: The Intelligence of Emotions* (Cambridge: Cambridge University Press, 2001).

11. Mark Johnson, *Moral Imagination: Implications of Cognitive Science for Ethics* (Chicago: University of Chicago Press, 1993), 4–5.

12. Mark Johnson, *The Meaning of the Body: Aesthetics of Human Understanding* (Chicago: University of Chicago Press, 2007), 1. See also the classic book by George Lakoff and Mark Johnson, *Metaphors We Live By* (Chicago: University of Chicago Press, 1980).

13. Johnson, *Meaning of the Body*, 1.

14. A nice summary of much of the recent research can be found in Guy Claxton, *Intelligence in the Flesh: Why Your Mind Needs Your Body Much More Than It Thinks* (New Haven: Yale University Press, 2015).

15. Charles Taylor, *A Secular Age* (Cambridge: Harvard University Press, 2007), 282.

16. John Vucetich, Michael Paul Nelson, and Chelsea Batavia, "The Anthropocene: Disturbing Name, Limited Insight," in *After Preservation: Saving American Nature in the Age of Humans*, ed. Ben Minteer and Stephen Pyne (Chicago: University of Chicago Press, 2015), 73.

17. Olivia Bina and Sofia Guedes Vaz, "Humans, Environment, and Economies: From Vicious Relationships to Virtuous Responsibility," *Ecological Economics* 72 (2011): 170, 178.

18. Alasdair MacIntyre, *After Virtue*, 2nd ed. (Notre Dame, IN: University of Notre Dame Press, 1984). See also his subsequent volumes *Whose Justice? Which Rationality?* (Notre Dame, IN: University of Notre Dame Press, 1988); *Three Rival Versions of Moral Inquiry: Encyclopedia, Genealogy, and Tradition* (Notre Dame, IN: University of Notre Dame Press, 1990); and *Dependent Rational Animals: Why Human Beings Need the Virtues* (Chicago: Open Court, 1999).

19. Philip Cafaro, "Economic Consumption, Pleasure, and the Good Life," *Journal of Social Philosophy* 32 (Winter 2001): 483.

20. Tim Hayward, "Climate Change and Ethics," *Nature Climate Change* (October 14, 2012): 846.

21. Ronald Sandler, *Environmental Ethics: Theory in Practice* (New York: Oxford University Press, 2018), 237.

22. See especially Smedes, *Choices*. See also Lewis Smedes, *Mere Morality: What God Expects from Ordinary People* (Grand Rapids: Eerdmans, 1983).

23. Bruce Birch and Larry Rasmussen, *Bible and Ethics in the Christian Life*, rev. ed. (Minneapolis: Augsburg Fortress, 1989).

24. See Allen Verhey's magnum opus, *Remembering Jesus: Christian Community, Scripture, and the Moral Life* (Grand Rapids: Eerdmans, 2002), 3–9.

25. Smedes, *Choices*, chap. 6. The following gives Smedes's full list of questions to determine whether you have been responsible: Have I used discernment? Have I interpreted the question? Did my action fit the situation? Does it support my commitments? Is it congruent with my roles? Have I used my imagination? Am I willing to go public? Am I willing to accept the consequences?

26. James K. A. Smith, *Imagining the Kingdom: How Worship Works* (Grand Rapids: Baker Academic, 2013), 31–32.

27. For more on this, see James K. A. Smith, *Desiring the Kingdom: Worship, Worldview, and Cultural Formation* (Grand Rapids: Baker Academic, 2009), part 1, and J. Smith, *Imagining the Kingdom*, part 1. On this point, see also the insightful and important work of Mark Johnson, for example, *Meaning of the Body* and *Moral Imagination*.

28. Jonathan Gottschall, *The Storytelling Animal: How Stories Make Us Human* (New York: Houghton Mifflin Harcourt, 2012). As Gottschall succinctly puts it, "Our life stories are who we are. They are our identity" (161).

29. Barbara Kingsolver, *Small Wonder: Essays* (New York: Harper Perennial, 2003), 40.

30. Smith, *Desiring the Kingdom*, 53. This emphasis on the importance of the imagination in shaping who we are as persons and cultivating ecological virtues is persuasively demonstrated in a very fine book by Matthew Dickerson and David O'Hara, *Narnia and the Fields of Arbol: The Environmental Vision of C. S. Lewis* (Lexington: University of Kentucky Press, 2009). The authors affirm that "Lewis argues and illustrates forcefully and frequently that care for creation is both a vital part of the Christian tradition and inseparable from true Christianity" (15).

31. This example is from my Hope College research student Lauren Madison.

32. Dr. Seuss, *The Lorax* (New York: Random House Books for Young Readers, 2012).

33. Smith, *Imagining the Kingdom*, 32.

34. MacIntyre, *After Virtue*, 216.

35. Stanley Hauerwas, *Truthfulness and Tragedy* (Notre Dame, IN: University of Notre Dame Press, 1977), 76.

36. See Stephen Crites, "The Narrative Quality of Experience," in *Why Narrative? Readings in Narrative Theology*, ed. Stanley Hauerwas and L. Gregory Jones (Grand Rapids: Eerdmans, 1989), 65–88. See also the seminal work of Paul Ricoeur, *Time and Narrative*, vols. 1–3 (Chicago: University of Chicago Press, 1990).

37. This section is from Steven Bouma-Prediger and Brian Walsh, *Beyond Homelessness: Christian Faith in a Culture of Displacement* (Grand Rapids: Eerdmans 2008), 210–11. Used with permission.

38. Stanley Hauerwas and David Burrell, "From System to Story: An Alternative Pattern for Rationality in Ethics," in Hauerwas and Jones, *Why Narrative?*, 186.

39. See, for example, Philip Cafaro, "Thoreau, Leopold, and Carson: Toward an Environmental Virtue Ethic," in *Environmental Virtue Ethics*, ed. Ronald Sandler and Philip Cafaro (Lanham, MD: Rowman & Littlefield, 2005), 31–44; Cafaro, "A Virtue Ethics Approach to Aldo Leopold's Land Ethic," *Environmental Ethics* 19 (Spring 1997): 53–67; Kathleen Dean Moore, "The Truth of the Barnacles: Rachel Carson and the Moral Significance of Wonder," *Environmental Ethics* 27 (Fall 2005): 265–77.

40. Gilbert Meilander, "Virtue in Contemporary Religious Thought," in *Virtue—Public and Private*, ed. Richard John Neuhaus (Grand Rapids: Eerdmans, 1986), 9.

41. Lewis, *Magician's Nephew*, 125.

42. The common term is *environmental virtue ethics*, hence the heading here, even though I argue later in this chapter for substituting the word *ecological* for *environmental*. So when describing the field, I use *environmental virtue ethics*, but when describing my own approach, I use the term *ecological virtue ethics*.

43. For example, Philip Cafaro says: "Environmental virtue ethics (EVE) first got off the ground in 1983, with Thomas Hill, Jr.'s 'Ideals of human excellence and preserving natural environments.'" Cafaro, "Introduction," in "Environmental Virtue Ethics," special issue, *Journal of Agriculture and Environmental Ethics* 23 (2010): 3.

44. Thomas Hill Jr., "Ideals of Human Excellence and Preserving Natural Environments," in Sandler and Cafaro, *Environmental Virtue Ethics*, 50–57.

45. Sandler and Cafaro, *Environmental Virtue Ethics*; Sandler, *Character and Environment: A Virtue-Oriented Approach to Environmental Ethics* (New York: Columbia University Press, 2007); Sandler, *Environmental Ethics: Theory in Practice* (New York: Oxford University Press, 2018).

46. Robert Hull, "All about EVE: A Report on Environmental Virtue Ethics Today," *Ethics and the Environment* 10 (Spring 2005): 89–110.

47. Philip Cafaro, "The Naturalist's Virtues," *Philosophy in the Contemporary World* 8 (Fall/Winter 2001): 85–99.

48. Cafaro, "Thoreau, Leopold, and Carson," in Sandler and Cafaro, *Environmental Virtue Ethics*, 31–44.

49. For a presentation of four major concerns, with a response to each, see Ronald Sandler, "Towards an Adequate Environmental Virtue Ethic," *Environmental Values* 13 (2004): 477–95.

50. For a list of objections to a virtue-oriented approach to environmental ethics, with corresponding responses, see Sandler, *Character and Environment*, 108–17.

51. Sandler, *Environmental Ethics*, 233.

52. Marilyn Holly, "Environmental Virtue Ethics: A Review of Some Current Work," *Journal of Agricultural and Environmental Ethics* 19 (2006): 393.

53. C. D. Meyers, "Nature, Virtue, and the Nature of Virtue: An Outline for an Environmental Virtue Ethics," *Southwest Philosophy Review* 26 (January 2010): 114.

54. Jason Kawall, "The Epistemic Demands of Environmental Virtue," *Journal of Agriculture and Environmental Ethics* 23 (2010): 109–28.

55. Sandler, *Environmental Ethics*, 233.

56. *Plurality* is the description of some form of many-ness, while *pluralism* is the affirmation of that reality. For example, to acknowledge religious plurality is to accept the existence of many different religions, while to espouse religious pluralism is to affirm that the reality of different religions is a good thing. The various epistemological debates are beyond the scope of this chapter. For an illuminating discussion of plurality and pluralism with respect to moral philosophy and ethics, see MacIntyre, *Whose Justice? Which Rationality?*

57. Sandler, *Environmental Ethics*, 233. See also Sandler, "Culture and the Specification of Environmental Virtue," *Philosophy and the Contemporary World* 10 (Fall-Winter 2003): 63–68.

58. For more on these epistemological issues, see Merold Westphal, *Whose Community? Which Interpretation?* (Grand Rapids: Baker Academic, 2009), and James K. A. Smith, *Who's Afraid of Postmodernism?* (Grand Rapids: Baker Academic, 2006).

59. Holmes Rolston III, "Environmental Virtue Ethics: Half the Truth but Dangerous as a Whole," in Sandler and Cafaro, *Environmental Virtue Ethics*, 72.

60. Rolston, "Environmental Virtue Ethics," in Sandler and Cafaro, *Environmental Virtue Ethics*, 76.

61. Holmes Rolston III, *A New Environmental Ethics: The Next Millennium for Life on Earth* (New York: Routledge, 2012), 115. Rolston acknowledges that despite his concerns, "the environmental virtue ethicists are right to remind us that we need to cultivate our human excellences, if we are to succeed in protecting life. We need benevolence and compassion toward other animals. We need respect for other life forms. We need gratitude for their presence on landscapes along with ourselves. We need humility to accept a limited share of Earth's resources—rather than trying to exploit as much as possible. We need wisdom . . . if we are to know who we are, where we are, and what we ought to do" (116).

62. For more on the decentering of the human in the book of Job, see Steven Bouma-Prediger, *For the Beauty of the Earth: A Christian Vision for Creation Care*, 2nd ed. (Grand Rapids: Baker Academic, 2010), 93–98.

63. Holly, "Environmental Virtue Ethics," 393.

64. Brian Treanor, "Environmentalism and Public Virtue," *Journal of Agriculture and Environmental Ethics* 23 (2010): 15. See also Hull, "All about EVE," 103.

65. For more on "the entrenched individualism of Western culture" as a significant challenge to environmental virtue ethics, see Sandra Jane Fairbanks, "Environmental Goodness and the Challenge of American Culture," *Ethics and the Environment* 15 (2010): 80–102.

66. Treanor, "Environmentalism and Public Virtue," 13.

67. For more on the various Christian scholars who have contributed to environmental virtue ethics, see the appendix to this book.

68. Wendell Berry, *Sex, Economy, Freedom, and Community* (New York: Pantheon, 1993), 34. See also Wendell Berry, *Home Economics* (Berkeley: Counterpoint, 1987), particularly the chapters "Getting Along with Nature" and "Two Economies."

69. *For the Beauty of the Earth* was first published by Baker Academic in 2001, with a second edition published in 2010.

70. The extensionist approach of Geoffrey Frasz.

71. The human-excellence approach of Ronald Sandler.

72. The human-exemplar approach of Philip Cafaro.

73. Berry, "Whatever Is Foreseen in Joy," in *This Day*, 20.

Chapter 2: Living with Amazement and Modesty

1. Rachel Carson, *The Sense of Wonder* (New York: Harper & Brothers, 1956), 88.

2. Norman Wirzba, "The Touch of Humility: An Invitation to Creatureliness," *Modern Theology* 24 (April 2008): 241. See also his excellent book *From Nature to Creation: A Christian Vision for Understanding and Loving Our World* (Grand Rapids: Baker Academic, 2015).

3. Rachel Carson describes a very similar experience of the wonder of the night sky in *Sense of Wonder*, 54–55.

4. "Humble humans from the humus" is a rendering of Gen. 2:5, which tells us that we are *'adam* because we are made from the *'adamah*. We are earth creatures from the earth.

5. Sigurd Olson, *Sigurd Olson's Wilderness Days* (New York: Knopf, 1972), 192.

6. Rachel Carson, *Silent Spring* (Boston: Houghton Mifflin, 1962).

7. For a short introduction to the life and writings of Rachel Carson, see Mary McCay, *Rachel Carson* (New York: Twayne, 1993). For a definitive biography, see Linda Lear, *Rachel Carson: Witness for Nature* (New York: Holt, 1997).

8. Carson, *Sense of Wonder*, 42–43.

9. Carson, *Sense of Wonder*, 45.

10. Carson, *Sense of Wonder*, 52.

11. Carson, *Sense of Wonder*, 68.

12. Annie Dillard, *Pilgrim at Tinker Creek* (New York: Harper & Row, 1974), 8.

13. Dillard, *Pilgrim at Tinker Creek*, 17.

14. Dillard, *Pilgrim at Tinker Creek*, 18.

15. Dillard observes, however, that although the secret of seeing "comes to those who wait for it, it is always, even to the most practiced and adept, a gift and a total surprise" (*Pilgrim at Tinker Creek*, 33). In other words, the virtue of wonder is not sufficient, for the secret of seeing is, in the end, a gift to be received with gratitude.

16. For more on wonder as a virtue, see Mary Oliver's poems "Messenger" and "When the Roses Speak, I Pay Attention," in *Thirst* (Boston: Beacon, 2006), 1, 9. See also the poems "Look and See" and "Mindful" in *Why I Wake Early* (Boston: Beacon, 2004), 26, 58–59.

17. Sam Keen, *Apology for Wonder* (New York: Harper & Row, 1969).

18. William Brown, *Sacred Sense: Discovering the Wonder of God's Word and World* (Grand Rapids: Eerdmans, 2015), 7.

19. Aristotle, *Nicomachean Ethics*, in *The Basic Works of Aristotle*, ed. Richard McKeon (New York: Random House, 1941), book 2, chapter 5.

20. Questions raised by my research student Lauren Madison in her paper "The Sense of Wonder and the Humility It Takes: How the Virtue of Humility Can Cultivate Wonder" (research paper, Hope College, 2013).

21. "World of Wonders" is the title of a song by the great Canadian singer, songwriter, and guitarist Bruce Cockburn, from the album *World of Wonders*, True North Records, 1985.

22. These examples are from my Hope College colleague David Myers.

23. Aristotle, *Nicomachean Ethics*, book 4, chapter 3.

24. Aristotle, *Nicomachean Ethics*, book 4, chapter 3.

25. Aristotle, *Nicomachean Ethics*, book 4, chapter 3.

26. *Sayings of the Desert Fathers*, trans. Benedicta Ward (Kalamazoo, MI: Cistercian Publications, 1975), 2.

27. *Sayings of the Desert Fathers*, 173.

28. See, e.g., Augustine, *City of God*, trans. Henry Bettenson, ed. David Knowles (New York: Penguin, 1972), section 19.

29. Bernard of Clairvaux, *The Steps of Humility and Pride*, trans. M. Ambrose Conway (Kalamazoo, MI: Cistercian Publications, 1980), 30.

30. Thomas Aquinas, *Summa Theologica* II-II, question 161.

31. Lisa Gerber, "Standing Humbly before Nature," *Ethics and the Environment* 7 (2002): 39–53.

32. For my translation and interpretation of this text, see Steven Bouma-Prediger, *For the Beauty of the Earth: A Christian Vision for Creation Care*, 2nd ed. (Grand Rapids: Baker Academic, 2010), 85–90.

33. Bernhard Anderson, *From Creation to New Creation* (Minneapolis: Fortress, 1994), 154.

34. Brown, *Sacred Sense*, 27–28. For an insightful discussion of wonder in additional texts in the Bible, see the fifteen other chapters in *Sacred Sense*. For a perceptive and more in-depth treatment of the Old Testament and the "ecology of wonder," see William Brown, *The Seven Pillars of Creation: The Bible, Science, and the Ecology of Wonder* (New York: Oxford University Press, 2010).

35. From the poem "God's Grandeur" in *The Poems and Prose of Gerard Manley Hopkins* (London: Penguin, 1985), 27.

36. Jeremy Begbie, *Resounding Truth: Christian Wisdom in the World of Music* (Grand Rapids: Baker Academic, 2007). See also his earlier works *Voicing Creation's Praise* (Edinburgh: T&T Clark, 1991) and *Theology, Music, and Time* (Cambridge: Cambridge University Press, 2000).

37. For scientific evidence supporting this poetic portrayal, see Peter Wohleben, *The Hidden Lives of Trees* (Vancouver: Greystone, 2016); Robert McFarlane, *Landmarks* (New York: Penguin, 2016).

38. See also Brown, *Sacred Sense*, chap. 11.

39. My translation and rendering of the poetic structure are informed by N. T. Wright's insightful literary analysis in *The Climax of the Covenant: Christ and the Law in Pauline Theology* (Minneapolis: Fortress, 1993), 104. For a more complete interpretation, see Bouma-Prediger, *For the Beauty of the Earth*, 99–104.

40. While these terms are usually thought to refer to astral or heavenly powers, the ubiquity and power of the emperor cult make it difficult to believe that Paul did not have Roman imperial rule in mind.

41. In the two parallel lines of the middle section of the poem, which thematically connect the two main strophes, the supremacy of Christ is reinforced ("And He is before all things / and all things hold together in Him / and He is the head / of the body, the church").

42. The cosmos holds together because, in the words of Brian Walsh, Christ is "nothing less than the ontological linchpin of creation." See Walsh's "Subversive Poetry and Life in the Empire," *Third Way* 23 (April 2000): 4. For more insight on this text, see Brian Walsh and Sylvia Keesmaat, *Colossians Remixed: Subverting the Empire* (Downers Grove, IL: IVP Academic, 2004).

43. In language reminiscent of Gen. 1:1 and Prov. 8:22, Christ is here proclaimed to be "the beginning." As with the term *firstborn*, the term *beginning* has to do with primacy, whether in time or with reference to sovereignty.

44. See, respectively, 1 Cor. 15:20, 23 and Rom. 8:29.

45. See, for example, Gen. 49:3, where the Hebrew word for *beginning* is translated as *firstborn*.

46. Joseph Sittler, "Called to Unity," in *Evocations of Grace*, ed. Steven Bouma-Prediger and Peter Bakken (Grand Rapids: Eerdmans, 2000), 39. Of all those in the twentieth century to champion the "cosmic Christ," none did so as well as Sittler, whose famous plenary speech at the 1961 meeting of the World Council of Churches in New Delhi, India, was an extended meditation on Col. 1:15–20.

47. This rendering is from Bouma-Prediger, *For the Beauty of the Earth*, 93–96. It was informed by the following works: Robert Gordis, *The Book of Job: Commentary, New Translation, and Special Studies* (New York: Jewish Theological Seminary of America, 1978); Gordis, *The Book of God and Man: A Study of Job* (Chicago: University of Chicago Press, 1965); Norman Habel, *The Book of Job* (Philadelphia: Westminster, 1985); Marvin Pope, *Job*, 3rd ed., Anchor Bible 15 (New York: Doubleday, 1973); and especially Carol Newsom's insightful commentary, "The Book of Job," in *The New Interpreter's Bible*, vol. 4 (Nashville: Abingdon, 1996).

48. For an insightful analysis of the human tendency to deny mortality and perpetuate evil, see Ernest Becker, *Denial of Death* (New York: Macmillan, 1973) and *Escape from Evil* (New York: Macmillan, 1975).

49. Perhaps the classic presentation of this question is Leo Tolstoy's short story, "The Death of Ivan Ilych," in *"The Death of Ivan Ilych" and Other Stories* (New York: Penguin, 1960).

50. For illumination on the phenomenon of sin, see Ted Peters, *Sin: Radical Evil in Soul and Society* (Grand Rapids: Eerdmans, 1995); Cornelius Plantinga Jr., *Not the Way It's Supposed to Be: A Breviary of Sin* (Grand Rapids: Eerdmans, 1995).

51. Aristotle, *Nicomachean Ethics*, book 3, chapter 10.

52. Ronald Sandler, *Character and Environment: A Virtue-Oriented Approach to Environmental Ethics* (New York: Columbia University Press, 2017), 50.

53. Sandler, *Character and Environment*, 50–51.

54. In chap. 1, I briefly described the five main approaches for developing a list of explicitly ecological virtues: exemplar, extensionist, agent benefit, human excellence, and means/ends.

55. Sandler, *Character and Environment*, 48–49.

56. Sandler, *Character and Environment*, 134.

57. Philip Cafaro, "The Naturalist's Virtues," *Philosophy in the Contemporary World* 8 (Fall/Winter 2001): 85–99. See also Philip Cafaro, "Thoreau, Leopold, and Carson: Toward an Environmental Virtue Ethics," in *Environmental Virtue Ethics*, ed. Ronald Sandler and Philip Cafaro (Lanham, MD: Rowman & Littlefield, 2005), 31–44.

58. For one example of this view, see Alan Weisman, *The World without Us* (New York: Picador, 2008).

59. See E. O. Wilson, *The Creation: An Appeal to Save the Earth* (New York: Norton, 2007) and my review of this book, "Hoping to Establish Common Ground for Saving Biodiversity," *Science* 314, no. 5804 (December 1, 2006): 1392–93.

60. For more on ecological literacy, see David Orr, *Ecological Literacy: Education and the Transition to a Postmodern World* (Albany: State University of New York Press, 1992). For a Christian approach to education for eco-literacy, see Steven Bouma-Prediger and Brian Walsh, "Education for Homelessness or Homemaking?: The Christian College in a Postmodern Culture," *Christian Scholar's Review* 32 (2003), reprinted in *Taking Every Thought Captive: Forty Years of the Christian Scholar's Review*, ed. Don King (Abilene, TX: Abilene Christian University Press, 2011), 133–45.

61. John Muir, *The Mountains of California* (San Francisco: Sierra Club Books, 1988), 191.

62. Muir, *Mountains of California*, 51–52.

63. John Muir, *My First Summer in the Sierra* (San Francisco: Sierra Clubs Books, 1998), 82–84.

64. Donald Worster, *A Passion for Nature: The Life of John Muir* (New York: Oxford University Press, 2008), 160.

65. Muir, *My First Summer in the Sierra*, 93.

66. Muir, *My First Summer in the Sierra*, 97.

67. Muir, *My First Summer in the Sierra*, 92.

68. Muir, *My First Summer in the Sierra*, 70.

69. Muir, *My First Summer in the Sierra*, 110.

70. Frederick Turner, *Rediscovering America: John Muir in His Time and Ours* (San Francisco: Sierra Club Books, 1985), 187.

71. Barbara Kingsolver, *Small Wonder: Essays* (New York: HarperCollins, 2002), 38–39.

72. Richard Louv, *Last Child in the Woods: Saving Our Children from Nature-Deficit Disorder* (Chapel Hill: Algonquin Books, 2006), 1.

73. Louv, *Last Child in the Woods*, 54–69.

74. Richard Louv, *The Nature Principle: Reconnecting with Life in a Virtual Age* (Chapel Hill: Algonquin Books, 2012), and *Vitamin N: The Essential Guide to a Nature-Rich Life* (Chapel Hill: Algonquin Books, 2016).

75. Muir, *Mountains of California*, 194.

Chapter 3: Living with Strength of Mind and Discernment

1. Bill McKibben, *The Comforting Whirlwind: God, Job, and the Scale of Creation* (Grand Rapids: Eerdmans, 1994), 89.

2. This story is taken from Wendell Berry's masterpiece, *Jayber Crow* (Washington, DC: Counterpoint, 2000), 334–63. This book, in my view, is Berry's finest novel and one of the best novels written in the last three decades. With parallels to Dante's *Divine Comedy*, it is an exceptionally insightful, profoundly moving, and often funny book about, among other things, faith, loss, place, home, heaven, hell, and love—most especially love.

3. Berry, *Jayber Crow*, 340.

4. Berry, *Jayber Crow*, 360.

5. See, for example, Plato, *Republic*, trans. G. M. A. Grube, rev. C. D. C. Reeve (Indianapolis: Hackett, 1992), book 4, 430e.

6. Plato, *Republic*, book 4, 435 and 441–42.

7. Aristotle, *Nicomachean Ethics*, in *The Basic Works of Aristotle*, ed. Richard McKeon (New York: Random House, 1941), book 3, chapters 10–11.

8. Aristotle, *Nicomachean Ethics*, book 3, chapter 11.

9. J. O. Urmson, *Aristotle's Ethics* (Oxford: Blackwell, 1988), 70.

10. Josef Pieper, *Four Cardinal Virtues* (Notre Dame, IN: University of Notre Dame Press, 1966), 145–46.

11. Thomas Aquinas, *Treatise on the Virtues*, trans. John Oesterle (Notre Dame: University of Notre Dame, 1984), question 64, article 1.

12. Thomas Aquinas, *Treatise on the Virtues*, question 61, article 1.

13. Pieper, *Four Cardinal Virtues*, 147–50.

14. Lewis Smedes, *A Pretty Good Person: What It Takes to Live with Courage, Gratitude, and Integrity* (San Francisco: Harper & Row, 1990), 103.

15. Henry David Thoreau, *Walden and Other Writings*, ed. Joseph Wood Krutch (New York: Bantam, 1981), 115.

16. Thoreau, *Walden and Other Writings*, 116.

17. William Cavanaugh, *Being Consumed* (Grand Rapids: Eerdmans, 2008), 19. He goes on to argue that since "consumer culture is one of the most powerful systems of formation in the contemporary world, arguably more powerful than Christianity," Christians must give undivided attention to moral formation.

18. Cavanaugh, *Being Consumed*, xi.

19. David Myers, *The Pursuit of Happiness: Who Is Happy and Why* (New York: William Morrow, 1992), 44.

20. Myers, *Pursuit of Happiness*, 46.

21. Pope Francis, *Laudato Si': On Care for Our Common Home*, in *Encyclical on Climate Change and Inequality* (New York: Melville, 2015), sections 222–23.

22. Diana Butler Bass, *Grateful: The Transformative Power of Giving Thanks* (New York: HarperOne, 2018), 52.

23. Bass, *Grateful*, 167. Lewis Smedes seconds this analysis and adds insight of his own in *Pretty Good Person*, chap. 1.

24. Aristotle, *Nicomachean Ethics*, book 6, chapter 5. For more on Aristotle's understanding of *phronēsis*, see Karl Clifton-Soderstrom's very fine book *The Cardinal and the Deadly: Reimagining the Seven Virtues and Seven Vices* (Eugene, OR: Cascade, 2015), 20–22.

25. Nicholas Wolterstorff, *Educating for Life: Reflections on Christian Teaching and Learning*, ed. Gloria Stronks and Clarence Joldersma (Grand Rapids: Baker Academic, 2002), 100.

26. David Orr, *Earth in Mind* (Washington, DC: Island Press, 1994), 49.

27. Orr, *Earth in Mind*, 49.

28. Orr, *Earth in Mind*, 50.

29. Orr, *Earth in Mind*, 50–51.

30. Orr, *Earth in Mind*, 52.

31. Susan Power Bratton, *Six Billion and More: Human Population Regulation and Christian Ethics* (Louisville: Westminster John Knox, 1992), 43.

32. Philip Kenneson, *Life on the Vine: Cultivating the Fruit of the Spirit in Christian Community* (Downers Grove, IL: InterVarsity, 1999), 227.

33. Kenneson, *Life on the Vine*, 226.

34. Kenneson, *Life on the Vine*, 232.

35. Kenneson, *Life on the Vine*, 233.

36. The literature on wisdom in the Bible is vast. For starters, see Roland Murphy, *The Tree of Life: An Exploration of Wisdom Literature* (Grand Rapids: Eerdmans, 2002); William Brown, *Character in Crisis: A Fresh Approach to the Wisdom Literature of the Old Testament* (Grand Rapids: Eerdmans, 1996); Stephen Barton, ed., *Where Shall Wisdom Be Found?* (Edinburgh: T&T Clark, 1999). For explicit connections between Wisdom literature and ethics, see William Brown, *Wisdom's Wonder: Character, Creation, and Crisis in the Bible's Wisdom Literature* (Grand Rapids: Eerdmans, 2014), and also Dave Bland and Sean Patrick Webb, *Creation, Character, and Wisdom: Rethinking the Roots of Environmental Ethics* (Eugene, OR: Wipf & Stock, 2016).

37. It should be noted that in all but one of the fifty-one New Testament texts that use Greek words for wisdom, the Greek is *sophia*, not *phronēsis*. (The exception is Luke 1:17.) But what is meant in these passages by *sophia* closely resembles the kind of practical wisdom spoken of previously. The distinction in the New Testament is not between Aristotle's notions of *sophia* and *phronēsis* but between divine wisdom and human wisdom. See Walter Bauer, William Arndt, and F. Wilbur Gingrich, *A Greek-English Lexicon of the New Testament*, 2nd ed. (Chicago: University of Chicago Press, 1979), 759–60.

38. Aristotle, *Nicomachean Ethics*, book 3, chapter 10.

39. Kathryn Blanchard and Kevin O'Brien, *An Introduction to Christian Environmentalism: Ecology, Virtue, and Ethics* (Waco: Baylor University Press, 2014), 68.

40. Philip Cafaro, "Thoreau, Leopold, and Carson: Toward an Environmental Virtue Ethics," in *Environmental Virtue Ethics*, ed. Ronald Sandler and Philip Cafaro (Lanham, MD: Rowman & Littlefield, 2005), 33. He notes that self-control also figured prominently in the life (and ethics) of Rachel Carson.

41. Philip Cafaro, "Gluttony, Arrogance, Greed, and Apathy: An Exploration of Environmental Vice," in Sandler and Cafaro, *Environmental Virtue Ethics*, 143.

42. Ronald Sandler, *Character and Environment: A Virtue-Oriented Approach to Environmental Ethics* (New York: Columbia University Press, 2007), 48, 82.

43. Sandler, *Character and Environment*, 60.

44. Peter Wenz, "Synergistic Environmental Virtues: Consumerism and Human Flourishing," in Sandler and Cafaro, *Environmental Virtue Ethics*, 207–8.

45. Michael Northcott, *The Environment and Christian Ethics* (Cambridge: Cambridge University Press, 1996), 314.

46. James Nash, "Toward the Revival and Reform of the Subversive Virtue: Frugality," *Annual of the Society of Christian Ethics* (1995): 141. Nash's essay is a classic statement that explains what frugality is, what it isn't, and why it is needed today.

47. Bill Shaw, "A Virtue Ethics Approach to Aldo's Leopold's Land Ethic," in Sandler and Cafaro, *Environmental Virtue Ethics*, 100–101.

48. Northcott, *Environment and Christian Ethics*, 315.

49. Ronald Sandler, "Global Warming and Virtues of Ecological Restoration," in *Ethical Adaptation to Climate Change*, ed. Allen Thompson and Jeremy Bendik-Keymer (Cambridge: MIT Press, 2012), 63, 70–77. See also Tim Hayward, "Climate Change and Ethics," *Nature Climate Change* 2 (December 2012): 843–48.

50. See Philip Cafaro, "The Naturalist's Virtues," *Philosophy in the Contemporary World* 8 (Fall/Winter 2001): 85–99.

51. Anders Melin, *Living with Other Beings: A Virtue-Oriented Approach to the Ethics of Species Protection* (Berlin: LIT, 2013), 150; see also 104–10.

52. Melin, *Living with Other Beings*, 151.

53. Blanchard and O'Brien, *Introduction to Christian Environmentalism*, 25.

54. Blanchard and O'Brien, *Introduction to Christian Environmentalism*, 35–37.

55. For more on this, see Wendell Berry, *Sex, Economy, Freedom, and Community* (New York: Pantheon, 1993), chaps. 1, 3, 7.

56. This story of Susan Drake Emmerich borrows from Steven Bouma-Prediger and Brian Walsh, *Beyond Homelessness: Christian Faith in a Culture of Displacement* (Grand Rapids: Eerdmans, 2010), 224–25. Used with permission.

57. This story is taken from Wendell Berry's brilliant and moving novel *Hannah Coulter* (Berkeley: Counterpoint, 2004).

58. Berry, *Hannah Coulter*, 84, 82.

Chapter 4: Living with Respect and Care

1. Pope Francis, *Laudato Si': On Care for Our Common Home*, in *Encyclical on Climate Change and Inequality* (New York: Melville, 2015), section 159.

2. Martin Luther King Jr., "The Most Durable Power," in *A Testament of Hope*, ed. James Washington (New York: HarperCollins, 1986), 11.

3. Aldo Leopold, *A Sand County Almanac* (New York: Ballantine, 1970), 72–74.

4. John Muir, *My First Summer in the Sierra* (San Francisco: Sierra Club, 1998), 148.

5. Annie Dillard, *Pilgrim at Tinker Creek* (New York: Harper & Row, 1974), 245.

6. See A. Pérez-Comas, "Mercury Contamination in Puerto Rico: The Ciudad Cristiana Experience," *Boletin de la Asociacion Media de Puerto Rico* 83, no. 7 (July 1991): 296–99, http://www.ncbi.nlm.nih.gov/pubmed/1817506.

7. Michael Weisskopf, "The Poisoning of Christian City," *Washington Post*, June 30, 1986, https://www.washingtonpost.com/archive/politics/1986/06/30/the-poisoning-of-christian-city/a6eee909-e12b-466d-b029-9416a04aaed4/?utm_term=.147a0ffe2658. A similar story has been more recently unfolding in Flint, Michigan, over contaminated water. See "The Flint Water Crisis: A Loss of Trust," CBS News, June 17, 2018, https://www.cbsnews.com/news/the-flint-water-crisis-a-loss-of-trust.

8. United Church of Christ Commission on Racial Justice, *Toxic Waste and Race in the United States: A National Report on the Racial and Socio-Economic Characteristics of Communities Surrounding Hazardous Waste Sites* (New York: United Church of Christ, 1987), https://www.nrc.gov/docs/ML1310/ML13109A339.pdf.

9. Dana A. Alston, ed., *We Speak for Ourselves: Social Justice, Race, and Environment* (London: Panos Institute, 1990), 9.

10. Charles Lee, "Evidence for Environmental Racism," *Sojourners*, February/March 1990, 25.

11. See also Robert Bullard, *Dumping in Dixie: Race, Class, and Environmental Quality*, 3rd ed. (Boulder, CO: Westview, 2000); Richard Hofrichter, ed., *Toxic Struggles* (Philadelphia: New Society, 1993); Gerald Visgilio and Dianna Whitelaw, eds., *Our Backyard: A Quest for Environmental Justice* (Lanham, MD: Rowman & Littlefield, 2003); Luke Cole and Sheila Foster, *From the Ground Up: Environmental Racism and the Rise of the Environmental Justice Movement* (New York: New York University Press, 2000). The contaminated water crisis in Flint, Michigan, is one of the better-known recent examples of environmental racism.

12. Rosemary Radford Ruether, *Sexism and God-Talk* (Boston: Beacon, 1983), 73.

13. For more on eco-feminism, see Steven Bouma-Prediger, *The Greening of Theology: The Ecological Models of Rosemary Radford Ruether, Joseph Sittler, and Jürgen Moltmann* (Atlanta: Scholars Press, 1995), chaps. 2 and 5.

14. See, for example, Carol Adams, ed., *Ecofeminism and the Sacred* (New York: Continuum, 1993); and Sallie McFague, *The Body of God* (Minneapolis: Augsburg Fortress, 1993).

15. See the EPA website at https://www.epa.gov/environmentaljustice.

16. The term *eco-justice* was coined in the early 1970s by the Board of Ministries of the American Baptist Churches as a way of defining its mission goals. The term was picked up by the Eco-Justice Project and Network of the Center for Religion, Ethics, and Social Policy at Cornell University (formed in 1974) and by the National Council of Churches. While in its early days eco-justice denoted justice to nonhuman creatures and systems and was a parallel to environmental justice, which focused on the unjust distribution of environmental hazards and the unequal enforcement of environmental regulations for humans, the term *eco-justice* now often includes both humans and the nonhuman world. In short, *eco-justice* is a more inclusive term than *environmental justice*.

17. Yi-Fu Tuan, *Topophilia* (New York: Columbia University Press, 1990), 4, 93. This understanding of love as affection is closer to the meaning of the Greek word *storgē*, though Tuan chooses to use the Greek word *philia* to convey what he means.

18. Tuan, *Topophilia*, 96–97.

19. Tuan, *Topophilia*, 99–100.

20. Keith Basso, *Wisdom Sits in Places* (Albuquerque: University of New Mexico Press, 1996).

21. Tuan, *Topophilia*, 101. Local patriotism is different from imperial patriotism—allegiance to a large territory such as a state or nation. See, for example, Wendell Berry, *Citizenship Papers* (Washington, DC: Shoemaker & Hoard, 2003).

22. Wes Jackson, *Becoming Native to This Place* (Washington, DC: Counterpoint, 1996), 3. See also William Vitek and Wes Jackson, *Rooted in the Land* (New Haven: Yale University Press, 1996). For a description of what a homecoming major might look like in Christian higher education, see Steven Bouma-Prediger and Brian Walsh, "Education for Homelessness or Homemaking?: The Christian College in a Postmodern Culture," *Christian Scholar's Review* 32 (Spring 2003); republished in *Taking Every Thought Captive*, ed. Don King (Abilene, TX: Abilene Christian University Press, 2011).

23. See, for example, the novels *Jayber Crow* (Berkeley: Counterpoint, 2000) and *Hannah Coulter* (Berkeley: Counterpoint, 2004); the nonfiction essays *The Gift of Good Land* (San Francisco: North Point, 1981) and *Home Economics* (Berkeley: Counterpoint, 1987); more recently *Our Only World* (Berkeley: Counterpoint, 2015); the poetry *New Collected Poems* (Berkeley: Counterpoint, 2012) and *This Day: Collected and New Sabbath Poems* (Berkeley: Counterpoint, 2013).

24. Wendell Berry, *It All Turns on Affection: The Jefferson Lecture and Other Essays* (Berkeley: Counterpoint, 2012).

25. Brian Walsh and I have described many of these same features of place in our book *Beyond Homelessness: Christian Faith in a Culture of Displacement* (Grand Rapids: Eerdmans, 2008).

26. E. O. Wilson, *Biophilia: The Human Bond with Other Species* (Cambridge: Harvard University Press, 1984), 1.

27. Wilson, *Biophilia*, 85.

28. Wilson, *Biophilia*, 116.

29. For example, William Frankena, *Ethics*, 2nd ed. (Englewood Cliffs, NJ: Prentice Hall, 1973), 64–65.

30. Leopold, *Sand County Almanac*, 197.

31. For an exhaustive list of biblical texts on justice, see Ronald J. Sider, ed., *Cry Justice: The Bible on Hunger and Poverty* (New York: Paulist Press, 1980).

32. Nicholas Wolterstorff, *Educating for Shalom* (Grand Rapids: Eerdmans, 2004), 143.

33. Cornelius Plantinga Jr., *Not the Way It's Supposed to Be: A Breviary of Sin* (Grand Rapids, Eerdmans, 1994), 10.

34. Sylvia Keesmaat and Brian Walsh, *Romans Disarmed: Resisting Empire, Demanding Justice* (Grand Rapids: Brazos, 2019).

35. James Dunn and Alan Suggate, *The Justice of God* (Grand Rapids: Eerdmans, 1993), 25.

36. Dunn and Suggate, *Justice of God*, 28.

37. Calvin DeWitt, *Caring for Creation* (Grand Rapids: Baker, 1998), 44. Perhaps the most powerful biblical reminder of our calling to be keepers of the earth is found in the flood narrative (Gen. 7–9). God makes a covenant with more than just humans. All creatures—indeed the earth itself—are in covenant fellowship with God.

38. This paragraph borrows from Bouma-Prediger and Walsh, *Beyond Homelessness*, 202–3.

39. For more on how creation itself bears witness to love and compassion, see Keesmaat and Walsh, *Romans Disarmed*.

40. Cornelius Plantinga Jr., "Contours of Christian Compassion," *Perspectives* 10 (February 1995): 11.

41. Allen Verhey, "Suffering and Compassion," *Perspectives* 10 (February 1995): 17–18. Verhey cautions, however, that all too often "modern 'compassion' wants to put an end to suffering—and by whatever means necessary" rather than truly suffering with another. Modern notions of compassion, in other words, often seek to eliminate all suffering, but thereby fail to realize that "technology does not provide an escape either from our mortality or altogether from our suffering." So we must be careful lest in our response to suffering we assume we can and must escape all suffering.

42. Plantinga, "Contours of Christian Compassion," 11. For an excellent discussion of compassion, see Henri Nouwen, *Compassion: A Reflection on the Christian Life* (New York: Doubleday, 1983). See also Martha Nussbaum's insightful discussion of compassion in *Upheavals of Thought: The Intelligence of Emotions* (Cambridge: Cambridge University Press, 2001).

43. For a sophisticated and informed use of this claim in New Testament ethics, see Allen Verhey, *Remembering Jesus: Christian Community, Scripture, and the Moral Life* (Grand Rapids: Eerdmans, 2002).

44. Tellingly, in the Greek text, all the second-person pronouns are plural, and all the verbs translated "love" in English are from *agapaō*.

45. See, for example, *Phaedrus* and *Symposium*, both by Plato.

46. C. S. Lewis, *The Four Loves* (New York: Harcourt Brace Jovanovich, 1960). Among Christians, this discussion by Lewis is perhaps most familiar. First, there is *erōs* or desire. This includes sexual desire but denotes desire more broadly. Second, there is *storgē* or affection, especially among members of the same family. Third, there is *philia* or the love between friends. Fourth and finally, there is *agapē* or the love of self-sacrifice. For another illuminating discussion of love, see Caroline Simon, *The Disciplined Heart: Love, Destiny, and Imagination* (Grand Rapids: Eerdmans, 1997).

47. Lewis Smedes, *Mere Morality: What God Expects from Ordinary People* (Grand Rapids: Eerdmans, 1983), 45.

48. These two loves are often, in the tradition of Anders Nygren, set over against each other. It should be clear that I do not see it that way. Like Smedes, I view them both—*erōs* and *agapē*—as God given.

49. Smedes, *Mere Morality*, 50.

50. Dietrich Bonhoeffer, *Letters and Papers from Prison*, trans. Reginald Fuller, Frank Clarke, and John Bowden, ed. Eberhard Bethge (New York: Macmillan, 1972), 381–82.

51. Smedes, *Mere Morality*, 50.

52. The first quote is from *A Testament of Hope*, ed. James Washington (New York: HarperOne, 2003), 14; the second quote is from the same volume, 11.

53. There are a number of kinds of justice. First, there is contractual or procedural justice. This is the justice of due process and fair transactions in the marketplace. Second, there is retributive or rectificatory justice. This is the justice of the criminal justice system, in two slightly different forms. Retributive justice is the rightness of convicted criminals getting what is due them—receiving proper penalty for an injustice committed. Rectificatory justice is setting things right by attempting to correct or rehabilitate the offender. Third, there is distributive justice. This is the justice of allocating scarce goods fairly. There are in the Western tradition five main answers to the question "Distribute according to what?" That is, there are five options with respect to the criterion of allocation: market value, common good, equality, merit, and need. For example, should we distribute that scarce kidney according to, respectively, who will pay the most, what will bring about the greatest good for the greatest number, what will bring the same good to all, whoever is most deserving, or whoever needs it most? Fourth and finally, there is substantive justice. This is the vision of the good society. This kind of justice specifies, with respect to rights or the legitimate claims to certain goods, what is legitimate, for whom, and with regard to which goods. For example, one's view of substantive justice determines whether adequate shelter is a right for homeless people. What lies at the heart of all these kinds of justice is the idea of fairness.

54. Nicholas Wolterstorff, *Justice in Love* (Grand Rapids: Eerdmans, 2011), chap. 7.

55. Wolterstorff, *Justice in Love*, 85–87. For a brief mention of the rights of nonhumans, see 138, 146. For a more in-depth discussion of justice, see Nicholas Wolterstorff, *Justice: Rights and Wrongs* (Princeton: Princeton University Press, 2008).

56. Smedes, *Mere Morality*, chap. 2.

57. Aristotle, *Nicomachean Ethics*, in *The Basic Works of Aristotle*, ed. Richard McKeon (New York: Random House, 1941), book 4, chapters 5, 9–13.

58. Kathryn Blanchard and Kevin O'Brien, *An Introduction to Christian Environmentalism: Ecology, Virtue, and Ethics* (Waco: Baylor University Press, 2014), 90.

59. Blanchard and O'Brien, *Introduction to Christian Environmentalism*, 87.

60. Blanchard and O'Brien, *Introduction to Christian Environmentalism*, 90.

61. Ronald Sandler, *Character and Environment: A Virtue-Oriented Approach to Environmental Ethics* (New York: Columbia University Press, 2007), 55.

62. Paul Haught, "Environmental Virtues and Environmental Justice," *Environmental Ethics* 33 (Winter 2011): 357–75.

63. Holmes Rolston III, *Environmental Ethics: Duties to and Values in the Natural World* (Philadelphia: Temple University Press, 1988), chaps. 1, 6.

64. See, for example, Lewis, *Four Loves*; Simon, *Disciplined Heart*; and Wolterstorff, *Justice in Love*.

65. Wolterstorff, *Justice in Love*, 33.

66. Wolterstorff, *Justice in Love*, 38.

67. Wolterstorff, *Justice in Love*, 101.

68. Wolterstorff, *Justice in Love*, 84.

69. Óscar Romero, *The Violence of Love*, trans. James R. Brockman (Maryknoll: Orbis, 2004), 130. Lewis Smedes seconds this understanding of love and justice. For Smedes, "fairness

needs love as the seed in the cold earth needs the nurture of the warming sun" and "love needs fairness as the flowing river needs its firm clay banks." Smedes, *A Pretty Good Person: What It Takes to Live with Courage, Gratitude, and Integrity* (San Francisco: Harper & Row, 1990), 157.

70. In reflecting on Jesus's silence about the motives for love, Wolterstorff comments:

Jesus says nothing at all about reasons or motives for loving the neighbor: all he says is that one should love one's neighbor as oneself. He nowhere rejects caring about some people because one is attached to them, caring about others because one feels compassion for them, caring about yet others because one finds oneself attracted to them, and so forth. In all such cases one is doing what Jesus commanded, caring about the other, seeking to promote her good and to secure her rights as ends in themselves. All of us find that there are "neighbors" who fall outside the orbit of the care evoked by our natural dynamics of attachment, attraction, compassion, identification, and the like. Our natural dynamics leave us indifferent to their good. In such cases, our care about them will have to be out of duty. Duty is the fall-back position. . . . If no natural dynamics motivate you to care about your neighbor, then care about him out of duty. (*Justice in Love*, 116–17)

71. See William Vitek and Wes Jackson, eds., *Rooted in the Land* (New Haven: Yale University, 1996); and Terry Tempest Williams, *Refuge: An Unnatural History of Family and Place* (New York: Vintage, 1992).

72. Geoffrey Frasz, "Benevolence as an Environmental Virtue," in *Environmental Virtue Ethics*, ed. Ronald Sandler and Philip Cafaro (Lanham, MD: Rowman & Littlefield, 2005), 121–34.

73. Philip Cafaro, "The Naturalist's Virtues," *Philosophy in the Contemporary World* 8 (Fall/Winter 2001): 85–99.

74. Cafaro, "Naturalist's Virtues," 93.

75. Philip Cafaro, "Gluttony, Arrogance, Greed, and Apathy: An Exploration of Environmental Vice," in Sandler and Cafaro, *Environmental Virtue Ethics*, 135–58.

76. Louke van Wensveen, "Cardinal Environmental Virtues: A Neurobiological Perspective," in Sandler and Cafaro, *Environmental Virtue Ethics*, 173–94.

77. Van Wensveen, "Cardinal Environmental Virtues," in Sandler and Cafaro, *Environmental Virtue Ethics*, 178.

78. Wangari Maathai, *Unbowed: A Memoir* (New York: Knopf, 2006), 137–38. See also Wangari Maathai, *Replenishing the Earth: Spiritual Values for Healing Ourselves and the World* (New York: Doubleday, 2010).

79. "The Nobel Peace Prize for 2004," NobelPrize.org, October 8, 2004, https://www.nobelprize.org/prizes/peace/2004/press-release.

80. Sigurd Olson, "Love of the Land," in *Reflections from the North Country* (Minneapolis: University of Minnesota Press, 1976), 125–29.

81. For other reflections by Olson, one early and one late in his life, see *Listening Point* (Minneapolis: University of Minnesota Press, 1958); and *Of Time and Place* (Minneapolis: University of Minnesota Press, 1982).

82. David Backes, *A Wilderness Within: The Life of Sigurd F. Olson* (Minneapolis: University of Minnesota Press, 1997), 291.

83. The quote is from a letter from Olson to George Laing in 1955, cited in Backes, *Wilderness Within*, 291.

84. Olson, *Reflections from the North Country*, 125.

85. Olson, *Reflections from the North Country*, 125.

86. Leopold, *Sand County Almanac*, 138.

87. Leopold, *Sand County Almanac*, 138–39.

88. For more on the life and legacy of Leopold, see the excellent work of Curt Meine, *Aldo Leopold: His Life and Work* (Madison: University of Wisconsin Press, 2010).

89. Leopold, *Sand County Almanac*, 139–40.

90. Leopold, *Sand County Almanac*, 261.

91. Leopold, *Sand County Almanac*, 251.

92. Leopold, *Sand County Almanac*, 239–40.

Chapter 5: Living with Fortitude and Expectation

1. Atticus Finch to Scout, in Harper Lee, *To Kill a Mockingbird* (New York: Harper & Row, 2006), 128.

2. Óscar Romero, *The Violence of Love*, trans. James R. Brockman (Maryknoll: Orbis, 2004), 206.

3. This story is taken from the unpublished paper "Courage and Hope as Imperative Ecological Virtues in Appalachia: A Case Study Approach," authored by my Hope College research student Lauren Madison. With her permission, I have edited it for the purpose of this chapter.

4. Witnesses of MTR mining have likened the experience to being immersed in a war zone. The blasts are harrowing and to be around them is to feel under attack. See Kyle T. Kramer, "Though the Mountains May Fall," *U.S. Catholic* 77, no. 4 (April 2012): 12–16; and David C. Holzman, "Mountaintop Removal Mining," *Environmental Health Perspectives* 119, no. 11 (November 1, 2011): 476–83.

5. One of the most commonly used arguments for MTR mining by the coal industry is the promise of economic prosperity. In the rhetoric of coal executives, environmentalists would rather save inanimate mountains than protect the livelihoods of living, breathing human beings. The coal industry claims that coal keeps the lights on at low cost, puts food on the table, and helps communities prosper.

6. To expose a seam of coal, the tops of the mountains are denuded and blasting holes are drilled in a grid. The holes are filled with explosives and then detonated in a series. See Sam Evans, "Voices from the Desecrated Places: A Journey to End Mountaintop Removal Mining," *Harvard Environmental Law Review* 34 (2010): 521–76.

7. Since the practice began in the 1960s, MTR mining has become an accepted means of extracting coal from the hills in which it resides. Hundreds of mountains in Appalachia have been destroyed. Their peaks are decapitated, reduced to rubble, and labeled "overburden" in industry terms—a telling word that suggests disposability and worthlessness.

8. Many of the human health risks that accompany MTR mining have to do with the wastes created by the process. After the coal is scraped away by giant excavators, the "overburden" must be dealt with. It is typically deposited in the valley below the mine site, filling headwater streams with debris, which can contaminate human water supplies with heavy metals such as selenium, arsenic, manganese, and lead. The pollution often causes extreme acidity, and clear streams turn bright orange. Once the coal has been extracted, the process of cleaning it creates a toxic sludge known as slurry, which is contained in pond-like impoundments or injected into old underground mining sites from which it can seep through coal seams into groundwater.

9. See Holzman. "Mountaintop Removal Mining," 476–83; and Laura Esch and Michael Hendryx, "Chronic Cardiovascular Disease Mortality in Mountaintop Mining Areas of Central Appalachian States," *Journal of Rural Health* 27, no. 4 (February 11, 2011): 350–57.

10. See Melissa M. Ahern et al., "The Association between Mountaintop Mining and Birth Defects among Live Births in Central Appalachia, 1996–2003," *Environmental Research* 111 (2011): 838–46; Melissa Ahern et al., "Residence in Coal-Mining Areas and Low-Birth-Weight Outcomes," *Maternal and Child Health Journal* 15 (2011): 974–79; and Nathaniel P. Hitt and Michael Hendryx, "Ecological Integrity of Streams Related to Human Cancer Mortality Rates," *EcoHealth* 7, no. 1 (2010): 91–104.

11. In Appalachia, coal truly is king. With over a century of operation in the region, coal mining has become the hallmark of Appalachia, as much a legacy of the culture as bluegrass music and home-style cooking. In the view of many coal supporters, to challenge the coal

industry's reign in the region is to threaten the Appalachian way of life. Those who do so are often held in contempt.

12. Rebecca Konyndyk DeYoung, "Courage," in *Being Good: Christian Virtues for Everyday Life*, ed. Michael W. Austin and R. Douglas Geivett (Grand Rapids: Eerdmans, 2012), 145–66. DeYoung's citations of Harry and James Potter are misleading if they suggest that courage for J. K. Rowling is necessarily aggressive. Harry only once uses an aggressive curse, and it fails. All of Harry's favorite wand spells are defensive. And Voldemort dies not from an act of aggression by Harry but from his own death curse, deflected by Harry's defensive response. A persuasive case can be made that in the Harry Potter books Rowling portrays precisely the kind of courage I describe in this chapter. I thank Brian Walsh for pointing this out and saving me from the wrath of Harry Potter fans.

13. Louke van Wensveen, *Dirty Virtues: The Emergence of Ecological Virtue Ethics* (Amherst, NY: Humanity Books, 2000), 132.

14. Aristotle, *Politics*, in *The Basic Works of Aristotle*, ed. Richard McKeon (New York: Random House, 1941), book 1, chapter 13.

15. Kristin M. Popik, "The Philosophy of Woman of St. Thomas Aquinas," *Faith and Reason* 5 (Spring 1979): 16–56.

16. DeYoung, "Courage," 148.

17. DeYoung, "Courage," 149.

18. DeYoung, "Courage," 151.

19. For more on this, see Josef Pieper, *The Four Cardinal Virtues* (Notre Dame, IN: University of Notre Dame Press, 1966), 115–41.

20. Thomas Aquinas, *Treatise on the Virtues*, trans. John Oesterle (Notre Dame, IN: University of Notre Dame Press, 1984), questions 49–67.

21. Aquinas, *Treatise on the Virtues*, question 60, article 5; question 61, articles 2 and 4.

22. Pieper, *Four Cardinal Virtues*, 126.

23. Pieper, *Four Cardinal Virtues*, 128.

24. Aquinas, *Treatise on the Virtues*, question 58, article 4.

25. Pieper, *Four Cardinal Virtues*, 124.

26. Pieper, *Four Cardinal Virtues*, 123.

27. Aquinas, *Treatise on the Virtues*, question 23, article 8.

28. Stanley Hauerwas, "The Difference of Virtue and the Difference It Makes: Courage Exemplified," *Modern Theology* 9 (July 1993): 256.

29. DeYoung, "Courage," 151.

30. For more on the power of nonviolence in history, see all three volumes of Gene Sharp, *The Politics of Nonviolent Actions* (Boston: Porter Sargent, 1973). For an attempt by Christians to combine the wisdom of the just-war tradition with pacifism, see *Just Peacemaking*, ed. Glen Stassen (Cleveland: Pilgrim Press, 2008). For a fascinating case study on courage and nonviolence, see Leilah Danielson, *American Gandhi: A. J. Muste and the History of Radicalism in the Twentieth Century* (Philadelphia: University of Pennsylvania Press, 2014), and Jeffrey Meyers, *The Way of Peace: A. J. Muste's Writings for the Church* (Eugene, OR: Cascade, 2016).

31. Lee, *To Kill a Mockingbird*, 128.

32. Emily Dickinson, "'Hope' Is the Thing with Feathers," in *The Poems of Emily Dickinson*, ed. R. W. Franklin (Cambridge: Belknap, 1999), 140.

33. Jonathan Lear, *Radical Hope: Ethics in the Face of Cultural Devastation* (Cambridge: Harvard University Press, 2006), 103.

34. Lear, *Radical Hope*, 113.

35. Lear, *Radical Hope*, 112.

36. David Orr, *Hope Is an Imperative: The Essential David Orr* (Washington, DC: Island Press, 2011), 324. This is from a chapter titled "Hope (In a Hotter Time)."

37. Orr, *Hope Is an Imperative*, 326.

38. Orr, *Hope Is an Imperative*, 326.

39. Orr, *Hope Is an Imperative*, 329–30.

40. Lewis Smedes, *A Pretty Good Person: What It Takes to Live with Courage, Gratitude, and Integrity* (San Francisco: Harper & Row, 1990), 41.

41. Smedes, *Pretty Good Person*, 42–43.

42. Lewis Smedes, *Standing on the Promises: Keeping Hope Alive for a Tomorrow We Cannot Control* (Nashville: Nelson, 1998), chaps. 2–4. *Keeping Hope Alive* (Nashville: Nelson, 1998) is a shorter version of *Standing on the Promises*.

43. Smedes, *Standing on the Promises*, 25.

44. William C. Mattison III, "Hope," in Austin and Geivett, *Being Good*, 110.

45. Orr, *Hope Is an Imperative*, xix.

46. For more on this, see N. T. Wright, *Surprised by Hope: Rethinking Heaven, the Resurrection, and the Mission of the Church* (New York: HarperOne, 2008), esp. chaps. 6–7.

47. Mattison, "Hope," 111–12. Not surprisingly, given its prominence in the Bible and in the life of the church, hope's centrality in Christian theology is evident in many places and with many people. Perhaps the most well-known contemporary theologian of hope is Jürgen Moltmann. See, for example, *Theology of Hope* (New York: Harper & Row, 1967) and his more recent volumes *The Coming of God: Christian Eschatology* (Minneapolis: Fortress, 1996) and *Ethics of Hope* (Minneapolis: Fortress, 2012).

48. This analysis of fortitude and its vices is not intended to imply moral culpability for people who suffer from mental-health issues such as anxiety disorder or chronic fatigue syndrome. These struggles are very real and more widespread than we often realize, so we must be careful not to lay blame on people for conditions over which they have little, if any, control. Many thanks to Brian Walsh for bringing this to my attention.

49. Ronald Sandler, *Character and Environment: A Virtue-Oriented Approach to Environmental Ethics* (New York: Columbia University Press, 2007), 49. See also Sandler's more recent book *Environmental Ethics: Theory in Practice* (New York: Oxford University Press, 2018), 226. Jennifer Welchman identifies courage as one of the "virtues of stewardship" in her essay "The Virtues of Stewardship," *Environmental Ethics* 21 (Winter 1999): 411–23.

50. Philip Cafaro, "Thoreau, Leopold, and Carson: Toward an Environmental Virtue Ethics," in *Environmental Virtue Ethics*, ed. Ronald Sandler and Philip Cafaro (Lanham, MD: Rowman & Littlefield, 2005), 31–44.

51. Geoffrey Frasz, "Benevolence as an Environmental Virtue," in Sandler and Cafaro, *Environmental Virtue Ethics*, 121–34.

52. Kathryn Blanchard and Kevin O'Brien, *An Introduction to Christian Environmentalism: Ecology, Virtue, and Ethics* (Waco: Baylor University Press, 2014), chap. 3.

53. Van Wensveen, *Dirty Virtues*, 133–34. By contrast, she describes "courage in an ecological age" as having three parts: earthiness, imaginative channeling, and vulnerability. We must acknowledge that we are earth creatures and that fear and grief are normal (healthy) responses to the peril and loss we feel about the world in which we live. We must resist the need to control or "master our fear" and instead use our imaginations to think of ways to creatively address the problems before us. And, third, in order to stand fast to defend what we cherish, we must accept our own vulnerability and make ourselves vulnerable (135–38).

54. On the indispensability of hope for living a human life, see Victor Frankl, *Man's Search for Meaning* (New York: Simon & Schuster, 1963); and Elie Wiesel, *Night* (New York: Bantam, 1958).

55. Søren Kierkegaard, *Sickness unto Death*, trans. Walter Lowrie (Princeton: Princeton University Press, 1941).

56. Kierkegaard's words, sadly, ring all too true as more and more Americans are committing suicide, in many cases because of the loss of meaning and hope. See Aaron Kheriaty, "Dying of Despair," *First Things*, August/September 2017, 21–25.

57. See, for example, Sally Curtin, Margaret Warner, and Holly Hedegaard, "Increase in Suicide in the United States, 1999–2014," *NCHS Data Brief*, no. 241, April 2016, https://www.re searchgate.net/profile/Sally_Curtin/publication/301564377_Increase_in_Suicide_in_the_Unit ed_States_1999-2014/links/571a31dc08ae408367bc84d6.pdf.

58. Charles Taliaffero, "Vices and Virtues in Religious Environmental Ethics," in Sandler and Cafaro, *Environmental Virtue Ethics*, 163.

59. Louke van Wensveen, "The Emergence of Ecological Virtue Language," in Sandler and Cafaro, *Environmental Virtue Ethics*, 21.

60. Blanchard and O'Brien, *Introduction to Christian Environmentalism*, 129–30.

61. Blanchard and O'Brien, *Introduction to Christian Environmentalism*, 140.

62. Jane Goodall, *Reason for Hope* (New York: Warner Books, 1999), 233.

63. Goodall, *Reason for Hope*, 234.

64. Goodall, *Reason for Hope*, 237.

65. Goodall, *Reason for Hope*, 242.

66. Goodall, *Reason for Hope*, 245.

67. Goodall, *Reason for Hope*, 251.

68. Jeff Biggers, "Daring Protestors Shut Down Obama Backed Strip Mine in West Virginia," Huffington Post, July 28, 2012, http://www.huffingtonpost.com/jeff-biggers/ramps-campaign _b_1714569.html.

69. As Silvio Marcacci puts it, "Building new coal is more expensive than building new renewable energy across the United States, and in many parts of the country, keeping existing coal plants open is more expensive than building new wind turbines (and solar, in some places)." Marcacci, "Utilities Closed Dozens of Coal Plants in 2017: Here Are the Six Most Important," *Forbes*, December 18, 2017, https://www.forbes.com/sites/energyinnovation/2017/12/18 /utilities-closed-dozens-of-coal-plants-in-2017-here-are-the-6-most-important/#42fad5295 aca.

70. As of 2017 in the United States, twenty-nine states have adopted renewable portfolio standards (RPS), which require utilities to sell a specified percentage or amount of renewable energy. This requirement can apply only to investor-owned utilities, but many states also include municipalities and electric cooperatives. Iowa was the first state to establish an RPS, and Hawaii has the most aggressive RPS requirement. In many states, standards are measured by percentages of kilowatt hours of retail electric sales. Iowa and Texas, however, require specific amounts of renewable energy capacity rather than percentages, and Kansas requires a percentage of peak demand. To learn more about RPS, see "State Renewable Portfolio Standards and Goals," National Conference of State Legislatures, http://www.ncsl.org/research/energy/renew able-portfolio-standards.aspx.

71. Renewable energy is gaining traction around the world, something a range of people are noticing, from civil engineers ("Renewable Energy Sources Gain Traction Globally—IEA," CCE News, November 16, 2017, http://cceonlinenews.com/2017/11/16/renewable-energy-sources -gain-traction-globally-iea) to business leaders (James Strapp, "Here's What More Than 41,000 People Think about Solar Energy," *Business Insider*, April 20, 2017, https://www.businessinsider. com/sc/public-opinions-about-solar-energy-2017-4) to politicians and diplomats at the United Nations (ESCAP, "Affordable and Clean Energy," https://www.unescap.org/sites/default/files /SDG%207%20Goal%20Profile_0.pdf).

72. Desmond Tutu, *God Has a Dream: A Vision of Hope for Our Time* (New York: Doubleday, 2004), viii–ix.

73. Tutu, *God Has a Dream*, 2.

74. This is one of the pivotal beliefs of Martin Luther King Jr. See, e.g., *A Testament of Hope*, ed. James Washington (New York: HarperCollins, 1986), 9, 14, 20.

75. Tutu, *God Has a Dream*, 19–20.

Chapter 6: Digging In

1. Pope Francis, *Laudato Si': On Care for Our Common Home*, in *Encyclical on Climate Change and Inequality* (New York: Melville, 2015), section 211.

2. Wendell Berry, *Sex, Economy, Freedom, and Community* (New York: Pantheon, 1993), 94–95. Some have taken up this challenge and offered insightful readings of Scripture "in light of the present fact of Creation." Indeed, that number continues to grow as Christians revisit the Bible, reread its texts, and reconsider their previously held views and practices. More work, however, needs to be done to make the fruit of these reflections on Scripture more widely available via liturgies, sermons, music, prayers, church school instruction, and the like. For a sample of such readings, see Richard Bauckham, *The Bible and Ecology: Rediscovering the Community of Creation* (Waco: Baylor University Press, 2010); Richard Bauckham, *Living with Other Creatures: Green Exegesis and Theology* (Waco: Baylor University Press, 2011); William Brown and S. Dean McBride, eds., *God Who Creates* (Grand Rapids: Eerdmans, 2000); William Brown, *Sacred Sense: Discovering the Wonder of God's Word and World* (Grand Rapids: Eerdmans, 2015); Ellen Davis, *Scripture, Culture, and Agriculture* (Cambridge: Cambridge University Press, 2009); Terence Fretheim, *God and the World* (Nashville: Abingdon, 2005); J. Richard Middleton, *The Liberating Image: The* Imago Dei *in Genesis 1* (Grand Rapids: Brazos, 2005); J. Richard Middleton, *A New Heaven and a New Earth: Reclaiming Biblical Eschatology* (Grand Rapids: Baker Academic, 2015); Douglas and Jonathan Moo, *Creation Care: A Biblical Theology of the Natural World* (Grand Rapids: Zondervan, 2018). I take up Berry's call to read Scripture "in light of the present fact of Creation," among other places, in my book *For the Beauty of the Earth: A Christian Vision for Creation Care*, 2nd ed. (Grand Rapids: Baker Academic, 2010).

3. Berry, *Sex, Economy, Freedom, and Community*, 96–98.

4. Berry, *Sex, Economy, Freedom, and Community*, 99.

5. Wendell Berry, *What Are People For?* (San Francisco: North Point, 1990), 98.

6. Berry, *Sex, Economy, Freedom, and Community*, 98.

7. Berry's views are available not only in his nonfiction but also in his novels, such as *Jayber Crow* (Berkeley: Counterpoint, 2000) and *Hannah Coulter* (Berkeley: Counterpoint, 2004), and in his poetry, such as his Sabbath poems collected in *This Day: Collected and New Sabbath Poems* (Berkeley: Counterpoint, 2013).

8. Joseph Sittler, *Gravity and Grace* (Minneapolis: Augsburg, 1986), 15.

9. The data on STREAM School are from my Hope College colleagues Sonja Trent-Brown and Stephen Scogin.

10. For more on virtue formation in higher education, see Perry Glanzer, "Moving beyond Value- or Virtue-Added: Transforming Colleges and Universities for Redemptive Moral Development," *Christian Scholar's Review* 39 (2010): 379–99; and also Shawn Floyd, "Morally Serious Pedagogy," *Christian Scholar's Review* 36 (Spring 2007): 245–61.

11. Place is important. Indeed, the formation of ecological virtues is not possible without love for a place. Affection for a place is, however, transferable. Learning to love the Adirondacks, for example, can provide the incentive and foster the skills for learning to love your own home place, wherever that is. For more on this, see Steven Bouma-Prediger and Brian Walsh, *Beyond Homelessness: Christian Faith in a Culture of Displacement* (Grand Rapids: Eerdmans, 2008), esp. chaps. 2, 5, 6.

12. Geoffrey Frasz, "Benevolence as an Environmental Virtue," in *Environmental Virtue Ethics*, ed. Ronald Sandler and Philip Cafaro (Lanham, MD: Rowman & Littlefield, 2005), 127.

13. Philip Cafaro, "The Naturalist's Virtues," *Philosophy in the Contemporary World* 8 (Fall/Winter 2001): 88.

14. One of the best recent examples of ecological attentiveness is David George Haskell, *The Forest Unseen: A Year's Watch in Nature* (New York: Penguin, 2012). Research indicates that time spent immersed in a natural setting improves creative reasoning and problem solving. See, for example, Ruth Ann Atchley, David Strayer, and Paul Atchley, "Creativity in the Wild:

Improving Creative Reasoning through Immersion in Natural Settings," *PLOS One* 7, no. 12 (December 2012), https://doi.org/10.1371/journal.pone.0051474.

15. Bouma-Prediger, *For the Beauty of the Earth*, 146–47.

16. Jerry Jenkins, Karen Roy, Charles Driscoll, and Christopher Buerkett, *Acid Rain in the Adirondacks: An Environmental History* (Ithaca, NY: Cornell University Press, 2007).

17. To those of us who teach, at any level from kindergarten through college, let's be honest: we are always shaping our students' characters in certain ways, whether we know it or not and whether they know it (or like it) or not. Our expectations for class attendance, rules on classroom behavior, and policies on plagiarism shape students and thus nurture their character. Our philosophy of grading influences student behavior, for example, by fomenting competition or fostering cooperation, and it ultimately forms character (for good or ill). So we should acknowledge that character formation is part of our job as educators, and we should more explicitly and intentionally construct our courses and plan our classes to foster certain virtues and extinguish certain vices.

Given this acknowledgment, I strongly encourage teachers to explore how they can nurture ecological virtue ethics in their classrooms. What stories of caring for creation might you reasonably include in your instruction (e.g., oral histories, written biographies)? What practices of nature stewardship could you weave into your teaching (e.g., group projects, homework assignments)? What exemplars of earthkeeping might fit easily into your curriculum (e.g., Aldo Leopold, Wangari Maathai)? What experiential learning opportunities might you incorporate into your classes (e.g., work in a community garden, trip to the local landfill)? We share a common home, our blue-green planet earth, thus we ought to educate so our students become better earthkeepers. This is especially the case for those of us who claim to follow Jesus, since earthkeeping is central to our faith.

18. Loren and Mary Ruth Wilkinson, *Caring for Creation in Your Own Backyard* (Vancouver: Regent College Publishing, 1992).

19. "Here" refers to things we can do around our own home, "there" refers to things we can do when traveling or on vacation, and "everywhere" refers to what we can do that will have a positive effect globally.

20. Leah Kostamo, *Planted: A Story of Creation, Calling, and Community* (Eugene, OR: Cascade, 2013); see also Craig Goodwin, *Year of Plenty: One Suburban Family, Four Rules, and 365 Days of Homegrown Adventure in Pursuit of Christian Living* (Minneapolis: Augsburg Fortress, 2011).

21. For more on sustainability at Hope College, see https://hope.edu/offices/sustainability.

22. One very helpful resource for trying to make wise decisions in our everyday lives is Michael Brower and Warren Leon, *The Consumer's Guide to Effective Environmental Choices: Practical Advice from the Union of Concerned Scientists* (New York: Three Rivers Press, 1999). This book has now been superseded by the latest from the Union of Concerned Scientists: *Cooler Smarter: Practical Steps for Low-Carbon Living* (Washington, DC: Island Press, 2012).

23. See, for example, David Orr, *Ecological Literacy: Education and the Transition to a Postmodern World* (Albany: State University of New York Press, 1992); see also David Orr, *Hope Is an Imperative: The Essential David Orr* (Washington, DC: Island Press, 2011).

24. For more on eco-literacy and ecological perception of place, see Bouma-Prediger, *For the Beauty of the Earth*, chap. 1. To learn about your own place, explore the local parks, go to the nearby nature centers, visit local farms and farmers' markets. Join a garden club, volunteer at the neighborhood school, become a member of a community-supported-agriculture farm. Pick up trash, help to eradicate invasive species, serve food at the community kitchen. The list is nearly endless.

25. Rachel Carson, *The Sense of Wonder* (New York: Harper & Brothers, 1956), 45. In this process, Carson emphasizes the importance of children having a companion, a mentor, a fellow explorer and wonderer. She writes, "If a child is to keep alive his inborn sense of

wonder without any such gift from the fairies, he needs the companionship of at least one adult who can share it, rediscovering with him the joy, the excitement and mystery of the world we live in."

26. David Orr, "The Intelligence of Ecological Design," Center for Ecoliteracy, June 29, 2009, https://www.ecoliteracy.org/article/intelligence-ecological-design.

27. Aldo Leopold, *A Sand County Almanac* (New York: Ballantine, 1966), 6.

28. Lisa Gerber, "Standing Humbly before Nature," *Ethics and the Environment* 7 (2002): 43.

29. Richard Mouw, *When the Kings Come Marching In* (Grand Rapids: Eerdmans, 1983), 65.

30. Nicholas Wolterstorff, *Lament for a Son* (Grand Rapids: Eerdmans, 1987), 85–86.

31. Desmond Tutu, *God Has a Dream: A Vision of Hope for Our Time* (New York: Doubleday, 2004), 128.

Appendix

1. Jay McDaniel, *Of God and Pelicans: A Theology of Reverence for Life* (Louisville: Westminster John Knox, 1989), 73–74.

2. James Nash, *Loving Nature: Ecological Integrity and Christian Responsibility* (Nashville: Abingdon, 1991), 63.

3. Nash, *Loving Nature*, 63.

4. Michael Northcott, *The Environment and Christian Ethics* (Cambridge: Cambridge University Press, 1996), 122–23.

5. Northcott, *Environment and Christian Ethics*, 314.

6. Michael Northcott, *Place, Ecology, and the Sacred: The Moral Geography of Sustainable Communities* (London: Bloomsbury, 2015), 80.

7. Northcott, *Place, Ecology, and the Sacred*, 78.

8. Willis Jenkins, *Ecologies of Grace: Environmental Ethics and Christian Theology* (New York: Oxford University Press, 2008), chap. 7. This originally appeared as "Biodiversity and Salvation: Thomistic Roots for Environmental Ethics," *Journal of Religion* 83 (July 2003): 401.

9. Jenkins, *Ecologies of Grace*, 139. For an insightful and nuanced discussion of Aquinas's views on "natural evils and ecological goods," see 144–48.

10. Jenkins, *Ecologies of Grace*, 140.

11. Jenkins, *Ecologies of Grace*, 148–49.

12. Jenkins, *Ecologies of Grace*, 149.

13. Seth Bible, "Pursuing Ecological Virtue: A Critical Analysis of the Environmental Virtue Ethics Models of Ronald Sandler, Louke van Wensveen, and Philip Cafaro" (PhD diss., Southeastern Baptist Theological Seminary, 2011).

14. Nancy Rourke, "The Environment Within: Virtue Ethics," in *Green Discipleship: Catholic Theological Ethics and the Environment*, ed. Tobias Winright (Winona, MN: Anselm Academic, 2011), 163–82.

15. Louke van Wensveen , "Environmentalists Read the Bible: The Co-creation of a Community, a Story, and a Virtue Ethic," in *Christian Ethics in Ecumenical Context: Theology, Culture, and Politics in Dialogue*, ed. Shin Chiba, George Hunsberger, Lester Edwin Ruiz, and Charles West (Grand Rapids: Eerdmans, 1995), 216. See also Louke van Wensveen, "Reviews and Prospects: The Emergence of a Grounded Virtue Ethic," in *Ecological Prospects: Scientific, Religious, and Aesthetic Perspectives*, ed. Christopher Chapple and Mary Evelyn Tucker (Albany: State University of New York Press, 1994).

16. Louke van Wensveen, "Christian Ecological Virtue Ethics: Transforming a Tradition," in *Christianity and Ecology: Seeking the Well-Being of Earth and Humans*, ed. Dieter Hessel and Rosemary Radford Ruether (Cambridge: Harvard University Press, 2000), 163, 165. At that Harvard conference, I responded to the paper that became the aforementioned chapter. My essay, "Response to Louke van Wensveen: A Constructive Proposal," follows hers in Hessel and Ruether, *Christianity and Ecology*, 173–82.

17. Louke van Wensveen, *Dirty Virtues: The Emergence of Ecological Virtue Ethics* (Amherst, NY: Humanity Books, 2000). An adaptation of chap. 1 from *Dirty Virtues* appears as "The Emergence of Ecological Virtue Language," in *Environmental Virtue Ethics*, ed. Ronald Sandler and Philip Cafaro (Lanham, MD: Rowman & Littlefield, 2005), 15–30.

18. Van Wensveen, *Dirty Virtues*, 5.

19. Van Wensveen, *Dirty Virtues*, 163–67.

20. Van Wensveen perceptively notes that "the biggest danger that threatens books on virtue is death by analysis"—that is, "Life-giving habits and attitudes that flourish in an atmosphere of spontaneity have a proclivity to wither when subjected to the light of critical inquiry." Despite this danger, she insists, reflection is important. And so the goal should be "a middle ground between death by analysis and death by lack of critical awareness." *Dirty Virtues*, 161–62.

21. Louke van Wensveen, "Cardinal Environmental Virtues: A Neurobiological Perspective," in Sandler and Cafaro, *Environmental Virtue Ethics*, 176.

22. Van Wensveen, "Cardinal Environmental Virtues," in Sandler and Cafaro, *Environmental Virtue Ethics*, 176.

23. Van Wensveen, "Cardinal Environmental Virtues," in Sandler and Cafaro, *Environmental Virtue Ethics*, 177.

24. Van Wensveen, "Cardinal Environmental Virtues," in Sandler and Cafaro, *Environmental Virtue Ethics*, 177.

25. Jame Schaefer, *Theological Foundations for Environmental Ethics: Reconstructing Patristic and Medieval Concepts* (Washington, DC: Georgetown University Press, 2009). See also Jame Schaefer, "Ethical Implications of Applying Aquinas' Notions of the Unity and Diversity of Creation to Human Functioning in Ecosystems" (PhD diss., Marquette University, 1994).

26. Kathryn Blanchard and Kevin O'Brien, *An Introduction to Christian Environmentalism: Ecology, Virtue, and Ethics* (Waco: Baylor University Press, 2014), 13.

27. Blanchard and O'Brien, *Introduction to Christian Environmentalism*, 170, 171–72.

Bibliography

Adams, Carol, ed. *Ecofeminism and the Sacred*. New York: Continuum, 1993.

Ahern, Melissa, Michael Hendryx, Jamison Conley, Evan Fedorko, Alan Ducatman, and Keith J. Zullig. "The Association between Mountaintop Mining and Birth Defects among Live Births in Central Appalachia, 1996–2003." *Environmental Research* 111 (2011): 838–46.

Ahern, Melissa, Martha Mullett, Katherine MacKay, and Candice Hamilton. "Residence in Coal-Mining Areas and Low-Birthweight Outcomes." *Maternal and Child Health Journal* 15 (2011): 974–79.

Alston, Dana A., ed. *We Speak for Ourselves: Social Justice, Race, and Environment*. London: Panos Institute, 1990.

Anderson, Bernhard. *From Creation to New Creation*. Minneapolis: Fortress, 1994.

Andrianos, Lucas. "Structural Greed and Creation: A Theological Reflection." *The Ecumenical Review* 63, no. 2 (2011): 312–29.

Anthony, R., C. Gamborg, M. Gjerris, and H. Rocklingsberg. "The Price of Responsibility: Ethics of Animal Husbandry in a Time of Climate Change." *Journal of Agricultural and Environmental Ethics* 24 (August 2011): 331–50.

Aquinas, Thomas. *Treatise on the Virtues*. Translated by John Oesterle. Notre Dame, IN: University of Notre Dame Press, 1984.

Aristotle. *Nicomachean Ethics*. In *The Basic Works of Aristotle*, edited by Richard McKeon. New York: Random House, 1941.

———. *Politics*. In *The Basic Works of Aristotle*, edited by Richard McKeon. New York: Random House, 1941.

Atchley, Ruth Ann, David Strayer, and Paul Atchley. "Creativity in the Wild: Improving Creative Reasoning through Immersion in Natural Settings." *PLOS One* 7, no. 12 (December 2012), https://doi.org/10.1371/journal.pone.0051474.

Attfield, Robin. *The Ethics of Environmental Concern*. 2nd ed. Athens: University of Georgia Press, 1983.

Augustine. *City of God*. Translated by Henry Bettenson. New York: Penguin, 1972.

Austin, Michael, and R. Douglas Geivett, eds. *Being Good: Christian Virtues for Everyday Life*. Grand Rapids: Eerdmans, 2012.

Backes, David. *A Wilderness Within: The Life of Sigurd F. Olson*. Minneapolis: University of Minnesota Press, 1997.

Bailey, Liberty Hyde. *The Holy Earth: The Birth of a New Land Ethic*. Berkeley: Counterpoint, 2015.

Barnett, Clive, Philip Cafaro, and Terry Newholm. "Philosophy and Ethical Consumption." In *The Ethical Consumer*, edited by Rob Harrison, Terry Newholm, and Deirdre Shaw, 11–24. London: Sage, 2005.

Barton, Stephen, ed. *Where Shall Wisdom Be Found?* Edinburgh: T&T Clark, 1999.

Bass, Diana Butler. *Grateful: The Transformative Power of Giving Thanks*. New York: HarperOne, 2018.

Basso, Keith. *Wisdom Sits in Places*. Albuquerque: University of New Mexico Press, 1996.

Bauckham, Richard. *The Bible and Ecology: Rediscovering the Community of Creation*. Waco: Baylor University Press, 2010.

———. *Living with Other Creatures: Green Exegesis and Theology*. Waco: Baylor University Press, 2011.

Bauer, Walter, William Arndt, and F. Wilbur Gingrich. *A Greek-English Lexicon of the New Testament*. 2nd ed. Chicago: University of Chicago Press, 1979.

Becker, Ernest. *Denial of Death*. New York: Macmillan, 1973.

———. *Escape from Evil*. New York: Macmillan, 1975.

Begbie, Jeremy. *Resounding Truth: Christian Wisdom in the World of Music*. Grand Rapids: Baker Academic, 2007.

———. *Theology, Music, and Time*. Cambridge: Cambridge University Press, 2000.

———. *Voicing Creation's Praise*. Edinburgh: T&T Clark, 1991.

Bendik-Keymer, Jeremy. "Species Extinction and the Vice of Thoughtlessness: The Importance of Spiritual Exercises for Learning Virtue." *Journal of Agricultural and Environmental Ethics* 23 (March 2010): 61–83.

Bernard of Clairvaux. *The Steps of Humility and Pride*. Translated by M. Ambrose Conway. Kalamazoo, MI: Cistercian Publications, 1980.

Berry, Wendell. *Citizenship Papers*. Washington, DC: Shoemaker & Hoard, 2003.

———. *The Gift of Good Land*. San Francisco: North Point, 1981.

———. *Hannah Coulter*. Berkeley: Counterpoint, 2004.

———. *Home Economics*. Berkeley: Counterpoint, 1987.

———. *It All Turns on Affection: The Jefferson Lecture and Other Essays*. Berkeley: Counterpoint, 2012.

———. *Jayber Crow*. Berkeley: Counterpoint, 2000.

———. *New Collected Poems*. Berkeley: Counterpoint, 2012.

———. *Our Only World*. Berkeley: Counterpoint, 2015.

———. *Sex, Economy, Freedom, and Community*. New York: Pantheon, 1993.

———. *This Day: Collected and New Sabbath Poems*. Berkeley: Counterpoint, 2013.

———. *What Are People For?* San Francisco: North Point, 1990.

Berryhill, W. Wade. "Creation, Liberation, and Property: Virtues and Values toward a Theocentric Earth

Ethics." *Regent University Law Review* 16 (2003–4): 1–52.

Bible, Seth. "Pursuing Ecological Virtue: A Critical Analysis of the Environmental Virtue Ethics Models of Ronald Sandler, Louke van Wensveen, and Philip Cafaro." PhD diss., Southeastern Baptist Theological Seminary, 2011.

Biermann, Joseph. *A Case for Character: Towards a Lutheran Virtue Ethics.* Minneapolis: Fortress, 2014.

Biggers, Jeff. "Daring Protestors Shut Down Obama-Backed Strip Mine in West Virginia." *Huffington Post,* July 28, 2012. http://www.huffingtonpost.com/jeff-biggers/ramps-campaign_b_1714569.html.

Bina, Olivia, and Sofia Guedes Vaz. "Humans, Environment, and Economies: From Vicious Relationships to Virtuous Responsibility." *Ecological Economics* 72 (December 2011): 170–78.

Birch, Bruce, and Larry Rasmussen. *Bible and Ethics in the Christian Life.* Revised and expanded ed. Minneapolis: Augsburg, 1989.

Blanchard, Kathryn, and Kevin O'Brien. *An Introduction to Christian Environmentalism: Ecology, Virtue, and Ethics.* Waco: Baylor University Press, 2014.

Bland, Dave, and Sean Patrick Webb. *Creation, Character, and Wisdom: Rethinking the Roots of Environmental Ethics.* Eugene, OR: Wipf & Stock, 2016.

Boesak, Allen. *Dare We Speak of Hope? Searching for a Language of Life in Faith and Politics.* Grand Rapids: Eerdmans, 2014.

Bonhoeffer, Dietrich. *Letters and Papers from Prison.* Translated by Reginald Fuller, Frank Clarke, and John Bowden. Edited by Eberhard Bethge. New York: Macmillan, 1972.

Bouma-Prediger, Steven. "Creation Care and Character: The Nature and Necessity of the Ecological Virtues." *Perspectives on Science and Christian Faith* 50 (1998): 6–21.

———. "Eschatology Shapes Ethics: New Creation and Christian Ecological Virtue Ethics." In *Rooted and Grounded: Essays on Land and Christian Discipleship,* edited by Ryan Harker and Janeen Bertsche Johnson, 144–54. Eugene, OR: Pickwick, 2016.

———. *For the Beauty of the Earth: A Christian Vision for Creation Care.* 2nd ed. Grand Rapids: Baker Academic, 2010.

———. *The Greening of Theology: The Ecological Models of Rosemary Radford Ruether, Joseph Sittler, and Jürgen Moltmann.* Atlanta: Scholars Press, 1995.

———. "Hoping to Establish Common Ground for Saving Biodiversity." *Science* 314, no. 5804 (December 1, 2006): 1392–93.

———. "Response to Louke van Wensveen: A Constructive Proposal." In Hessel and Ruether, *Christianity and Ecology,* 173–82.

———. "What Kind of Person Would Do Something like That?" *International Journal of Christianity & Education* 20 (March 2016): 20–31.

Bouma-Prediger, Steven, and Peter Bakken. *Evocations of Grace: Joseph Sittler's Writings on Ecology, Theology, and Ethics.* Grand Rapids: Eerdmans, 2000.

Bouma-Prediger, Steven, and Brian Walsh. *Beyond Homelessness: Christian Faith in a Culture of Displacement.* Grand Rapids: Eerdmans, 2008.

———. "Education for Homelessness or Homemaking? The Christian College in a Postmodern Culture." *Christian*

Scholar's Review 32 (Spring 2003): 281–96. Reprinted in *Taking Every Thought Captive: Forty Years of the Christian Scholar's Review*, edited by Don King, 133–45. Abilene, TX: Abilene Christian University Press, 2011.

Bratton, Susan Power. *Six Billion and More: Human Population Regulation and Christian Ethics*. Louisville: Westminster John Knox, 1992.

Bright, Alan, Brett Bruyere, Philip Cafaro, Bruce Martin, and Robin Mittelstaed. "Assessing the Development of Environmental Virtue in 7th and 8th Grade Students in an Expeditionary Learning Outward Bound School." *Journal of Experiential Education* 31 (March 2009): 341–58.

Brooks, David. *The Road to Character*. New York: Random House, 2015.

———. *The Social Animal: The Hidden Sources of Love, Character, and Achievement*. New York: Random House, 2011.

Brower, Michael, and Warren Leon. *The Consumer's Guide to Effective Environmental Choices: Practical Advice from the Union of Concerned Scientists*. New York: Three Rivers Press, 1999.

Brown, William. *Character in Crisis: A Fresh Approach to the Wisdom Literature of the Bible*. Grand Rapids: Eerdmans, 1996.

———. *Sacred Sense: Discovering the Wonder of God's Word and World*. Grand Rapids: Eerdmans, 2015.

———. *The Seven Pillars of Creation: The Bible, Science, and the Ecology of Wonder*. New York: Oxford University Press, 2010.

———. *Wisdom's Wonder: Character, Creation, and Crisis in the Bible's Wisdom Literature*. Grand Rapids: Eerdmans, 2014.

Brown, William, and S. Dean McBride, eds. *God Who Creates*. Grand Rapids: Eerdmans, 2000.

Bruner, Daniel, Jennifer Butler, and A. J. Swoboda. *Introducing Evangelical Ecotheology: Foundations in Scripture, Theology, History, and Praxis*. Grand Rapids: Baker Academic, 2014.

Bullard, Robert. *Dumping in Dixie: Race, Class, and Environmental Quality*. 3rd ed. Boulder, CO: Westview, 2000.

Cafaro, Philip. "Economic Consumption, Pleasure, and the Good Life." *Journal of Social Philosophy* 32 (Winter 2001): 471–86.

———. "Environmental Virtue Ethics Special Issue: Introduction." *Journal of Agricultural and Environmental Ethics* 23 (March 2010): 3–7.

———. "Gluttony, Arrogance, Greed, and Apathy: An Exploration of Environmental Vice." In Sandler and Cafaro, *Environmental Virtue Ethics*, 135–58.

———. "The Naturalist's Virtues." *Philosophy in the Contemporary World* 8 (Fall/Winter 2001): 85–99.

———. "Thoreau, Leopold, and Carson: Toward an Environmental Virtue Ethics." In Sandler and Cafaro, *Environmental Virtue Ethics*, 3–17.

———. *Thoreau's Living Ethics: Walden and the Pursuit of Virtue*. Athens: University of Georgia Press, 2004.

———. "Thoreauvian Patriotism as an Environmental Virtue." *Philosophy in the Contemporary World* 2 (Summer 1995): 1–7.

———. "A Virtue Ethics Approach to Aldo Leopold's Land Ethic." *Environmental Ethics* 19 (Spring 1997): 53–67.

Cafaro, Philip, and Joshua Colt Gambrel. "The Virtue of Simplicity." *Journal of Agricultural and Environmental Ethics* 23 (March 2010): 85–108.

Cahill, Lisa Sowle. "The Ethical Implications of the Sermon on the Mount." *Interpretation* 41 (April 1987): 144–56.

Callicott, Baird. *Beyond the Land Ethic: More Essays in Environmental Philosophy*. Albany: State University of New York Press, 1999.

Carson, Rachel. *The Sense of Wonder*. New York: Harper & Brothers, 1956.

———. *Silent Spring*. Boston: Houghton Mifflin, 1962.

Cavanaugh, William. *Being Consumed: Economics and Christian Desire*. Grand Rapids: Eerdmans, 2008.

Cessario, Romanus. *The Moral Virtues and Theological Ethics*. Notre Dame, IN: University of Notre Dame Press, 1991.

Chapman, Robert L. "The Goat-Stag and the Sphinx: The Place of the Virtues in Environmental Ethics." *Environmental Values* 11 (May 2002): 129–44.

Chapple, Christopher, and Mary Evelyn Tucker, eds. *Ecological Prospects: Scientific, Religious, and Aesthetic Perspectives*. Albany: State University of New York Press, 1994.

Claxton, Guy. *Intelligence in the Flesh: Why Your Mind Needs Your Body Much More Than It Thinks*. New Haven: Yale University Press, 2015.

Clifton-Soderstrom, Karl. *The Cardinal and the Deadly: Reimagining the Seven Virtues and the Seven Vices*. Eugene, OR: Cascade, 2015.

Coeckelbergh, Mark. "Environmental Virtue: Motivation, Skill, and (In)formation Technology." *Environmental Philosophy* 8 (Fall 2011): 141–69.

Cole, Luke, and Sheila Foster. *From the Ground Up: Environmental Racism and the Rise of the Environmental Justice Movement*. New York: New York University Press, 2000.

Cooper, David, and Simon James. *Buddhism, Virtue, and the Environment*. Burlington, VT: Ashgate, 2005.

Couenhoven, Jesse. "Against Metaphysical Imperialism: Several Arguments for Equal Partnerships between the Deontic and Aretaic." *Journal of Religious Ethics* 38 (September 2010): 521–44.

Crites, Stephen. "The Narrative Quality of Experience." In Hauerwas and Jones, *Why Narrative?*, 65–88.

Cunningham, David. *Christian Ethics: The End of the Law*. New York: Routledge, 2008.

Curtin, Sally, Margaret Warner, and Holly Hedegaard. "Increase in Suicide in the United States, 1999–2014." *NCHS Data Brief*, no. 241 (April 2016).

Danielson, Leilah. *American Gandhi: A. J. Muste and the History of Radicalism in the Twentieth Century*. Philadelphia: University of Pennsylvania Press, 2014.

Davis, Ellen. *Scripture, Culture, and Agriculture*. Cambridge: Cambridge University Press, 2009.

Dawson, David. "Applying Stories of the Environment to Business: What Business People Can Learn from the Virtues in Environmental Narratives." *Journal of Business Ethics* 58, no. 1 (2005): 37–49.

Deane-Drummond, Celia. *Eco-Theology*. London: Anselm Academic, 2008.

———. "Environmental Justice and the Economy: A Christian Theologian's View." *Ecotheology* 11 (September 2006): 294–310.

DeWitt, Calvin. *Caring for Creation*. Grand Rapids: Baker, 1998.

DeYoung, Rebecca Konyndyk. "Courage." In Austin and Geivett, *Being Good*, 145–66.

————. *Glittering Vices: A New Look at the Seven Deadly Sins and Their Remedies*. Grand Rapids: Brazos, 2009.

Dickerson, Matthew, and David O'Hara. *Narnia and the Fields of Arbol: The Environmental Vision of C. S. Lewis*. Lexington: University of Kentucky Press, 2009.

Dickinson, Emily. *The Poems of Emily Dickinson*. Edited by R. W. Franklin. Cambridge: Belknap, 1999.

Dillard, Annie. *Pilgrim at Tinker Creek*. New York: Harper & Row, 1974.

Doran, Chris. *Hope in the Age of Climate Change*. Eugene, OR: Cascade, 2017.

Dunn, James, and Alan Suggate. *The Justice of God*. Grand Rapids: Eerdmans, 1993.

Edwards, Denis. *Partaking of God: Trinity, Evolution, and Ecology*. Collegeville, MN: Liturgical Press, 2014.

Emerson, Ralph Waldo. *Nature and Other Essays*. Mineola, NY: Dover Publications, 2009.

Esch, Laura, and Michael Hendryx. "Chronic Cardiovascular Disease Mortality in Mountaintop Mining Areas of Central Appalachian States." *Journal of Rural Health* 27 (February 11, 2011): 350–57.

Evans, Sam. "Voices from the Desecrated Places: A Journey to End Mountaintop Removal Mining." *Harvard Environmental Law Review* 34 (2010): 521–76.

Fairbanks, Sandra Jane. "Environmental Goodness and the Challenge of American Culture." *Ethics and the Environment* 15 (Fall 2010): 79–102.

Farley, Benjamin. *In Praise of Virtue: An Exploration of the Biblical Virtues in a Christian Context*. Grand Rapids: Eerdmans, 1995.

Ferkany, Matt, and Kyle Powys Whyte. "The Importance of Participatory Virtues in the Future of Environmental Education." *Journal of Agricultural and Environmental Ethics* 25 (June 2012): 419–34.

Firth, Dan, Paul Knights, and David Littlewood. "Eco-Minimalism as a Virtue." *Environmental Ethics* 33 (Winter 2011): 339–56.

Floyd, Shawn. "Morally Serious Pedagogy." *Christian Scholar's Review* 36 (Spring 2007): 245–61.

Foot, Philippa. *Virtues and Vices and Other Essays in Moral Philosophy*. Berkeley: University of California Press, 1978.

Francis (Pope). *Laudato Si': On Care for Our Common Home*. In *Encyclical on Climate Change and Inequality*. New York: Melville House, 2015.

Frankena, William. *Ethics*. 2nd ed. Englewood Cliffs, NJ: Prentice-Hall, 1973.

Frankl, Victor. *Man's Search for Meaning*. New York: Simon & Schuster, 1963.

Frasz, Geoffrey. "Benevolence as an Environmental Virtue." In Sandler and Cafaro, *Environmental Virtue Ethics*, 121–34.

————. "Environmental Virtue Ethics: A New Direction for Environmental Ethics." *Environmental Ethics* 15 (Fall 1993): 259–74.

————. "What Is Environmental Virtue Ethics That We Should Be Mindful of It?" *Philosophy in the Contemporary World* 8 (Fall/Winter 2001): 5–14.

Fretheim, Terence. *God and the World*. Nashville: Abingdon, 2005.

Gerber, Lisa. "Standing Humbly before Nature." *Ethics and the Environment* 7 (2002): 39–53.

Glanzer, Perry. "Moving beyond Value- or Virtue-Added: Transforming Colleges and Universities for Redemptive Moral Development." *Christian Scholar's Review* 39 (2010): 379–99.

Goodall, Jane. *Reason for Hope: A Spiritual Journey.* New York: Warner Books, 1999.

Goodwin, Craig. *Year of Plenty: One Suburban Family, Four Rules, and 365 Days of Homegrown Adventure in Pursuit of Christian Living.* Minneapolis: Augsburg Fortress, 2011.

Gordis, Robert. *The Book of God and Man: A Study of Job.* Chicago: University of Chicago Press, 1965.

———. *The Book of Job: Commentary, New Translation, and Special Studies.* New York: Jewish Theological Seminary of America, 1978.

Gottschall, Jonathan. *The Storytelling Animal: How Stories Make Us Human.* New York: Houghton Mifflin Harcourt, 2012.

Goudzwaard, Bob, and Craig Bartholomew. *Beyond the Modern Age: An Archaeology of Contemporary Culture.* Downers Grove, IL: IVP Academic, 2017.

Habel, Norman. *The Book of Job.* Philadelphia: Westminster, 1985.

Hansen, James. *Storms of My Grandchildren: The Truth about the Coming Climate Catastrophe and Our Last Chance to Save Humanity.* New York: Bloomsbury, 2009.

Harak, G. Simon. *Virtuous Passions: The Formation of Christian Character.* New York: Paulist Press, 1993.

Haskell, David George. *The Forest Unseen: A Year's Watch in Nature.* New York: Penguin, 2012.

Hauerwas, Stanley. *Character and the Christian Life.* San Antonio: Trinity University Press, 1985.

———. "The Difference of Virtue and the Difference It Makes." *Modern Theology* 9 (July 1993): 249–64.

———. *Truthfulness and Tragedy.* Notre Dame, IN: University of Notre Dame Press, 1977.

Hauerwas, Stanley, and David Burrell. "From System to Story: An Alternative Pattern for Rationality in Ethics." In Hauerwas and Jones, *Why Narrative?*, 158–90. Grand Rapids: Eerdmans, 1989.

Hauerwas, Stanley, and L. Gregory Jones, eds. *Why Narrative? Readings in Narrative Theology.* Grand Rapids: Eerdmans, 1989.

Hauerwas, Stanley, and Charles Pinches. *Christians among the Virtues: Theological Conversations with Ancient and Modern Ethics.* Notre Dame, IN: University of Notre Dame Press, 1997.

Haught, Paul. "Environmental Virtues and Environmental Justice." *Environmental Ethics* 33 (Winter 2011): 357–75.

———. "Hume's Knave and Nonanthropocentric Virtues." *Journal of Agricultural and Environmental Ethics* 23 (March 2010): 129–43.

Hayward, Tim. "Climate Change and Ethics." *Nature Climate Change* 2 (December 2012): 843–48.

———. "Ecological Citizenship: Justice, Rights and the Virtue of Resourcefulness." *Environmental Politics* 15 (June 2006): 435–46.

Hessel, Dieter, and Rosemary Radford Ruether, eds. *Christianity and Ecology: Seeking the Well-Being of Earth and Humans.* Cambridge: Harvard University Press, 2000.

Hiebert, Theodore. "Reclaiming the World: Biblical Resources for the Ecological Crisis." *Interpretation* 65 (October 2011): 341–52.

Hill, Thomas, Jr. "Comments on Frasz and Cafaro on Environmental Virtue Ethics." *Philosophy in the Contemporary World* 8 (Fall/Winter 2001): 59–62.

———. "Finding Value in Nature." *Environmental Values* 15 (2006): 331–41.

———. "Ideals of Human Excellence and Preserving Natural Environments." *Environmental Ethics* 5 (Fall 1983): 211–24.

Hitt, Nathaniel, and Michael Hendryx. "Ecological Integrity of Streams Related to Human Cancer Mortality Rates." *EcoHealth* 7 (2010): 91–104.

Hoang, Bethany Hanke, and Kristen Deede Johnson. *The Justice Calling: Where Passion Meets Perseverance.* Grand Rapids: Brazos, 2016.

Hofrichter, Richard, ed. *Toxic Struggles.* Philadelphia: New Society Press, 1993.

Holly, Marilyn. "Environmental Virtue Ethics: A Review of Some Current Work." *Journal of Agricultural and Environmental Ethics* 19 (August 2006): 391–424.

Holmes, Arthur. *Shaping Character: Moral Education in the Christian College.* Grand Rapids: Eerdmans, 1991.

Holzman, David. "Mountaintop Removal Mining." *Environmental Health Perspectives* 119 (November 1, 2011): 476–83.

Hopkins, Gerard Manley. *The Poems and Prose of Gerard Manley Hopkins.* London: Penguin, 1985.

Horrell, David, Cherryl Hunt, and Christopher Southgate. *Greening Paul: Rereading the Apostle in a Time of Ecological Crisis.* Waco: Baylor University Press, 2010.

Hughes, William. "Elizabeth Telfer, Food for Thought: Philosophy and Food." *Journal of Agricultural and Environmental Ethics* 11 (1998): 55–58.

Hull, Robert. "All about EVE: A Report on Environmental Virtue Ethics Today." *Ethics and the Environment* 10 (Spring 2005): 89–110.

Hursthouse, Rosalind. "Environmental Virtue Ethics." In *Working Virtue: Virtue Ethics and Contemporary Moral Problems,* edited by Rebecca L. Walker and Philip J. Ivanhoe, 155–71. New York: Oxford University Press, 2007.

Irwin, T. H. "Splendid Vices? Augustine for and against Pagan Virtues." *Medieval Philosophy and Theology* 8 (September 1999): 105–27.

Jackson, Wes. *Becoming Native to This Place.* Washington, DC: Counterpoint, 1996.

Jenkins, Jerry, Karen Roy, Charles Driscoll, and Christopher Buerkett. *Acid Rain in the Adirondacks: An Environmental History.* Ithaca, NY: Cornell University Press, 2007.

Jenkins, Willis. "Biodiversity and Salvation: Thomistic Roots for Environmental Ethics." *Journal of Religion* 83 (July 2003): 401–20.

———. *Ecologies of Grace: Environmental Ethics and Christian Theology.* New York: Oxford University Press, 2008.

Johnson, Mark. *The Meaning of the Body: Aesthetics of Human Understanding.* Chicago: University of Chicago Press, 2007.

———. *Moral Imagination: Implications of Cognitive Science for Ethics.* Chicago: University of Chicago Press, 1993.

Kawall, Jason. "The Epistemic Demands of Environmental Virtue." *Journal of Agricultural and Environmental Ethics* 23 (March 2010): 109–28.

———. "Inner Diversity: An Alternative Ecological Virtue Ethics." *Philosophy in the Contemporary World* 8 (Fall/Winter 2001): 27–35.

———. "Reverence for Life as a Viable Environmental Virtue." *Environmental Ethics* 25 (Winter 2003): 339–58.

Keen, Sam. *Apology for Wonder.* New York: Harper & Row, 1969.

Keesmaat, Sylvia, and Brian Walsh. *Romans Disarmed: Resisting Empire,*

Demanding Justice. Grand Rapids: Brazos, 2019.

Kenneson, Philip. *Life on the Vine: Cultivating the Fruit of the Spirit in Christian Community.* Downers Grove, IL: InterVarsity, 1999.

Kheriaty, Aaron. "Dying of Despair." *First Things*, August/September 2017, 21–25.

Kierkegaard, Søren. *Sickness unto Death.* Translated by Walter Lowrie. Princeton: Princeton University Press, 1941.

King, Don, ed. *Taking Every Thought Captive.* Abilene, TX: Abilene Christian University Press, 2011.

King, Martin Luther, Jr. *A Testament of Hope.* Edited by James Washington. New York: HarperCollins, 1986.

Kingsolver, Barbara. *Small Wonder: Essays.* New York: Harper Perennial, 2003.

Koetje, David, ed. *Living the Good Life on God's Good Earth.* Grand Rapids: Faith Alive, 2006.

Kohak, Erazim. *The Embers and the Stars: A Philosophical Inquiry into the Moral Sense of Nature.* Chicago: University of Chicago Press, 1984.

———. *The Green Halo: A Bird's Eye View of Ecological Ethics.* Chicago: Open Court, 2000.

Kostamo, Leah. *Planted: A Story of Creation, Calling, and Community.* Eugene, OR: Cascade, 2013.

Kotva, Joseph, Jr. *The Christian Case for Virtue Ethics.* Washington, DC: Georgetown University Press, 1996.

Kramer, Kyle. "Though the Mountains May Fall." *U.S. Catholic* 77, no. 4 (April 2012): 12–16.

Kruschwitz, Robert, and Robert Roberts, eds. *The Virtues: Contemporary Essays on Moral Character.* Belmont, CA: Wadsworth, 1987.

Lakoff, George, and Mark Johnson. *Metaphors We Live By.* Chicago: University of Chicago Press, 1980.

Lane, Belden. *Backpacking with the Saints: Wilderness Hiking as Spiritual Practice.* Oxford: Oxford University Press, 2015.

———. *The Solace of Fierce Landscapes: Exploring Desert and Mountain Spirituality.* Oxford: Oxford University Press, 1998.

Lanier, Jaron. *You Are Not a Gadget.* New York: Knopf, 2010.

Lear, Jonathan. *Radical Hope: Ethics in the Face of Cultural Devastation.* Cambridge: Harvard University Press, 2006.

Lear, Linda. *Rachel Carson: Witness for Nature.* New York: Holt, 1997.

Lee, Charles. "Evidence for Environmental Racism." *Sojourners*, February–March, 1990, 22–25.

Lee, Harper. *To Kill a Mockingbird.* New York: Harper & Row, 2006.

Leopold, Aldo. *A Sand County Almanac.* New York: Ballantine, 1970.

Lewis, C. S. *The Four Loves.* New York: Harcourt Brace Jovanovich, 1960.

———. *The Magician's Nephew.* New York: Macmillan, 1978.

Liederbach, Mark, and Seth Bible. *True North: Christ, the Gospel, and Creation Care.* Nashville: B&H Academic, 2012.

Light, Andrew, and Eric Katz, eds. *Environmental Pragmatism.* London: Routledge, 1986.

Lindamann, Monica. "Environmental Virtue Education: Ancient Wisdom Applied." Master's thesis, University of North Texas, 2005.

Loder, Reed Elizabeth. "Gratitude and the Environment: Toward Individual and Collective Ecological Virtue." *Journal Jurisprudence* 10 (2011): 383–435.

Louv, Richard. *Last Child in the Woods: Saving Our Children from Nature Deficit Disorder.* Chapel Hill: Algonquin, 2006.

———. *The Nature Principle: Reconnecting with Life in a Virtual Age*. Chapel Hill: Algonquin, 2012.

———. *Vitamin N: The Essential Guide to a Nature-Rich Life*. Chapel Hill: Algonquin, 2016.

Maathai, Wangari. *Replenishing the Earth: Spiritual Values for Healing Ourselves and the World*. New York: Doubleday, 2010.

———. *Unbowed: A Memoir*. New York: Knopf, 2006.

MacIntyre, Alasdair. *After Virtue: A Study in Moral Theory*. 2nd ed. Notre Dame, IN: University of Notre Dame Press, 1984.

———. *Dependent Rational Animals: Why Human Beings Need the Virtues*. Chicago: Open Court, 1999.

———. *Three Rival Versions of Moral Inquiry: Encyclopedia, Genealogy, and Tradition*. Notre Dame, IN: University of Notre Dame Press, 1990.

———. *Whose Justice? Which Rationality?* Notre Dame, IN: University of Notre Dame Press, 1988.

Madison, Lauren. "Courage and Hope as Imperative Ecological Virtues in Appalachia: A Case Study Approach." Summer research paper, Hope College, 2012.

———. "The Sense of Wonder and the Humility It Takes: How the Virtue of Humility Can Cultivate Wonder." Summer research paper, Hope College, 2013.

Marcacci, Silvio. "Utilities Closed Dozens of Coal Plants in 2017: Here Are the Six Most Important." *Forbes*, December 18, 2017, https://www.forbes.com/sites/energyinnovation/2017/12/18/utilities-closed-dozens-of-coal-plants-in-2017-here-are-the-6-most-important/#1c9d4a005aca.

Mattison, William, III. "Hope." In Austin and Geivett, *Being Good*, 107–25.

McCay, Mary. *Rachel Carson*. New York: Twayne, 1993.

McConnell, Terrance. *Gratitude*. Philadelphia: Temple University Press, 1993.

McDaniel. Jay. *Of God and Pelicans: A Theology of Reverence for Life*. Louisville: Westminster John Knox, 1989.

McFague, Sallie. *The Body of God*. Minneapolis: Augsburg Fortress, 1993.

McFarlane, Robert. *Landmarks*. New York: Penguin, 2016.

McKibben, Bill. *The Comforting Whirlwind: God, Job, and the Scale of Creation*. Grand Rapids: Eerdmans, 1994.

Meilander, Gilbert. *Faith and Faithfulness*. Notre Dame, IN: University of Notre Dame Press, 1981.

———. *The Theory and Practice of Virtue*. Notre Dame, IN: University of Notre Dame Press, 1984.

———. "Virtue in Contemporary Religious Thought." In *Virtue—Public and Private*, edited by Richard John Neuhaus, 7–29. Grand Rapids: Eerdmans, 1986.

Meine, Curt. *Aldo Leopold: His Life and Work*. Madison: University of Wisconsin Press, 2010.

Melin, Anders. *Living with Other Beings: A Virtue-Oriented Approach to the Ethics of Species Protection*. Berlin: LIT, 2013.

Meyers, C. D. "Nature, Virtue, and the Nature of Virtue: An Outline for an Environmental Virtue Ethics." *Southwest Philosophy Review* 26 (January 2010): 109–17.

Meyers, Jeffrey. *The Way of Peace: A. J. Muste's Writings for the Church*. Eugene, OR: Cascade, 2016.

Middleton, J. Richard. *The Liberating Image: The* Imago Dei *in Genesis 1.* Grand Rapids: Brazos, 2005.

———. *A New Heaven and a New Earth: Reclaiming Biblical Eschatology.* Grand Rapids: Baker Academic, 2014.

Miller, Peter, and Laura Westra, eds. *Just Ecological Integrity: The Ethics of Maintaining Planetary Life.* Lanham, MD: Rowman & Littlefield, 2002.

Moltmann, Jürgen. *The Coming of God: Christian Eschatology.* Minneapolis: Fortress, 1996.

———. *Ethics of Hope.* Minneapolis: Fortress, 2012.

———. *Theology of Hope.* New York: Harper & Row, 1967.

Moo, Jonathan, and Robert White. *Let Creation Rejoice: Biblical Hope and Ecological Crisis.* Downers Grove, IL: IVP Academic, 2014.

Moore, Kathleen Dean. "The Truth of the Barnacles: Rachel Carson and the Moral Significance of Wonder." *Environmental Ethics* 27 (Fall 2005): 265–77.

Mouw, Richard. *When the Kings Come Marching In.* Grand Rapids: Eerdmans, 1983.

Muir, John. *The Mountains of California.* San Francisco: Sierra Club, 1988.

———. *My First Summer in the Sierra.* San Francisco: Sierra Club, 1998.

Murphy, Roland. *The Tree of Life: An Exploration of Wisdom Literature.* Grand Rapids: Eerdmans, 2002.

Myers, David. *The Pursuit of Happiness: Who Is Happy and Why.* New York: William Morrow, 1992.

Nash, James. *Loving Nature: Ecological Integrity and Christian Responsibility.* Nashville: Abingdon, 1991.

———. "Toward the Revival and Reform of the Subversive Virtue: Frugality." *Annual of the Society of Christian Ethics* (1995): 137–60.

Newsom, Carol. "The Book of Job." In *The New Interpreter's Bible.* Vol. 4. Nashville: Abingdon, 1996.

Noddings, Nel. *Caring: A Feminine Approach to Ethics and Moral Education.* Berkeley: University of California Press, 1984.

Northcott, Michael. *The Environment and Christian Ethics.* New York: Cambridge University Press, 1996.

———. *Place, Ecology, and the Sacred: The Moral Geography of Sustainable Communities.* London: Bloomsbury, 2015.

Nouwen, Henri. *Compassion: A Reflection on the Christian Life.* New York: Doubleday, 1983.

Nussbaum, Martha. *Upheavals of Thought: The Intelligence of Emotions.* Cambridge: Cambridge University Press, 2001.

Oliver, Mary. *Thirst.* Boston: Beacon, 2006.

———. *Why I Wake Early.* Boston: Beacon, 2004.

Olson, Sigurd. *Listening Point.* Minneapolis: University of Minnesota Press, 1958.

———. *Of Time and Place.* Minneapolis: University of Minnesota Press, 1982.

———. *Reflections from the North Country.* Minneapolis: University of Minnesota Press, 1976.

———. *Sigurd Olson's Wilderness Days.* New York: Knopf, 1972.

———. *The Singing Wilderness.* Minneapolis: University of Minnesota Press, 1956.

O'Neill, John. "Environmental Virtues and Public Policy." *Philosophy in the Contemporary World* 8 (Fall/Winter 2001): 125–36.

Orr, David. *Earth in Mind: On Education, Environment, and the Human Prospect.* Washington, DC: Island Press, 1994.

———. *Ecological Literacy: Education and the Transition to a Postmodern World.* Albany: State University of New York Press, 1992.

———. *Hope Is an Imperative: The Essential David Orr.* Washington, DC: Island Press, 2007.

———. "The Intelligence of Ecological Design." Center for Ecoliteracy, June 29, 2009, https://www.ecoliteracy.org/article/intelligence-ecological-design.

Outka, Gene. *Agape: An Ethical Analysis.* New Haven: Yale University Press, 1972.

Patterson, John. "Maori Environmental Virtues." *Environmental Ethics* 16 (Winter 1994): 397–409.

Pérez-Comas, A. "Mercury Contamination in Puerto Rico: The Ciudad Cristiana Experience." *Boletín de la Asociación Médica de Puerto Rico* 83, no. 7 (1991): 269–99, http://www.ncbi.nlm.nih.gov/pubmed/1817506.

Peters, Ted. *Sin: Radical Evil in Soul and Society.* Grand Rapids: Eerdmans, 1995.

Pieper, Josef. *The Four Cardinal Virtues.* Notre Dame, IN: University of Notre Dame Press, 1966.

Pincoffs, Edward. *Quandaries and Virtues: Against Reductionism in Ethics.* Lawrence: University of Kansas Press, 1986.

Pipher, Mary. *The Green Boat: Reviving Ourselves in Our Capsized Culture.* New York: Riverhead Books, 2013.

Plantinga, Cornelius, Jr. "Contours of Christian Compassion." *Perspectives* 10 (February 1995): 9–11.

———. *Not the Way It's Supposed to Be: A Breviary of Sin.* Grand Rapids: Eerdmans, 1995.

Plato. *Republic.* Translated by G. M. A. Grube. Revised by C. D. C. Reeve. Indianapolis: Hackett, 1992.

Pope, Marvin. *Job.* 3rd ed. Anchor Bible 15. New York: Doubleday, 1973.

Popik, Kristin. "The Philosophy of Woman of St. Thomas Aquinas." *Faith and Reason* 5 (Spring 1979): 16–56.

Porter, Jean. *The Recovery of Virtue: The Relevance of Aquinas for Christian Ethics.* Louisville: Westminster John Knox, 1990.

Rasmussen, Larry. "New Wineskins." *Interpretation* 65 (October 2011): 364–76.

Ricoeur, Paul. *Time and Narrative.* Vols. 1–3. Chicago: University of Chicago Press, 1990.

Rolston, Holmes, III. "Can and Ought We to Follow Nature?" *Environmental Ethics* 1 (Spring 1979): 7–30.

———. *Environmental Ethics: Duties to and Values in the Natural World.* Philadelphia: Temple University Press, 1988.

———. "Environmental Virtue Ethics: Half the Truth but Dangerous as a Whole." In Sandler and Cafaro, *Environmental Virtue Ethics*, 61–78.

———. *A New Environmental Ethic: The Next Millennium for Life on Earth.* New York: Routledge, 2012.

Romero, Óscar. *The Violence of Love.* Translated by James R. Brockman. Maryknoll: Orbis, 2004.

Rourke, Nancy. "The Environment Within: Virtue Ethics." In *Green Discipleship: Catholic Theological Ethics and the Environment,* edited by Tobias Winright, 163–82. Winona, MN: Anselm Academic, 2011.

———. "Prudence Gone Wild: Catholic Environmental Virtue Ethics." *Environmental Ethics* 33 (Fall 2011): 249–66.

Ruether, Rosemary Radford. *Sexism and God-Talk*. Boston: Beacon, 1983.

Russell, Daniel, ed. *The Cambridge Companion to Virtue Ethics*. Cambridge: Cambridge University Press, 2013.

Sahni, Pragati. *Environmental Ethics in Buddhism: A Virtues Approach*. New York: Routledge, 2008.

Sandler, Ronald. *Character and Environment: A Virtue-Oriented Approach to Environmental Ethics*. New York: Columbia University Press, 2007.

———. "Culture and the Specification of Environmental Virtue." *Philosophy in the Contemporary World* 10 (Fall /Winter 2003): 63–68.

———. *Environmental Ethics: Theory in Practice*. Oxford: Oxford University Press, 2018.

———. "Ethical Theory and the Problem of Inconsequentialism: Why Environmental Virtue Ethicists Should Be Virtue-Oriented Ethicists." *Journal of Agricultural and Environmental Ethics* 23 (March 2010): 167–83.

———. "The External Goods Approach to Environmental Virtue Ethics." *Environmental Ethics* 25 (Fall 2003): 279–93.

———. "Global Warming and Virtues of Ecological Restoration." In Thompson and Bendik-Keymer, *Ethical Adaptation to Climate Change*, 63–79.

———. "A Theory of Environmental Virtue." *Environmental Ethics* 28 (Summer 2006): 247–64.

———. "Towards an Adequate Environmental Virtue Ethic." *Environmental Values* 13 (2004): 477–95.

Sandler, Ronald, and Philip Cafaro, eds. *Environmental Virtue Ethics*. Lanham, MD: Rowman & Littlefield, 2005.

Sayings of the Desert Fathers. Translated by Benedicta Ward. Kalamazoo, MI: Cistercian Publications, 1975.

Schaefer, Jame. "Ethical Implications of Applying Aquinas' Notions of the Unity and Diversity of Creation to Human Functioning in Ecosystems." PhD diss., Marquette University, 1994.

———. *Theological Foundations for Environmental Ethics: Reconstructing Patristic and Medieval Concepts*. Washington, DC: Georgetown University Press, 2009.

Schrader-Frechette, Kristin. *Environmental Justice: Creating Equality, Reclaiming Democracy*. New York: Oxford University Press, 2002.

Schut, Michael. *Simpler Living, Compassionate Life: A Christian Perspective*. Denver: Living the Good News Press, 1999.

Seuss, Dr. *The Lorax*. New York: Random House Books for Young Readers, 2012.

Sharp, Gene. *The Politics of Nonviolent Actions*. Boston: Porter Sargent, 1973.

Shaw, Bill. "A Virtue Ethics Approach to Aldo Leopold's Land Ethic." In *Environmental Virtue Ethics*, 93–106.

Sider, Ronald J., ed. *Cry Justice: The Bible on Hunger and Poverty*. New York: Paulist Press, 1980.

Simon, Carol. *The Disciplined Heart: Love, Destiny, and Imagination*. Grand Rapids: Eerdmans, 1997.

Singer, Peter. *Animal Liberation: A New Ethics for Our Treatment of Animals*. New York: New York Review, 1975.

Sittler, Joseph. "Called to Unity." In *Evocations of Grace: Joseph Sittler's Writings on Ecology, Theology, and Ethics*, edited by Steven Bouma-Prediger and Peter Bakken, 38–50. Grand Rapids: Eerdmans, 2000.

———. *Gravity and Grace*. Minneapolis: Augsburg, 1986.

Smedes, Lewis. *Choices: Making Right Decisions in a Complex World*. San Francisco: Harper & Row, 1986.

———. *Mere Morality: What God Expects from Ordinary People.* Grand Rapids: Eerdmans, 1983.

———. *A Pretty Good Person: What It Takes to Live with Courage, Gratitude, and Integrity.* San Francisco: Harper & Row, 1990.

———. *Standing on the Promises: Keeping Hope Alive for a Tomorrow We Cannot Control.* Nashville: Nelson, 1998.

Smith, James K. A. *Desiring the Kingdom: Worship, Worldview, and Cultural Formation.* Grand Rapids: Baker Academic, 2009.

———. *Imagining the Kingdom: How Worship Works.* Grand Rapids: Baker Academic, 2013.

———. *Who's Afraid of Postmodernism?* Grand Rapids: Baker Academic, 2006.

———. *You Are What You Love: The Spiritual Power of Habit.* Grand Rapids: Brazos, 2016.

Smith, Pamela. "The Ecotheology of Annie Dillard: A Study in Ambivalence." *Cross Currents* 45, no. 3 (Fall 1995): 341–58.

Stafford, Sue P. "Intellectual Virtue in Environmental Virtue Ethics." *Environmental Ethics* 32 (Winter 2010): 339–52.

Stassen, Glen, ed. *Just Peacemaking.* Cleveland: Pilgrim Press, 2008.

Statman, Daniel, ed. *Virtue Ethics: A Critical Reader.* Washington, DC: Georgetown University Press, 1997.

Sterba, James. "A Morally Defensible Aristotelian Environmental Ethics: Comments on Gerber, O'Neill, Frasz, and Cafaro on Environmental Virtue Ethics." *Philosophy in the Contemporary World* 8 (Fall/Winter 2001): 63–66.

Stone, Christopher. *Earth and Other Ethics: The Case for Moral Pluralism.* New York: Harper & Row, 1987.

Swanton, Christine. "Heideggerian Environmental Virtue Ethics." *Journal of Agricultural and Environmental Ethics* 23 (March 2010): 145–66.

Taliaffero, Charles. "Vices and Virtues in Religious Environmental Ethics." In Sandler and Cafaro, *Environmental Virtue Ethics,* 159–72.

Taylor, Charles. *A Secular Age.* Cambridge: Harvard University Press, 2007.

Taylor, Paul. *Respect for Nature: A Theory of Environmental Ethics.* Princeton: Princeton University Press, 1986.

Thompson, Allen. "Radical Hope for Living Well in a Warmer World." *Journal of Agricultural and Environmental Ethics* 23 (March 2010): 43–49.

———. "The Virtue of Responsibility for the Global Climate." In Thompson and Bendik-Keymer, *Ethical Adaptation to Climate Change,* 203–21.

Thompson, Allen, and Jeremy Bendik-Keymer, eds. *Ethical Adaptation to Climate Change: Human Virtues of the Future.* Cambridge: MIT Press, 2012.

Thompson, Paul. "Agrarian Philosophy and Ecological Ethics." *Science and Engineering Ethics* 14 (2008): 527–44.

Thoreau, Henry David. *Walden and Other Writings.* Edited by Joseph Wood Krutch. New York: Bantam, 1981.

Tolstoy, Leo. *"The Death of Ivan Ilych" and Other Stories.* New York: Penguin, 1960.

Treanor, Brian. "Environmentalism and Public Virtue." *Journal of Agricultural and Environmental Ethics* 23 (March 2010): 9–28.

———. "Narrative Environmental Virtue Ethics: Phronesis without a Phronimos." *Environmental Ethics* 30 (Winter 2008): 361–79.

Tuan, Yi-Fu. *Topophilia: A Study of Environmental Perception, Attitudes, and Values*. New York: Columbia University Press, 1990.

Tucker, Mary Evelyn, and John Grim, eds. *Religions of the World and Ecology*. Cambridge: Harvard University Press, 1998–2004.

Turner, Frederick. *Rediscovering America: John Muir in His Time and Ours*. San Francisco: Sierra Club, 1985.

Tutu, Desmond. *God Has a Dream: A Vision of Hope for Our Time*. New York: Doubleday, 2004.

Union of Concerned Scientists. *Cooler Smarter: Practical Steps for Low-Carbon Living*. Washington, DC: Island Press, 2012.

United Church of Christ Commission on Racial Justice. *Toxic Waste and Race in the United States: A National Report on the Racial and Socio-Economic Characteristics of Communities surrounding Hazardous Waste Sites*. New York: United Church of Christ, 1987.

Urmson, J. O. *Aristotle's Ethics*. Oxford: Blackwell, 1988.

van Tongeren, Paul. "Temperance and Environmental Concerns." *Ethical Perspectives* 10 (2003): 118–28.

van Wensveen, Louke. "Attunement: An Ecological Spin on the Virtue of Temperance." *Philosophy in the Contemporary World* 8 (Fall/Winter 2001): 67–78.

———. "Cardinal Environmental Virtues: A Neurobiological Perspective." In Sandler and Cafaro, *Environmental Virtue Ethics*, 173–94.

———. "Christian Ecological Virtue Ethics: Transforming a Tradition." In Hessel and Ruether, *Christianity and Ecology*, 155–71.

———. *Dirty Virtues: The Emergence of Ecological Virtue Ethics*. Amherst, NY: Humanity Books, 2000.

———. "The Emergence of Ecological Virtue Language." In Sandler and Cafaro, *Environmental Virtue Ethics*, 15–30.

———. "Environmentalists Read the Bible: The Co-creation of a Community, a Story, and a Virtue Ethic." In *Christian Ethics in Ecumenical Context: Theology, Culture, and Politics in Dialogue*, edited by Shin Chiba, George Hunsberger, Lester Edwin Ruiz, and Charles West, 205–16. Grand Rapids: Eerdmans, 1995.

———. "Reviews and Prospects: The Emergence of a Grounded Virtue Ethic." In *Ecological Prospects: Scientific, Religious, and Aesthetic Perspectives*, edited by Christopher Chapple and Mary Evelyn Tucker, 211–23. Albany: State University of New York Press, 1994.

Van Wieren, Gretel. *Restored to Earth: Christianity, Environmental Ethics, and Ecological Restoration*. Washington, DC: Georgetown University Press, 2013.

Verhey, Allen. *Remembering Jesus: Christian Community, Scripture, and the Moral Life*. Grand Rapids: Eerdmans, 2002.

———. "Suffering and Compassion." *Perspectives* 10 (February 1995): 17–21.

Visgilio, Gerald, and Dianna Whitelaw, eds. *Our Backyard: A Quest for Environmental Justice*. Lanham, MD: Rowman & Littlefield, 2003.

Vitek, William, and Wes Jackson. *Rooted in the Land*. New Haven: Yale University Press, 1996.

Vucetich, John, Michael Paul Nelson, and Chelsea Batavia. "The Anthropocene: Disturbing Name, Limited Insight." In *After Preservation: Saving American Nature in the Age of Humans*, edited by Ben Minteer and Stephen Pyne,

66–73. Chicago: University of Chicago Press, 2015.

Walsh, Brian. "Subversive Poetry and Life in the Empire." *Third Way* 23, April 2000, 20.

Walsh, Brian, and Sylvia Keesmaat. *Colossians Remixed: Subverting the Empire.* Downers Grove, IL: IVP Academic, 2004.

Weisman, Alan. *The World without Us.* New York: Picador, 2008.

Weisskopf, Michael. "The Poisoning of Christian City." *Washington Post*, June 30, 1986, https://www.washingtonpost.com/archive/politics/1986/06/30/the-poisoning-of-christian-city/a6eee909-e12b-466d-b029-9416a04aaed4/?utm_term=.147a0ffe2658.

Welchman, Jennifer. "The Virtues of Stewardship." *Environmental Ethics* 21 (Winter 1999): 411–23.

Wenz, Peter. "Synergistic Environmental Virtues: Consumerism and Human Flourishing." In Sandler and Cafaro, *Environmental Virtue Ethics*, 197–213.

Westphal, Merold. *Whose Community? Which Interpretation?* Grand Rapids: Baker Academic, 2009.

Westra, Laura. *Living in Integrity: A Global Ethic to Restore a Fragmented Earth.* Lanham, MD: Rowman & Littlefield, 1998.

White, John R. "Ecological Value Cognition and the American Capitalist Ethos." *Environmental Philosophy* 3 (Fall 2006): 44–51.

Wiesel, Elie. *Night.* New York: Bantam, 1958.

Wilkens, Steve, and Mark Sanford. *Hidden Worldviews: Eight Cultural Stories That Shape Our Lives.* Downers Grove, IL: IVP Academic, 2009.

Wilkinson, Loren, ed. *Earthkeeping in the Nineties: Stewardship of Creation.* Revised edition. Grand Rapids: Eerdmans, 1991.

Wilkinson, Loren, and Mary Ruth Wilkinson. *Caring for Creation in Your Own Backyard.* Vancouver: Regent College Publishing, 1992.

Wilkinson, Loren, Peter DeVos, Calvin DeWitt, Eugene Dykema, Vernon Ehlers, Derk Pereboom, and Aileen Van Beilen. *Earthkeeping: Christian Stewardship of Natural Resources.* Grand Rapids: Eerdmans, 1980.

Williams, Terry Tempest. *Refuge: An Unnatural History of Family and Place.* New York: Vintage, 1992.

Wilson, E. O. *Biophilia: The Human Bond with Other Species.* Cambridge: Harvard University Press, 1984.

———. *The Creation: An Appeal to Save the Earth.* New York: Norton, 2007.

Wilson, Jonathan. *God's Good World: Reclaiming the Doctrine of Creation.* Grand Rapids: Baker Academic, 2013.

———. *Gospel Virtues: Practicing Faith, Hope, and Love in Uncertain Times.* Downers Grove, IL: InterVarsity, 1998.

Wirzba, Norman. *From Nature to Creation: A Christian Vision for Understanding and Loving Our World.* Grand Rapids: Baker Academic, 2015.

———. *Living the Sabbath: Discovering the Rhythms of Rest and Delight.* Grand Rapids: Brazos, 2006.

———. *The Paradise of God: Renewing Religion in an Ecological Age.* New York: Oxford University Press, 2003.

———. "The Touch of Humility: An Invitation to Creatureliness." *Modern Theology* 42 (April 2008): 225–44.

Wohlleben, Peter. *The Hidden Lives of Trees.* Vancouver: Greystone, 2016.

Wolterstorff, Nicholas. *Educating for Life: Reflections on Christian Teaching and Learning.* Edited by Gloria Stronks and Clarence Joldersma. Grand Rapids: Baker Academic, 2002.

———. *Educating for Shalom*. Grand Rapids: Eerdmans, 2004.

———. *Hearing the Call: Liturgy, Justice, Church, and World*. Edited by Mark Gornik and Gregory Thompson. Grand Rapids: Eerdmans, 2011.

———. *Journey toward Justice: Personal Encounters in the Global South*. Grand Rapids: Baker Academic, 2013.

———. *Justice in Love*. Grand Rapids: Eerdmans, 2011.

———. *Justice: Rights and Wrongs*. Princeton: Princeton University Press, 2008.

———. *Lament for a Son*. Grand Rapids: Eerdmans, 1987.

Worster, Donald. *A Passion for Nature: The Life of John Muir*. New York: Oxford University Press, 2008.

Wright, N. T. *After You Believe: Why Christian Character Matters*. New York: HarperOne, 2010.

———. *The Climax of the Covenant: Christ and the Law in Pauline Theology*. Minneapolis: Fortress, 1993.

———. *Surprised by Hope: Rethinking Heaven, the Resurrection, and the Mission of the Church*. New York: HarperOne, 2008.

Scripture Index

Subject and Name Index

DISCARD